PROTOCOL IN MAHABHARATA

PROTOCOL IN MAHABHARATA

D.D. Aggarwal

KALPAZ PUBLICATIONS
DELHI–110 052

PROTOCOL IN MAHABHARATA

Rs. 790

ISBN: 81-7835-177-3

Published in 2003 in India by
Kalpaz Publications
C–30, Satyawati Nagar
Delhi–110 052
E-mail: kalpaz@hotmail.com

Lasertypesetting by: Varsha Graphics, Delhi
Printed at: Chawla Offset Printers, Delhi

Contents

Preface

Like geological excavations, which reveal new facts of past civilisation, classical texts also yield new facets, when subjected to continued study. Having been involved with protocol at high levels, this book is an effort to find out the modern concepts of protocol in various fields, available in Mahabharata, an ocean of such deliberations, demolishing the British contention that India lacked even primary concepts of protocol before their arrival.

Protocol in Mahabharata centres around the multiple levels of protocol relating to hierarchical order as well as code of conduct prevailing in society at the specified period. Its violation was looked upon as sacrilegious and punishable.

On the cosmic level, God is the most supreme. He has three powers of Brahma (Creator), Vishnu (Maintainer) and Mahesh (Annihilator) and under them are various gods and their subordinates (Ganas), similar to the system of governance in Mahabharata times and even existing today. Like present day system, the Mahabharata narrates the laws of peace; duties of the raja; international agreements, immunity to raja's representatives (like ambassadorial immunities); spy system in raja's own kingdom and in other countries; relation of the raja with his subjects and other rajas; existence of Samitis and Sabhas, advisors and staff manned by persons of verified capability and integrity.

With protocol as the principal focus point, this book depicts the flexibility of caste system, the status of different varnas and ashramas; personal and family laws; crime and punishment; sages and preceptors and their relationship with the pupils and disciples and the most important the protocol in Heaven and among the Olympian gods of Indian mythology, particularly the deliberations between Lord Krishna and Arjuna forming

Bhagwat Gita and between Bhishma and Yudhishtra covering all aspects of human life, including a glimpse of the life of men, women and gods and the elements of protocol in their relationships in the Puranic era through this book. Mention may also be made that like the present day system of king as suzerain and the vassal states under him, in ancient times also there was Chakravarty raja and other small rajas under him but governing their states autonomously. These rajas used to come for helping the Chakravarty raja in time of need and used to have his protection in case of disputes with other rajas.

D.D. Aggarwal

Introduction

When the British came to India, they had come as traders and had been writing letters to Indian Governors putting 'their heads on their feet' etc. but after the battles of Plassy and Buxar, they started ruling India and called Indians barbaric and owed it to themselves to civilise Indians. They had at that time seen Muslim rule existing for over 600 years, when there was no law of governance and jurisprudence as in Muslim rule, all this was as per 'Shariat'. Ancient Hindu literature had all been destroyed by Muslims. So English did not by then have the knowledge of Hindu vedas, shastras, samritis and puranas, which are oceans of knowledge. So much so that English, thought they had taught protocol to the world, whereas in our ancient historically proved Maurya and Gupta periods, India was a seat of learning for the entire universe. It was the most advanced, most educated, most resourceful country of the world, superb in the matter of protocol in all aspects.

Mahabharata is the treasury of Hindu philosophy of 'Karma' and 'Dharma'; the fate and action and protocolic relation not only amongst the human beings, but between the gods, the animals and birds and even the rivers and mountains. Modern concepts of protocol look poorer when we go deep into the spiritual, political, administrative, social and international protocol imbibed in Mahabharata alone.

In Spiritual Protocol, it Narrates

1. Ishwar-Jeeva relation — how human being could reach God by bhakti and yoga.
2. Protocolic relations between gods themselves, there being Vishnu at the top of hierarchy; then Shiva and Brahma; then the gods like Indra, Sun, Moon, Varuna, Brihaspati, etc., and then their subordinates. It speaks of full realm in the universe beyond the universe of human beings.

3. Gods used to take their shares personally in the havans; they used to witness the Mahabharata war; Krishana playing with gopis.

4. There were frequent visits to this universe by gods and of the other lokas by human beings. So much so that godly weapons had been used in the battles in this universe.

5. Gita and the dialogue between Bhishma and Yudhisthra are spiritual discourses covering all aspects.

In Political Protocol, it Explains

1. Duties of a raja.

2. Raja was responsible mainly for the protection of the life and property of the people.

3. Relations of the raja with the praja. Besides protection of the praja from foreign aggression and internal criminals, the raja was required to see that rains took place in time. By holdnig yagyas etc. they kept the rain god pleased. The crops were in abundance; all essential commodities were available at reasonable prices and at full measurement.

4. The raja had to see that people of all varnas had been following their respective Dharmas. The raja's men had not been harassing the people and the praja in turn respected their raja and were prepared to give their all for the sake of the raja. There was thus a father and the son relation between the raja and the praja.

5. The raja was even normally considered to be responsible to care for the ultimate salvation of his people.

In Administrative Protocol, there is Mention of

1. Raja having council of ministers to run the Government. He was also to have a Sabha or a Samiti and was obliged to consult them in all important matters and abide by their advice and in case of any difference of opinion due to which the raja did not accept the advice, he had to give convincing reasons for the same.

2. With a view to keep himself apprised of what had been happening in his kingdom, the raja used to have a net of spies, who were people of his confidence. They had direct access to the raja and they were to report every matter even if it may not be to the taste of the raja.

3. The raja had his employees. They were responsible to run the Government. There is even the procedure laid down for their recruitment, verification of the antecedents, family, conduct etc.

4. In all functions, the seating arrangement was made as per laid down 'order of precedence'. Such an arrangement was as per the capability of persons attending such meetings. In the Aswamedha Yagya performed by Yudhisthra, even gods had attended that yagya and the seating arrangement in order of priority was made for gods, rishis, munis, and others as per their capability and not varnas.

5. Raja's men could not harass the people. Then there was even a vigilance organisation to oversee the working of the other government servants.

6. Qualifications had been laid down for the recruitment of employees. There was punishment laid down for each crime—even for the minutest. There were even reward/punishment one had to face for all good and bad deeds in this universe. Also laid down was the procedure to resort to repentence; it was duly recognised and was kept in view while deciding the cases against such people. There was a procedure laid down for conducting the legal proceedings such as receipt of a petition, defence by the defendants; evidence/witness by both sides; enquiry, where considered necessary and then the award of judgement. There was even provision for appeal and the raja was the highest court of appeal and his judgement was accepted by all.

7. The raja was responsible for providing roads, gardens, hospitals, gurukulas etc. for the benefit of the people and their maintenance was by his employees. There was laid down rajbhag from agricultural products, other cess on industrial produce, market tax, river tax, customs duty etc. monitored by the raja's men.

8. There is mention of the hierarchical system in bureaucracy, with raja being at the top, then the ministers, and then the other officers and staff. They were from various fields of life.

The Social Protocol was based on the Fundemantal of Varnas and Ashramas. These Interalia Provided that

1. People of all varnas at first went to gurukulas for education and after preliminary education for all, they got further education as per their options. This option was nothing else but the varna, one chose to adopt for being followed by him such as if one, who wanted to read further, he became brahmin; who was interested in governance, was taught the warfare, use of arms and goverance etc. became kshatriya; one, who was interested in agriculture, trade, industry, got training in that vocation and became vaish and one, who could not fit in any of the above vocations, became shudra. Since the varnas had been opted by each as per his capability, no one had grudge against the people of other varnas and resorted to the Dharma of their varnas only. The concept of Dharma changed from person to person and varna to varna, e.g., killing may be adharma for the human beings but it was Dharma of the raja to kill the enemies, criminals etc.; collection of wealth was not allowed by the people of all varnas except vaish and so on.

2. As far as possible, the marriage had to take place within the people of same varna so that there was affinity in the husband and wife.

3. In social gatherings, people of all varnas gathered.

4. There was laid down duty of the husband, wife, father, mother, sons, daughters, brothers and friends. Any action not recognised as such was treated as adharma and punishment laid down for the same.

5. Woman was granted an honourable place in the society. They used to go to battle fields and did all other jobs with their husbands.

6. There were representatives of the people of all varnas in the Sabha/Samiti duly elected by them. In this way the public had a say in the governance. Even raja was either directly elected or approved by the sabha.

7. Brahmins were given protocolic respect by all. The raja was honoured by all. Even brahmins could not kill a raja. When Parshurama killed Sahasarbahu raja, his father told him that brahmins' job was to excuse others and not to kill even if the

guilty was the raja himself and he had to repent for it.

8. Every person was recognised by the present capability and not by the varna. Once a rishi had put his pupil on asan in his absence. The pupil was basically a shudra. At that time Balrama came there and he could not tolerate a shudra sitting on rishi's asan. He killed him. Then the rishi did not approve of raja's action and the raja had to repent for it. So, in the social structure even the raja was not above the social, religious rules.

9. What to speak of living beings, there is a mention of protocolic relation between the living human beings and the deads, who were remembered by performing 'Shradhas'.

In International Protocol, there was Detailed Description of—

1. How the ambassadors/representatives of one raja had to be treated by another raja. Such representatives could convey any message of his master even if it was not assimilable by the raja and he could not be harmed. It shows the ambassadorial immunities, then existing.

2. Each raja had his spies in the kingdom of other rajas. They operated secretly and were to convey everything of raja's interest in that kingdom. Pandavas and Kaurvas had been knowing each other's position and decisions during the war. Even otherwise, the Kaurvas had been keeping themselves abreast of all happenings in their vassal states.

3. There was a system of many autonomous rajas and a chakraverty raja over them. The chakravarty raja used to get annual contribution/presents from the vassal states and in turn the chakravarty raja protected such vassal states from other aggressions.

4. The rajas had fear of invasion by others. But in such invasions, the victorious raja generally left the defeated raja to rule himself after payment of some presents or compensation by the defeated raja and accepting suzerainty of the victorious raja. Such suzerainty was also established in periodical gatherings like Aswamedha Yagyas, where all vassal rajas used to come and offer presents in recognition of the suzerainty of the chakravarty raja.

5. In case of wars/battles, there were detailed laws of war laid down. Such laws in present day are, therefore, nothing new for India. At the time of start of Mahabharata, detailed laws of war to be followed by each side had been laid down. Such rules in fact were already in existence but were re-written at that time such as the fighting shall be during the day only and after sun-set there shall be no fighting and there was even meeting of the people of both sides. There was a rule of one person fighting with one person ; a man on chariot fighting with another man on chariot; a person with one type of armament fighting with another man too with the same kind of armament, such as the two shall fight with dhanushban, sword, gada etc. as mutually settled; a person without chariot, without arm, without kawach etc. was not attacked. There had, however, been breaches at times such as Abhimanyu had been killed by six persons fighting with one when he had defeated all individually and then he was killed when his chariot had been broken and he was without arm. Kauravas had done so when Darona, Karna etc. were there who knew all laws of war but then it was taken as a breach of laws of war and was quoted as such when subsequently Pandavas too caused such breaches, as according to the laws of war itself if one party resorted to breach of the laws of war, the other was free to resort to the same too.

6. There was detailed provision how international agreements should be entered into after each battle/war and otherwise too between two friendly rajas; between a victorious and a defeated raja and for other purposes of transport, visits etc. by the people of one raja to the kingdom of another raja. Such agreements were never broken and any breach led to battles only such as Kauravas agreed to hand over their rajya to Pandavas after they returned from exile for 13 years in forests but on Pandavas religiously having passed the period in forests with all attached sufference for such living, the Kaurvas did not fulfil their part of agreement in returning their kingdom resulting in the war of Mahabharata.

Mahabharata can be easily divided into five parts—one dealing with the births etc. of Kaurvas and Pandavas and the rule of their ancestors. Second is defeat in gambling and passage of 13 years by Pandavas in forests. Third is the Mahabharata war and Krishana's narration of Gita to Arjuna to prepare him for the war pronouncing the theory of 'Karma' and 'Dharma'. The fourth is the dialogue of Bhishma and Yudhisthra after the war when Yudhisthra was worried about crores of people having been killed in the battle and his resolve not to accept the rajya of the kingdom after so many killings and then the fifth and the last is Yudhisthra accepting to govern and the post-government happenings.

I have tried to narrate all important happenings in this book and have incorporated certain portions for the sake of maintaining continuity of the reading even though they may not be relating to protocolic aspect. In this way this book has come out to be a mini-Mahabharata and may be of interest to the readers.

In the end, as per tradition, I am grateful to my wife, my son, and other members of the family but for whose co-operation, I may not have been able to do this job.

in discharging the duties pertaining to that varna. Then, there were the ashramas, applicable to the people of each varna; the first one being the brahmcharya. During this period, one was sent to gurukula. In the gurukula, one attained education remaining completely devoted to the guru; going out for 'bhiksha' and handing over, whatever had been received, to the guru and then eating as given by the guru. The disciples were obedient to the guru to the core. They did not have any passions, greed, etc., and all in the gurukula were treated equally; even though one may be a rajkumar and another a son of a vaisha and so on. The gurus were selfless and used to impart education befitting each one to the best of their capability. Except for a few cases where the guru, being a Rajguru, imparted education to the wards of brahmins and kshatriyas only, the gurukulas were open to the people of all varnas and once in a gurukula, all were treated equally. Instances of a few of the devoted disciples have been given with a view to show that even without caring for their lives, the disciples used to do as directed by the guru. The guru too at times used to put the disciple to very had tests, with a view to test his obedience to the guru, his interest in particular vocation of studies and the fulfilment of the directions. Through these tests, the entire philosophy of life was told like in one of these tests given to a disciple, the disciple saw many things in Nagloka. He narrated all that he saw to the guru and the guru then interpreted to the disciple, the meaning of whatever he saw, e.g., the nature, the formation of days and nights, twelve months, six seasons and the year. In this way, it shows that in ancient times, the people were aware of the principle of formation of days, nights, seasons, months, year, etc., by virtue of their knowledge of the movement of stars. Since gurus/brahmins were selfless, they had been respected by all and no one could afford to annoy them as they had the power in whatever they said and this could become a curse. It is said that one should not even in light mood cause any annoyance to the brahmins as they had the biggest armament in their speech, which could be used as a revenge against the persons, who spoke ill of brahmins.

न चाप्येवं त्वया भूयः क्षेप्तव्या ब्रह्मवादिनः
न चावमान्या दर्पात्तु ते वाग्वज्रा भृशकोपनाः। (31/32)

After this, there is the narration of incidents of happenings within gods, relation of gods within themselves and the requirement of their behaviour and position vis-a-vis others, e.g., Indra, Garuda, Vishnu, Agni, Varuna etc. Narada had been the link between various gods. At that time there was frequent exchange of views between the gods and the people of this universe. The rajas of this universe had been going to fight on

1
Adi Parva

As usual the book starts with the worship of God

नारायणं नमस्कृत्य नरं चैव नरोत्तमम्,
देवीं सरस्वतीं व्यासं ततो जयमुदीरयेत् (1/1)

There is indication of the contents in the grantha, e.g., the soul and its three gunas, satoguna, rajoguna and tamoguna and the five ingredients which go into the making of a being (जीव). As Ramcharitmanas is narrated by Shiva to Parvati and Shrimad Bhagwat by Shukdeva to Parikshit, Mahabharata composed by Ved Vyasa has been narrated by Ugrashravaji to rishis and then by Rishi Vaisampayanji to Janmejaya, the son of Parikshit after Parikshit had been bitten by Takshak and died and Janmejya had succeeded him. Janmejaya had engaged Som-shrava, the son of Shrutshrava as his Purohit. At first the book narrates the relation between the guru and the disciple. In ancient times, the children were sent to gurukula for education. Then after the preliminary education, essential for boys of all varnas, one could opt the varna of his choice. One, who wanted to study vedas and shastras further, became brahmin and his job was to teach others; one, who had a taste for warfare and was brave, became kshatriya and was given the education of usage of armaments, diplomacy and the art of governance; one, who had interest in trade, industry etc., became a vaisha and one, who could not fit in any of these three varnas, became shudra. In this way, the distribution of the mankind in four functional vocations was as per one's option (वर्ण), which in turn was as per his capability and once a varna had been opted, it became his Dharma to act accordingly as per tenets pertaining to the dischange of duty as per that Dharma, enunciated in vedas and samritis. Since the varna had been opted by each one according to his capability, he had no grudge behalf of the gods against the asuras.

After Parikshit had died as a result of snake bite, his son Janmejaya undertook to kill all snakes. When many of them had been killed, the Takshak sought refuge under Indra. Then Indra too was called to be killed in the Havan. Then Manu, an ancestor of Janmejaya had to come and ask Janmejaya to stop killing snakes as that was one specie of the beings and any specie could not completely be wiped off by a human being as every specie had a job to be performed and on the elimination of that specie, the universe would suffer because of the non-performance of the job entrusted to that specie.

On Janmejaya having asked why Takshak had killed his father, Ugrashrava narrated that once during hunting, Parikshit became thirsty and on his having seen rishi in an ashrama, he asked for being served with water but the rishi being in samadhi could not attend to him. The raja having been annoyed, put a dead snake in his neck and went away. Some of rishi's disciples, who saw this happening, told Shringi, son of the rishi, who was away taking bath in river, about the raja having put snake in the neck of his father. Without ascertaining the facts, Shringi passed on a curse that Parikshit would be bitten by a Takshak after seven days. When rishi came to know of such a curse having been passed by his son on the raja, he rebuked him saying that passing of a curse on the raja, who was responsible for protecting the praja, was wrong as in that case the praja would suffer having been unprotected in the absence of the raja and that passing of the curse was something exceeding one's power. The rishi then came to the raja and apprised him about the curse having been passed on him by his son. The Raja then handing over the rajya to his son, proceeded to the bank of Ganga.

This Would Indicate that—

1. There existed the division of mankind on functional basis into varnas — brahmin, kshatriya, vaish as shudras and each one had to perform his job treating this as his Dharma.

2. The brahmin was to pardon the wrong-doers and the job of punishing the wrong-doer was that of the raja.

3. In case raja himself was the culprit then he could be punished by the people or God.

4. People had the power of punishing the raja by dethroning him or going out from his rajya.

5. The raja, being the protector of his praja, was not to be killed as in his absence, the entire praja would suffer and in that case the curse-passer would be answerable.

6. The brahmins had the power of passing the curse on any one but this power had to be exercised with great precaution and prudence when there was no alternative to passing the curse to redress the wrong.

7. Anyone, who exceeded his powers, had to repent for the same.

8. According to the institution of ashramas, the raja had to hand over the rajya to his eldest son and proceed to forests in vanprastha. Here too on the rishi having apprised the raja of the curse passed on him by his son, the raja adopted vanprastha handing over the rajya to his son Janmejaya.

9. In the institution of vanprastha, the father was obliged to hand over the rajya to the son, lest he should on having grown up, snatch it by force causing bad relation between them as in the case of Shahjahan and Aurangzeb. So, to avoid such a situation arising, the concept of vanprastha had been provided. This not only saved the situation of father and son dispute but also enabled the father to attain salvation after having already attained the other three accomplishments—Dharma, Artha, and Kama (attainment of Dharma, wealth and satisfaction of ambitions).

10. Raja Parikshit was a popular king. He knew all about Dharma but sometimes the happen-to-be matters mar the intellect of the person. So did Parikshit become a victim of circumstances. He was thirsty and expected a warm welcome from the rishi being a very popular raja but on his not having been entertained, he felt distressed and took the wrong action of putting the dead snake in the neck of the rishi not-knowing that the rishi might be in samadhi.

Janmejaya undertook to burn all snakes in havan kund. In ancient days, we had the power to call all snakes at a place through mantras, so much so that even Indra got frightened when he had been summoned through mantra for being burnt on account of his having given refuge to a snake. Here the names of all types of snakes have been given indicating that in our ancient times, people had full knowledge of the various species of all beings or the zoology.

Ved Vyasa too came to Janmejaya after the yagya was over. Janmejaya worshipped him as he was a rishi as also the ancestor of Kuru Vansha. On Janmejaya having requested for narrating about the dissensions in Kauravas and Pandavas leading to Mahabharata, Ved Vyasa entrusted the job of narrating the entire history to Vaisampayanji. Before starting the narration of Mahabharata, Vaisampayanji, as per protol, at first paid respects to his guru Ved Vyasa, then to other rishis etc. and then started narrating the katha after certifying the bonafides of Janmejaya as a fit man to hear the katha. In Hindu Dharma, everyone is not eligible to listen to a Dharmik Katha like the katha was not narrated to a man, who did not have belief in it; who did not understand it or who had no respect for the same in his mind and so on. So Vaisampayanji first checked up his bonafides and then started narrating the same. At first he told the importance of Mahabharata as unless one knows the importance of a katha, he would not develop respect and belief for the same. There is a mention of the importance of brahmins and cows in the grantha. It is the abstract of all shastras and fit for being heard by the gentlemen, as it is considered to be most auspicious in all religions. It shows that there were more than one Dharrna at that time and all religions had their own faults etc. but each had faith in Mahabharata. It may be because it narrates the solutions of problems in all kinds of situations—spiritual, political, administrative and social—and anyone memorising it attains salvation, the last ambition of people of all Dharmas. In those times, all people performed as per their Varna Dharma and anyone not complying with the verdict of shastras was punished by the raja, who was the protector of his people and was responsbile to ensure the compliance of their respective Dharmas by all. If raja himself was adharmik, then he was dethroned or killed by praja. There was time when all rajas had become leisurely and did not care for the well-being of the people. They were rather causing all sorts of cruelties to the public for extraction of money. In such a situation, none had been performing as per tenets of his Dharma. So God came incarnate as Parshurama and annihilated all rajas, several times. Then the further generations of kshatriyas realised their Dharma and the society came on correct track. If raja complied with all canons of Dharma, then there would not be any chronic illness, no famines, no shortage of rains, no early deaths etc. as had been the case during Rama rajya, Yudhisthra rajya etc. This is the speciality in Hindu Dharma and, therefore, no where in the universe, has such a perfection been achieved. There is mention of Raja Puru and his son Dushyant and grandson Bharata having ruled the entire universe surrounded by four oceans.

पौरवाणाम् वशंकरो दुष्यन्तो नाम वीर्यवान्,

पृथिव्याश्चतुरन्ताया गोप्ता भरतसत्तम। (68/3)

This is a geographical fact even today. Those rajas had guaranteed independent living to all people in universe and ruled as per tenets of vedas/shastras, ensuring the attainment of Dharma, wealth and satisfaction of all ambitions and caring for their achievement of salvation too. Raja Dushyant had all these good points. Once when he went to a forest for hunting, he saw Shakuntala in the Ashram of Rishi Kanav. The rishi was not there at that time and he got attracted towards her. But he did not make any advances and told her that she was very charming and he felt attracted towards her but she should tell him who she was as the kshatriyas would not get attracted towards rishi's daughter. This was the culture in ancient India. He proposed himself if as was apparent from her beauty, she was an kshatriya girl as otherwise he had full control on his passions and he could never be attracted towards a brahmin girl. Shakuntala then disclosed that she was Menaka's and Viswamitra's daughter. Viswamitra being an kshatriya, Dushyant could propose himself to her if she accepted. On her acceptance only, they had gandharva marriage (Love marriage).

Before agreeing to her marriage, she indicated that she considered rishi as his father as he had brought her up like his daughter and she shall be married with the choice of the father only. She said a lady could never be independent. In childhood, she is dependent on the father and then on her husband and in the end on her children. So she could not accept any proposal for marriage without the knowledge of her father. Dushyanta, however, told that if she loved him, they could marry and indicated that there ware eight kinds of marriages.

1. Arranged marriage by father.
2. Marriage after holding a yagya and finding an eligible bachelor there.
3. Boy and girl living together and then getting married.
4. Marriage of girl on token receipt.
5. Marriage of girl in consideration of money.
6. Love marriage in which boy and girl marry of their volition.

7. Kidnapping and then marrying.

8. Winning the girl in battle.

He, therefore, persuaded her to accept love marriage as she also loved him.

Next day he left for his capital and forgot her because of some rishi's curse passed on Shakuntala, when she, having lost in the remembrance of Dushyant, could not entertain him in her ashram, as was the prescribed duty of any house-hold person in those days.

When rishi came back, he accepted the marriage as he knew Dushyant was an eligible raja for marriage with Shakuntala and he too would not have been able to find a better match for her. Shakuntala gave birth to raja Bharata, who again was the ruler of universe and on his name only India is called 'Bharat'.

After sometime, Rishi Kanva sent her to Dushyant as she could not be kept in the ashram for long after marriage. In the context of another marriage of Yayati and Devyani too, there is mention that marriage of an kshatriya with the daughter of a brahmin was forbidden and, therefore, inspite of Devyani (daughter of a brahmin) having developed liking for Yayati, a raja, the marriage, was not accepted unless the father of Devyani on her persuation, agreed for the same. In this way, although our rules of varna are strict with a view to maintain morality and also on biological consideration, but could be relaxed in deserving cases. Devyani had developed disliking for raja's daughter and the raja had to agree to the dictates for the satisfaction of guru's daughter as he could not afford to annoy the brahmin on the principle that one should leave one person of family for protecting the family; one family for the good of the village ; one village for the good of the janpada, and the universe for attaining salvation. This was the sense of sacrifice in our people in ancient times. Also it is said that one should be above all passions as even the entire wealth of the universe and all ladies of the land are insufficient to quench one's thirst of satisfying the passions. So, it is better to sacrifice fulfilment of passions and be content. In the context of handing over the throne, the principle, as per theory of primogenitor, was that only eldest son could become the raja but the raja could nominate a younger son too if the elders were not obedient to raja or were not capable of becoming raja.

Subsequently in that dynasty, raja Vichatravirya died in young age without any children. Then his mother asked his widow wife to bear child from her brother-in-law Ved Vyasa, and told that in this situation such bearing was allowed. So with the union of Ved Vyasa and Ambika, a widow of Vichatravirya, one son Dharitrashtra was born but since Ambika had closed her eyes, out of shock, at the time of conception, her son was to be blind. So another widow, again with union of Ved Vyasa, gave birth to Pandu and in the chain, a maid servant with the union of Ved Vyasa gave birth to Vidur. Although Dhritrashtra was eldest, he could not succeed in view of his being blind. Therefore, Pandu became raja. Pandu too had gone to forests after sometime and during his absence, Dharitrashtra officiated as raja, as a stop gap arrangement, as the kingdom could not be left without the raja. In the forest, Pandu got five sons—Yudhishthra, Bhima and Arjuna from his wife Kunti and Nukula and Sehdeva from Madri. After that he died while in forests and Madri burnt herself with Pandu. Kunti with five boys come to Hastinapur. The sons were brought up in the mahal and were imparted education by Guru Dronacharya along with one hundred sons of Dharitrashtra. This shows that there was the tradition of satee even in our ancient period of Ramayana or Mahabharata. Also that all Pandavas had born out of the union of Kunti and Dharmraj, Indra and Air and Madri and Aswani Kumars, shows that some procedure of aid (artificial insinuation by donor) might be available in those days too. On the death of Pandu, all Pandavas along with other brothers had slept on earth for 12 nights and there was mourning in entire Hastinapur for those days. Such a mourning for 12 nights exists even today. After the mourning period was over, Ved Vyasa had told his mother Satyawati that the period of peaceful living was over and a bad time was going to come. This was the forecast, which our munis could know by their knowledge and used to come true. He would have seen the friction to come up in Kaurvas and Pandavas, particularly because of the bad deeds of Duryodhana and other Kaurvas. He, therefore, advised Satyawati to go to forest in her last days.

In gurukula itself, Duryodhana had started feeling jealous of Bhima's bravery and Arjuna's skill in operating bows and arrows and had always been finding opportunities to harm them.

1. Once Duryodhana mixed poison in the food of Bhima but he still survived.

2. Again Duryodhana arranged to tie Bhima with a tree surrounded by snakes but still he came out alive although snakes had bitten him there but the effect of snakes' poison had undone the effect of poison taken by Bhima.

3. Kunti had known Duryodhana's designs on them but Vidur checked her from raising the issue as he knew that it was not the proper time for any agitation. It could be done only after the Pandvas had grown up. Vidur, however, had known that there could not be friendship between a rich and another poor man; an intelligent person with another foolish one; and one brave and another weak person. So there was no possibility of reconciliation between Kaurvas and Pandvas.

4. To show what they had learnt from the guru, a meeting was held. Arjuna was superb in operation of bow and arrow. There Karna appeared on the scene but he, being the son of a mean family, could not contest with kshatriyas and was, therefore, discarded. Duryodhana having seen in him a match against Arjuna, owned him and made him the Raja of Angadesha.

5. Kaurvas arranged construction of Lakshagriha and pursuaded Pandavas to go for an outing and stay there for a few days. When Pandavas went there, it was put on fire. However, Vidur had sensed the plan and had apprised Pandavas of the same as also sent an expert to dig a tunnel enabling Pandavas to go out of the griha. This was how Pandavas were saved and another lady, who had come to pass her night with five children was burnt. Kaurvas were happy to find all six burnt there and they even performed last rites, taking them to be Kunti and Pandavas.

6. The importance of gurus had deteriorated in those days. One Eklavya had come to Darona to learn the operation of bow and arrow but, not being a kshatriya, Darona refused to entertain him. He made a statue of Darona and learnt operation of bow and arrow from him. He became expert and came to Darona to offer guru dakshina. Since Darona did not want any one to excel Arjuna in dhanurvidya, Darona asked for right hand thumb in guru dakshina as without that thumb, he would not be able to operate the bow. Eklavya had to give the thumb in guru dakshina. In this way, Eklavya was deprived of operating the bow. This is the extent to which gurus had downgraded themselves in values in those days.

After the education was over, Yudhishthra had been appointed as Yuvraj as, he being the eldest son of Pandu, was the rightful successor to the throne.This, however, did not suit Duryodhana, who wanted to become Yuvraj. Then Yudhisthra became very popular in the praja by his just treatment. It was in this situation that Kaurvas made plan of killing the Pandvas but they were saved by Vidur, and Pandava, started living in forests in-cognito. Dharitrashtra was a party to the Lakshagriha plan as he himself had started feeling jealous of the bravery and popularity of Pandavas in Hastinapur and in other countries. Dharitrashtra then consulted Kanika, a mantri, in the matter. Kanika advised him that :

1. The raja should always be prepared to punish the undesirable elements.
2. The raja should not allow his deficiencies to be exposed.
3. The raja should keep a watch on the deficiencies of others.
4. the raja should attack the enemy after knowing his weaknesses.
5. The raja should accomplish after starting a job.
6. The raja should eliminate another raja wishing to conquer him.
7. The enemy should be attacked and killed in his bad times and when he is in trouble.
8. The enemy should not be underestimated as even a small enemy can harm the mightier raja.
9. The enemy should be killed even when he seeks refuge, when defeated, as in case he is allowed to go free, he would again attack. This is what had happened when Prithvi Raj spared Mohammed Ghori when he was defeated several times and ultimately he was successful in defeating Prithvi Raj when he had been killed. If Prithvi Raj had killed him and his commanders, he would not have dared again visit and attack India. This is how Mohammdans created terror in the minds of Hindus by killing lacs of them and ruled for over 600 years.
10. In respect of enemy, the raja should operate all the four cardinal principles of sam, dam, dand and bhed (साम, दाम, दण्ड, भेद)—This is how English had been able to have entire India at their feet.
11. The raja should at first kill the enemy and then all his relatives as had been done by Akbar, who after killing Hemu, defeated in battle, killed all his family members too.
12. For war and for defeating the enemy, any action is fair. This is the extent to which the Indian culture had degraded in Mahabharata time as such an action is against the Yudhniti propounded by vedas and shastras.

13. The raja should be very friendly with the enemy to win his confidence and kill him when he is completely downtrodden by circumstances and when the time is favourable to the raja.

14. The raja should win over the greedy by payment of money to the extent of his requirement, by bravery when it is feasible, by creating division in brothers to make the enemy weak and wining over a few to his side or by entering into friendship agreement with the comparatively brave raja so that he does not harm him but still the raja should be alert from all the rajas, particularly those around him.

15. The raja should appoint his spies in the territories of all other rajas so that he is able to know about any plan against him.

16. The raja should also keep spies in his kingdom, in markets, gambling places, sports complexes etc. with a view to keep him apprised of what was happening in his kingdom and that none was planning to dethrone him.

17. The raja should be very kind and benevolent in talking but very strict mentally. Even when he plans to do most dreadful actions, he should be smiling.

18. The raja should not have confidence even in his wives, sons etc. and proper watch be kept on them so that their plans/designs, if any, against the raja, could be known.

19. The raja should give all sorts of assurances to his people but should not comply with all of them.

20. The raja should never appear in rage and in pride and should always appear normal to all the people.

21. In case of trouble, the raja should adopt any method, which might be helpful in taking him out of that trouble and when he is relieved of the trouble, he should speak of Dharma.

22. The raja should attack the enemy when the enemy's force is weak; suffering from some ailment; is thrust in mud; is hungry or thirsty.

23. The raja should try to stop the supply line of the enemy's force and then sit alert. The force shall surrender after sometime when their supplies are not recouped.

24. The raja should be on the look out when the enemy is down in rejoicing or in pleasures etc. and attack at that time. This is how Mohammed Ghori attacked on Prithiviraj when he was enjoying with Sanyogita, and Aurangzeb's commander attacked on Shambaji, when he was down with drinks.

25. The raja should not let his designs/plans be known to his friends and foes.

26. The raja should not appear dreaded even when he is in danger. He should rather appear as if nothing had happened.

27. A raja, who becomes sympathetic to an enemy, who had been punished, is calling his death. He should not, therefore, spare such a punished enemy.

28. The raja should take time in complying with assurances, if anyone given but not feasible so that the assured person is always hopeful of getting the assured benefit and at the same time does not get anything.

29. The raja should keep his preparations on without anyone knowing the same.

30. He advised Dharitrashtra to keep the Pandavas in good humour and at the same time try to harm them or annihilate them.

31. The Pandavas being very brave, they should, therefore, be dealt with in such a way that he should not repent in the end, the Minister advised. With this the Minister went to his home and the raja was upset about how to eliminate the fear of Pandavas.

Then Dharitrashtra, Shakuni, Karna, Dushashana etc. met and made a plan to burn the Pandavas along with their mother Kunti and the outcome was the plan of Lakshagriha but Vidur could sense this plan and saved Pandavas from the clutches of this sedition. Lakh, jute etc. inflammable material had been used in the construction of Lakshgriha, which shows the expertise in these chemicals in ancient times. The expert dug a tunnel in shortest time— a civil engeneering job of that time. On Lakshagriha having been put on fire and taking the Pandavas, as having been killed, Dharitrashtra had showingly been in shock but internally he was happy and performed all last rites.

Having gone out from the Lakshagriha to deep forests, Bhima took all on his shoulders and in hands and went far off. On night when they were sleeping in forests, a rakshas Hidamb saw them and was happy to find them as he was a man-eater. He sent his sister Hidamba to check up who they were. Hidamba went there incognito as a beautiful girl and fell in love with Bhima, who appeared very brave to her. She proposed herself to him but he could not agree in the situation in which he had been placed. After some time the rakshas came there and there was a great fight in which the rakshas was killed. Kunti then agreed to the proposal for marriage but on the condition that Bhima would go to her house in the day and would come back in the night. Here a point has been made that in case of a lady asking for the marriage, the gent may agree to the proposal but it is seen that in this way Pandavas would have so many marriages, which may not be correct even for the rajas. This, however, had been a practice of that time that rajas had many wives. Bhima got one son Ghatotkachha out of that union. Kunti and brothers then went away from there to a village on direction from Ved Vyasa. In that village, one person was sent daily turn-by-turn for being eaten by a rakshas. Then came the turn of the house in which Pandavas were staying. They were husband, wife, one son and one daughter. Each had been justifying his going to rakshas and they had been crying. Kunti enquired and offered Bhima to be sent. Bhima went and killed the rakshas. All felt a sigh of relief. But it is strange that the raja of the area did not remedy the grievance of the villagers, when there were so much duty-bound rajas in those days.

Then the Pandavas came to know of the svayamber of Daropadi and many brahmins were going there for alms. They also told Pandavas to accompany them as Pandavas too had been living there as brahmins.

On the way, they met Gandharvaraj Chitrath, who had been enjoying bath in Ganga along with many ladies and other people were not allowed to be there. On seeing Pandavas, Chitrath got enraged and a battle ensued. In the battle, Gandharvaraj was defeated. Chitrath gave Pandavas, Chaksushi mantra, by which one could see anything in all the three lokas. He also gave many precious horses and wealth but Arjuna asked if Chitrath wanted to give those horses, wealth and mantra by being pleased or to save his life, then he would not accept the same. This was kshatriya-like and not Brahman-like as Chitrath had offered these things to him seeing him as a brahmin. Then Chitrath told that this was out of the friendship developed between them and then the same had been accepted. Having reached Drupada's capital, Pandavas stayed at the house of a potter. Next day there was the svayamber in which Pandavas sat with the brahmins. Krishana had been there and recognised them but none else could recognise them. Darupada had put the condition of marriage with a person, who could shoot the fish above a chakra, seeing the same from water below. This condition was with a view that such a condition could be fulfilled by Arjuna only and Darupada wanted Daropadi to be married to Arjuna only after having seen his expertise in Dhanurvidya. In the svayamber, all rajas, including Duryodhana etc., tried their luck but were not successful. Then Karna came there. He could probably do the job but then Daropadi refused to marry a Soot's son. Such a refusal was based on the condition of svayamber itself and Karna should not have come forward as he did not fulfil this condition :

एतन्महत् कर्म करोति यो वै कुलेन रूपेण बलेन युक्तः
तस्माद्य भार्या भगिनी ममेयंकृष्णा भवित्री न मृषा ब्रवीमि।

(84/36)

One, who is from a **higher family,** handsome, brave and with good moral character, and performed the job, shall have Daropadi in marriage. So Karna, although could fulfil the job of the target but being from of Soot family, did not qualify to contest, but he contested, possibly because at that point of time, he was raja of Angadesh. Seeing Karna, Daropadi said.

दृष्टवा तु तं द्रोपदी वाक्यमुच्चै-
र्जगाद नाहं वरयामि सूतम् (186/23)

Then Arjuna came forward from amongst the brahmins. Krishana and Balrama could recognise him but none else. Arjuna performed the job and Daropadi accepted him in marriage. All brahmins and kshatriyas were surprised on a brahmin having performed the job. The kshatriyas could not tolerate it and they created law and order situation there but Arjuna and Bhima subdued them all. They took Daropadi and went to the place of their stay. Daropadi's brother had followed them with a view to know their whereabouts and after listening to their talks, he could make out that they were kshatriyas. He told so to his father Darupada too. In this way, marriage was a gamble.

On the other side, when Arjuna and Bhima went to their place, Bhima told his mother that they had brought 'Biksha'. The mother, as usual, told them to distribute amongst themselves without actually seeing that they referred to Daropadi as 'Bhiksha'. Subsequently seeing Daropadi, she said, she had passed a wrong order and felt sorry. Daropadi was satisfied to have got the husband of her choice. She took her in the house. Yudhishthra, to fulfil what mother had said, thought over it but asked Arjuna to marry Daropadi as he had won her in svayamber. But Arjuna told that he could not marry when his elder brothers were still unmarried.

Then seeing everyone attracted towards Daropadi and with a view to avoid any dissension amongst the brothers, it was agreed that she would marry them all.

"सर्वेशां द्रोपदी भार्या भविष्यति हि नः शभा।" (190/16)

In the evening, Pandavas brought Bhiksha and Kunti entrusted it to Daropadi to take herself first and then to give to Pandavas. Daropadi obeyed the mother-in-law.

Next day they were called by Darupada at his house for celebrating the marriage. Then the introduction was made and Darupada was happy to know that they were Pandavas by their behaviour in mahal like the rajkumars. He also promised to get them their rajya back. He then arranged for Arjuna and Daropadi's marriage. Then Yudhishthra told that they all had to marry with Daropadi. This appeared very surprising as according to custom, one raja could have several queens but not the vice-versa. Drupada, however, agreed for marrying Daropadi with anyone of them. Yudhisthra told that Dharma is in a very minute form and people do not know it well. He only told that his mother had ordered them all to marry with Daropadi and they had decided to do as their mother wished. Then Ved Vyasa came there. They all (Pandvas and Drupada family) paid him respects. Vyasa accepted the respects and in turn blessed them and sat on the asan. He asked everyone to tell his opinion in the matter. Darupada told it as non-dharmik and against tradition as well. Daristdumana also raised a point of order as to how the elder brothers could cohabit with the wife of his younger brother. Yudhisthra told that it was not adharmik, as in Puranas also there is mention of one Jatila (Gautam gotra girl) had married seven persons. Similarly Kundu Muni's daughter too had married ten persons, who were brothers. Kunti also agreed with what Yudhishthra had said. Vyasa then called Darupada in isolation and told that, as narrated by Yudhishthra, such a marriage was not against the tenets of Dharma. Vyasa then told what had happened in previous life of Daropadi, when Shiva had fixed her as the wife of five gods in next life. These five Pandavas were those gods and Daropadi, that lady in previous life. So, the marriage was already destined. Darupada then agreed for the marriage after he had himself seen through a shakti what had happened in previous life. In this way in the ancient times, we had some power to know what had happened in the past. Might be there was some recording system at that time too, which had been played before Darupada. Also Daropadi is the Laxmi of Swarga, who had born out of fire and was thus not an ordinary girl. She was, therefore, already destined to be married with five

Pandavas. Then Yudhishthra first married Daropadi according to vedic tradition. Similarly, each of the five Pandavas married Daropadi each day. Daropadi used to pass night with her husband and appeared as a virgin, the next day. After marriage, Darupada handed over a lot of dowry in marriage to each of the five Pandavas. So the system of dowry had been there in ancient India too but it was given not under pressure or on any consideration but of his own volition by the parents of the daughter. Krishana also presented many valuables in the marriage in view of Kunti being his aunt (बुआ). So it was also a recognised tradition for the meternal uncle to give valuables in the marriage of the wards of the sister. This tradition still continues.

Kaurvas also came to know through their spies that they were Pandavas, who were considered to have been burnt in Lakshagriha. Similarly, all other rajas too came to know of this fact through their spies. It shows that there was a strong spy system working for each raja as per shastras. Duryodhana etc. then prepared themselves to attack on Pandavas and kill them while they were without any power but Shakuni forbade them telling that Pandavas were very powerful and now they also had the help of Darupada with them. It was then decided that they should accept and welcome Pandavas in Hastinapur as it was difficult to conquer the fort of Darupada which had walls all around; there was canal and trenches on all sides and then walls further to trenches. There was a lot of foodgrains stock in the fort and it was protected by brave men. It was, therefore, difficult to conquer that town. This shows how experts our people in ancient times were to have erected such safe forts and towns. Then an agreement was arrived at between Kaurvas and Pandavas. When Vidur came to know of the marriage of Pandavas with Daropadi, he told Dharitrashtra, who expressed happiness on Pandavas having been alive and arranged for their reception in Hastinapur. But again Duryodhana and Dharitrashtra, not actually being happy, proposed to attack Pandavas and kill them when they were not with any force but then Bhishma etc. did not approve of it and allotted Khandava Desh to them for being ruled. Pandavas shifted there and made their capital at Indraprastha. They brought a lot of wealth by conquerring many rajas and became quite well off. Indra also sent Vishwakarma to construct the capital for Pandavas. A very beautiful town was constructed. Narada then came there. Yudhishthra etc. welcomed him and paid their respects as per protocol and entrusted entire rajya to him. Narada was happy. He asked Pandavas that Daropadi was the wife of all of them. They should, therefore, make such rules that no dissensions arose amongst them because of her. He also referred to some cases of such dissenssions. Pandavas then made a rule :

ऐकेकस्य गृहे कृष्णा वसेद वर्षमकल्मषा
द्रोपद्या न सहासीनानन्योन्यं योऽभिदर्शयेत
स नो द्वादश वर्षाणि ब्रह्मचारी वने वसेत। (211/29)

(Daropadi shall pass one year with each of them in turn and in case one of the brothers sees Daropadi sitting with another brother in isolation, then he shall go to forest for 12 years and live like a Brahamchari). Because of this rule, there was no dissension amongst the Pandavas. After some time, the cows of a brahmin had been stolen in this rajya. He came crying to the mahal and held raja responsible for the theft. Arjuna immediately prepared himself to bring the thieves to book but at the store of the armaments, Yudhisthra had been in loneliness with Daropadi. He could not wait and gate-crashed to take the arms. He then saved the cows of the brahmin. Here is a matter of protocol as it is said to be the duty of the raja that no thefts took place in his kingdom. Arjuna, even at the cost of breach of the understanding between the brothers not to enter the room when any of the Pandavas was with Daropadi in isolation, entered their place and so had to go out to forests for 12 years.

अरक्षितारं राजानं बलिषड्भात्रहारिणम्
तमाहु सर्वलोकस्य समग्रं पापचारणिम्।। (212/9)

(A raja, who even after taking one-sixth part of products, is not able to protect the people, is a sinner in the kingdom) Although Arjuna had offered to undergo the punishment, Yudhishtra defended his action as :

1. He had entered his room after asking him, and
2. By entering the room to take dhanush to bring back brahmin's cows, he had actually served the king i.e. Yudhishthra and, therefore, he was not to be punished.

But Arjun still left for the forests to fulfil the understanding. On the way, Arjuna while taking bath in Ganga, was caught by Ulapi, the daughter of a Nagaraja. Arjuna brought her out of the water. Ulupi then became a beautiful girl and offered herself to Arjuna but Arjuna said that he had to pass twelve years in forests as a brahmchari and so could not accept the offer. Ulupi, however, told that the rule of remaining brahmchari was with reference to Daropadi and any offer from any other girl would not involve any breach of the understanding. Arjuna then yielded and by their union one son Iravana was born. Arjuna continued in the forests. During this time, he met Krishana at Prabhas Tiratha. From there they both went to Dwarka. Dwarka was appropriately decorated to welcome Arjuna and Dwarkavasis had come in lakhs to have a glimpse of Arjuna. Arjuna paid respects to elders, embraced his equals and loved affectionately the youngers. He spent many days with Krishana. The punishment to Arjuna was to live in forests for twelve years as brahmchari but as interpreted by Ulupi, the punishment must, in spirit, have been with reference to remaining away from Daropadi only. So that purpose was served here if Arjuna wooed anyone during that period as also if he lived in the town also away from Indraprastha. Here he met Subhadra, Krishana's sister, and they got attracted towards each other. He enquired from Krishana. Krishana knew that Balrama wanted Subhadra to be married with Duryodhana and Krishana wanted her marriage with Arjuna so he arranged Subhadra being kidnapped by Arjuna. With this Balrama and other people of Dwarkapuri got enraged and wanted to give a fight to Arjuna but Krishana pacified them and marriage was formally celebrated, as kidnapping other girl by kshatriyas with the consent of the girl is allowed in religion. Arjuna stayed there for an year. Abhimanyu was born there. After twelve years, Arjuna and Subhadra came to Indraprastha. Arjuna paid respects to Yudhishthra and Bhima, his elders and embraced youngers. He then broke the news of marriage with Subhadra. Initially Daropadi was not happy and rebuked Arjuna but Arjuna, after accepting his mistake, pacified her. Subhadra was then accepted in the family. After some time, Krishana too came there with many soldiers, dowry etc. Yudhishthra sent Nakula and Sehdeva to receive him. Here question arises that according to protocol, Yudhishthra, a raja, should have gone to receive another raja Krishana. Thus why Nakula and Sehdeva were sent ? The answer can, possibly be that Krishana had come there not as a raja but as the brother of Yudhisthra's younger brother's wife. So the formality could be fulfilled by Nakula and Sehdeva and Yudhishthra had been acting as the guardian of Arjuna. So he needed not go there. Krishana was received in Indraprastha with all protocols. Krishana paid respects to elders, Yudhishthra and Bhima, and embraced Arjuna, Nakula and Sehdeva. He offered a very rich dowry to the people of the groom from bride's side. This was accepted by Yudhisthra as usual as per vedic tenets. Then Krishana stayed there with Arjuna and others for a long time.

Abhimanyu was made well-versed in dhanush vidya by Arjuna himself, who was expert in this vocation. Here dhanurvidya has been told of four types :

मन्त्रमुक्तं, पाणिमुक्तं मुक्तामुक्तं तथैवच
अमुक्तं च धनुर्वेदे चतुष्पाच्छस्त्रमीरितम्। (220/72)

1. मन्त्रमुक्तं : This is by mantras only.
2. पाणिमुक्तं : When arrow is shot from bow by hands.
3. मुक्तामुक्तं : When Mantra and hands, both are used.
4. आमुक्तं :· This is not operated but by seeing it alone, the enemy runs away.

This shows that there were various kinds of armaments like rockets, bombs, missiles etc. existing at that time and the battles were not only by use of bow and arrows. Our armament technology of the present time is yet to catch up to that standard. Daropadi also gave birth to five children—one each from her five husbands. Prativindhya from Yudhishthra, Sutsome from Bhima; Shrutkarma from Arjuna, Shatanika from Nakula and Shrutsena from Sehdeva. They were all very brave.

The praja was very happy under the kingship of Yudhisthra. All the brothers had brought lot of wealth from various countries after conquering them and made those countries their vassals. Once, when Arjuna and Krishana were in Khandava forest, a brahmin came and asked for being fed. He said he was in fact Agni god and in her food, she would eat Khandava forests by being burnt but this forest was protected by Indra's men. A fight between Krishana/Arjuna and Indra was, therefore, involved. They agreed for it. Khandava forest was burnt and the battle ensued. Krishana and Arjuna defeated Indra and other gods. They gave lot of armaments to them. This entire story would infact lead to conclude that Pandavas had been allotted the forests in their kingdom and they required some clear area for urban and rural habitation. Krishana and Arjuna would, therefore, have cleared the forests for this purpose and would have entered into the contract for planning and creating the town for their capital, subsequently called Indraprastha,with 'Mayasur'. In this way, farms, gardens were provided and capital structured. This is called clearance of Khandava forests. Mayasura, having been saved from being killed, had offered to do some job but then as per vedic protocol, Arjuna told that in case he wanted to help because his life had been saved, then he shall not ask for any help. He, therefore, directed him to serve Krishana as that would be treated as his service too. But Krishana asked him to construct the capital for Pandavas. Then only Indraprastha was constructed, where water was there but it appeared dry and where it appeared dry, there was water;

where there was door, it did not look like a door and where there was no door, it appeared as if there was a door and so on. So this was a unique mahal in the capital. In fact Pandavas had created such mahals and so much of other wealth in a very short time, that it caused jealousy to Kaurvas, particularly Duryodhana and Dharitrashtra and this became the reason for Mahabharata war. After some time, Krishana went to Dwarka after getting a protocolic send off from Indraprastha.

After some time, Narada muni came there. He was worshipped by Pandavas and made to sit on sinhasan as per protocol. Narada asked Yudhisthra so many questions that indirectly he coached him of all the requirements of a raja :

1. Whether the earnings are sufficient to meet his requirements ?
2. Whether he has been treating brahmins, kshatriyas, vaishas and shudras well as they deserved to be treated?
3. Whether he has been utilising the time properly ?
4. Whether he keeps a watch on the designs of the other rajas ?
5. Whether his ministers etc. are not in league with the enemies ?
6. Whether he is able to differentiate between friends and foes ?
7. Whether he has kept lethargy under control ?
8. Whether he takes care of kisans and labourers and they have not been ignored ?
9. Whether he is able to keep secrecy, where required ?
10. Whether he takes quick action on remunerative projects.
11. Whether the evaluation of products is got done by reliable persons ?
12. Whether the gurus in gurukulas are sufficiently learned?
13. Whether there is sufficient stock of foodgrains in the forts and the same were also sufficiently equipped and protected by brave persons ?
14. Whether he has made sufficient arrangement of spies and out of spies whether atleast twenty percent are under his strict surveillance ?
15. Whether the Purohit is obedient, from high family, well-educated and whether he respects him ?

16. Whether capable pandits have been engaged for sacrificial yagyas etc. ?
17. Whether all his ministers are noble, capable and honest?
18. Whether all persons have been provided jobs according to their capability ?
19. Whether the collectors have not been harassing the farmers in evaluating crop and collecting the rajbhag?
20. Whether ministers etc. have cordiality and affection for the raja?
21. Whether he honoured the learned ones according to their capability ?
22. Whether the praja respected him like their father or not ?
23. Whether he attacked the enemy when he was on a weak wicket ?
24. Whether before attacking the enemy, he assesed his capability and the topography of enemy's area ?
25. Whether he kept on bribing the braves in enemy's army ?
26. Whether his army is well equipped with elephants, horses, chariots, treasures, suppliers, doctors and spies ?
27. Whether he had been creating the famine conditions in the area of the enemy ?
28. Whether his foodgrains stock, armaments, means of transport, main gates are all in tact or not ?
29. Whether his staff does not indulge in drinks, gambling etc. ?
30. Whether he is able to meet his expenses within 1/4th, half or 3/4th of the receipts ?
31. Whether his accountants and treasurers have been presenting the accounts to him or not ?
32. Whether he has not engaged greedy, thieves, enemies or incapable persons in Government jobs ?
33. Whether there are water ponds in the rajya for storing rain water?
34. Whether the villages are managed by capable panchas or not ?
35. Whether like towns, villages are also properly protected or not?
36. Whether in the rajya the women are duly protected or not ?
37. Whether he gets up after sleeping upto midnight and then

thinking of the well-being of the people or not ?

38. Whether he gets up in time and finishes his daily chorus in time or not ?

39. Whether the brahmins take their food in the mahal or not ?

40. Whether there are no back-biters in his ministers and high officials ?

41. Whether he keeps on listening to religious discourses from capable persons or not ?

42. Whether he feels obliged to the persons doing good to the rajya?

43. Whether he is aware of all the penal codes etc. or not ?

These are indirectly the jobs required to be done by a raja. Subsequently Yudhisthra worshipped Narada and answered his questions.

Narada also explained the management in Brahma Loka, Indra Sabha, Kuber Sabha, Yamraj Sabha etc. so that Yudhisthra could also make up deficiencies, if any, in his sabha compared to those of the above sabhas. Narada then advised him for conducting Rajsuya Yagya.

Yudhisthra had been thinking over holding the yagya. He consulted his brothers and Krishana on the matter. Krishana told him that for conducting Rajsuya Yagya, he had to have all rajas under him as vassals or his friends. In that connection at least one Jarasandha was there, who would not bow before him and in that case it would be difficult to perform the yagya. Therefore, first thing was to go to each raja and check up his position in this regard and to arrange for fighting with Jarasandha. Krishana then went to Jarasandha along with Arjuna and Bhima incognito as brahmins and asked for dual fight. He agreed for dual fight with Bhima. The fighting continued for a fortnight and when they were both tired, Krishana got hold of a 'sarkunda' and tore it through and through. Bhima could understand that Jarasandha would die when he is torn. He acted accordingly and killed Jarasandha. His son was coronated. As per vedic tenets, after defeating the raja, the kingdom was handed over to him after getting some wealth as compensation and making him his vassal state, or in case of death, his son was coronated as in Bali's place Sugreeva had been coronated and in Ravana's place Vibheesana had been coronated. So Jarasandha's son Sehdeva had been coronated as a raja of the vassal state under Indraprastha. Then the Pandavas went across to all rajas and collected presents and their submission to Indraprastha rajya. The yagya was then arranged in which all rajas, including Shishupal, Dharitrashtra, Bhishma, Daronacharya, Duryodhana etc. had joined and all had brought lots of presents. There was none, who had brought less than one thousand gold mohars. Yudhisthra had alloted duties to his brothers, e.g., Dushasana was entrusted with the arrangement and distribution of eatables; Sanjaya was to look after various rajas; Bhishma and Darona were there to monitor the entire proceedings; acceptance, accounting and distribution of jewels, diamonds etc. was for Kripacharya; Vidur was entrusted with the distribution of wealth; Krishana was to wash the feet of all rishis and brahmins ; Nakula was to take care of Dharitrashtra, Jayadhratha etc; Duryodhana accepted the presents given by various rajas; Aswatthama was to welcome the brahmins. Like this, each was entrusted with some job befitting his capability. This division of labour indicates the management expertise of the people in those days.

At the start of the yagya, a question of protocol arose as to who should be worshipped first. Yudhisthra asked Bhishma, as he was the eldest and most learned person in the family as also in the gathering. He suggested Krishana being worshipped first. So Yudhishthra started worshipping Krishana but although all rajas accepted it, Shishupal said Krishana was simply a gawala. He was neither a raja/kshatriya nor a brahmin. Then how he was number one to be worshipped. Then Bhishma told that he was in fact God incarnate and, therefore, he deserved the first pooja. Shishupal, however, inspired all rajas to revolt but then Krishana went on listening to the rebukes and when he had completed one hundred, Krishana called his chakra and cut Shishupal in two pieces. (Krishana had undertaken to Shishupal's mother that he shall excuse his hundred abuses). Then he was immediately cremated and yagya continued and finished. Lots of alms were given to brahmins and others, who deserved; lakhs of brahmins took meals, and so on. It was a great rejoicing and all gods accepted 'havi' in the yagya themselves. All rajas accepted Yudhisthra as their chakravarti raja. All this pomp and show and honour of Pandavas, however, created jealousy in the mind of Duryodhana, who already had always been jealous of them. He desired to see the mahal and lifted his clothes thinking of existence of water, when it was dry and fell in the water, when he thought it was dry. He bowed thinking there was a door but it was not and ran into wall when he thought there was door and so on. On such omissions, Pandavas and Daropadi laughed but Yudhisthra checked them and called for clothes to be changed. Although so many rajas etc. had come there but why all these omissions took place in the case of Duryodhana only might be due to the fact that, he being very jealous of Pandavas, was not alert while walking and was almost lost, or in other's cases such omissions went unnoticed.

2
Sabha Parva

After the completion of the yagya, all went to their houses. Duryodhana also went to Hastinapur but he was very much in rage on accont of jealousy for Pandavas and because of his omissions, which made him a laughing stock in Indraprastha. He consulted Shakuni as to how to finish Pandavas. He wanted to fight but Shakuni told that Pandavas were rather brave and could not be subdued in battle. He told him that with the approval of Dharitrashtra, a sabha could be arranged in which Yudhishthra would be invited for gambling and since he was not good at it, he would lose his all as Shakuni was the master of the gambling and playing the dice. They accordingly made Dharitrashtra agree for it although it was opposed by Bhishma, Darona, Vidur etc. At first Dharitrashtra too objected to it but due to the affinity of his sons, he gave in. Vidur was sent to call up Pandavas for the gambling. Although Yudhishthra did not agree and thought gambling was bad but since Dharitrashtra had called them, he agreed. In the gambling, he lost all his wealth. Then he put his brothers and himself at stake and then Daropadi was lost in the stake. They called Daropadi in the sabha. The Purohit, who went there was asked by Daropadi whether Yudhisthra had put her on stake first or himself first. He told it was Yudhishthra first. Then she said Yudhishthra having lost himself could not put her at stake. He had no answer to it. Then Dushashana came and he too was asked the same question. He was also told that since she was in periods, she could not go in the sabha of the elders but Dushashana caught her by hairs and took her to the sabha. All felt ashamed on this operation of Kaurvas but could not speak. Daropadi put the same question in the sabha but none could reply. Yudhishthra only said that he had put Daropadi at stake and lost her. Yudhisthra's reply should have met the question of Daropadi as even after Yudhisthra had lost himself, Daropadi continued to be his wife. Ofcourse whether

Yudhisthra could put Daropadi at stake without her cousent is a moot question in modern era but in ancient India husband could perhaps do it. Then the infamous action of removal of Daropadi's clothes was carried out but the clothes would not end. Dushashana then gave up the play. Then when Daropadi had been crying, Dharitrashtra asked her for two boons. She at first asked herself to be released from 'Dasatava' and then her husbands. She was asked to have one more boon but she refused. Then Dharitrashtra of his own, returned all the lost kingdom and wealth to Pandavas. The Pandavas thereupon went back paying their respects to all in the sabha.

When they had left, Shakuni and Duryodhana again overpowered Dharitrashtra seeing that Pandavas had again got everything back, to again call them for gambling on one condition only that whosoever lost would undergo twelve years exile in forests and one year more during which if they could be traced, they would have to repeat it. Pandavas were called back and put to gambling and they again lost so they prepared to go in exile to forests.

Questions now arise as to how Bhishma, Vidur etc., being against gambling and the bad way adopted time and again by Kaurvas, agreed for gambling after initial hesitation. Why Pandavas, being Dharmatama, agreed for gambling knowing that it was ethically a bad play? Why answer to Daropadi's question was not given by anyone? The gambling was restricted to wealth, then how the elders permitted the brothers and self and ultimately Daropadi, being put at stake? How, when Daropadi was brought in the sabha by catching from hairs, none objected to it, rather all seeing it kept quiet and how all agreed for Daropadi's clothes being removed in the sabha? How again Pandavas agreed for gambling when they had once seen its result in the hands of Shakuni ? Correct, Bhishma, Darona etc. had undertaken to be loyal to throne but the throne cannot order such immoral happenings and such happenings having been tolerated is a blot on the intellect and morality of the people, seen with highest esteem and honour. Also Daropadi could pass a curse on the evil doers being a pious lady but she chose to fight out the entire happenings. But for the help by the almighty in extending Daropadi's clothes, the position would have been very embarrasing for all Hindus and for would be and had been chakravarty rajas and queen Daropadi. The action, as it was, had been against all protocols and ethics of morality. But this all had to happen as Kaurvas and Pandavas had ultimately to end up in Mahabharata war in which all rajas had to take part and had mostly to die. This had even been anticipated by

Vyasa, who had visited the yagya and had told Yudhisthra :

> त्वामेकं कारणं कृत्वा कालेन भरतर्षभ,
> समेतं पार्थिवं क्षत्रं क्षयं यास्ति भारतः।
> दुर्योधनापराधेन भीमार्जुन बलेन च। (46/12)

(Meaning that Yudhisthra being the medium, there shall be a war of all rajas in which almost all shall perish. That happening shall be because of the fault of Duryodhana and bravery of Arjuna and Bhima. Eversince then Yudhisthra had been quiet upset).

3
Van Parva

In the beginning of the parva, (Vanparva and Viratparva), the poet, as per protocol, again remembers the almighty god as is done in the beginning of each project. So each volume of the Grantha is a project for this purpose.

नारायणं नमस्कृत्य नरं चैव नरोत्तमम्,
देवीं सरस्वतीं व्यासं ततो जयमुदीरयेत्। (1/1)

(Here Shri Krishana and Saraswati have been remembered before starting writing/reading Mahabharata. As already indicated, the dialogue between Janmejaya and Vaisampayanji is going on. Pandavas and Daropadi had gone to forests for thirteen years after having been defeated in gambling. Vaisampayanji tells about how the Pandavas passed their time of thirteen years in forests. Hearing of the Pandavas going to forests, the residents of Hastinapur and Indraprastha felt distressed and vowed to accompany them to the forests. This is exactly what had happened when Rama had gone to forests. Although Yudhisthra pursuaded them to return to their houses, yet some brahmins did accompany them and remained with them for the entire period. The residents had been criticising Bhishma, Dharitrashtra, Darona, Kripacharya etc. for having arranged the gambling and thus entraping Pandavas and forcing them to go out to forests for thirteen years. During the last one year, the Pandavas had to live in hiding and if they could be traced during that one year, the period of exile shall restart. In this way, Kaurvas from their side had bade good bye to Pandavas for good. The residents were out in praise as the Pandavas had been ruling according to tenets of vedas, where everyone was happy and in peace. In such a situation, the praja too are prepared to sacrifice their all for the sake of the raja. The people, who knew of their Dharma had inter alia stated that out of over-ambitiousness, man falls for passions and this leads to arising of thirst for everything in the universe and in case of non-fulfilment of this thirst, one starts doing non-religious works leading to his decay in the universe. Such, it was stated, was the condition of Kaurvas, who would in course of time come to a state of decay. Similarly, the thirst for wealth is also ever-increasing and does not end till one feels content with what one has. If one feels content and choses the way of Dharma, one adopts, yagya, study of Dharma, alms-giving, tapasya, truthfulness, excuse and control over passions and self.

God helps those, who pass their time as per Dharma. Many brahmins had accompanied Pandavas to forests. Then there arose the problem of feeding them all. They remembered Surya, who provides food to all. Surya gave them one utensil, which would give meals to as many people as they wished. Possibly in the forests, Pandavas would have reached a place where there would have been many fruit, trees and because of sun, the fruits would have ripened which Pandavas and brahmins could take. Thus because of Surya, they managed meals for the entire period of exile.

This only confirms that one does get the result of the labour put in by him. Pandavas got fruits from the trees in the forests.

On Pandavas having left for forests, Dharitrashtra felt sad about it although it was all his creation. Possibly he agreed for the gambling as per Duryodhana's wish. So the bad men would always plead for adharmik things and afterwards because of what public and other elders would have told that it was not a good action, he would have started repenting over his actions. One should, therefore, adequately examine the implications of such important decisions before complying with the same lest one should repent later on. In such a situation, only guru or a saintly man can console the repenting person. Here Vidur did this job by coaching Dharitrashtra about what Dharma is and how far it plays a part in man's life. He also told that Duryodhana etc. were on wrong path and the raja should not have acted on their advice. Now the possible way of undoing the wrong already done was to restore the Pandavas with their rajya on their return after completion of the period of exile. It was, however, still too much for Dharitrashtra to absorb as he was too much lost in the affection for his sons that he even expelled Vidur from the rajya. Even Duryodhana etc. did not sit quietely and planned to kill Pandavas in forests in isolation. When they were going to proceed, Muni Vyasa reached there and checked them from taking such an action as Pandavas were enough, even alone, to defeat them all.

Krishana also came to meet the Pandavas in forests. He told that gambling was bad and should have been avoided. He told that he could not know all this happening as he was away to fight with Salve, an asura, otherwise he would not have allowed this situation to come as he knew that Kaurvas were out to destroy Pandavas somehow and capture Indraprastha. Mentioning Salve, Krishana told that his capital was like a fort, with hillocks on all sides; then trenches had been provided; then there was a place for the army to fight and adequate arms fitted there with tunnels to recoup the eatables and armaments in to the fort. Then was arrangement for playing band whenever there was any invasion so that entire town could rise to face the enemy. Drinking was not allowed during battle as they could be subdued by the enemy being unconscious after being drunk. As a war strategy, all bridges connecting the town with mainland had been destroyed and all boats captured so that the enemy could not reach the town. Also all wells had been dried up or possibly poisoned so that the enemy would not use these. Entry passes had been introduced and anyone going out and entering the town had to had the entry pass. Many cavalry men and troops had been posted on all roads so that the enemy's men could not enter the town. All troops had been fully paid and were given new uniforms and armaments so that they were able to face the enemy with full force. Further, all men of Dwarka took part in the battle. This was the Bhartiya rule but it had been lost sight of during Rajput peiod when fighting was only for troops and it did not matter, who the ruler was for other people of the community. On reaching Dwarka, Krishana also started for fighting with Salve after worshipping Shiva and with the blessings of brahmins.

Here Krishana had been shown worshipping Shiva like Rama had worshipped Shiva before attacking on Lanka. This is to eliminate the difference between Shaivaites and Vaishnavaites.

तै प्रहृष्टात्मभिवीरै राशीर्भि नन्दितः
वाचयित्वा द्विजश्रेष्ठान् प्रणम्य शिरसा भवन्
शैव्य सग्रीव युक्तेन रथेनानादयन् दिशः,
प्रध्माप्य शंखप्रवरं पांचजन्यमहं नृप। (20.12/13)

Krishana's army included troops, elephants, horses, chariots and on foot. Krishana's sarthi had been awfully injured in the bettle field but he still continued to control the chariot. Such was the devotion of the sarthis for the master in those days. That is why Arjuna had chosen Krishana as his sarthy in Mahabharata.

Krishana went back after meeting Pandavas in the forests asking them to prepare themselves for the war after completion of the period of exile. Then, Marcandey, a rishi, had come there. On Daropadi asking him why there had been suffering inspite of her husbands being brave and very capable rajas, Marcandey told that Kaurvas were in rage and Pandavas were peace-loving; prepared to excuse even the ill-doers. Such persons had to suffer but ultimately they would be the winners. Marcandey told that :

1. Neither rage nor power to excuse is superior but these have to be exercised according to the environ and the position in which one is placed.

2. The person in rage may harm others as he cannot decide about the good or bad part in anything.

3. Such persons even suffer for themselves, as those, who have been harmed, would harm them in course of time and those, who have been benifitted would leave them.

4. One is in rage for the sake of having a luxurious life but such a life cannot give contentment to the people and there shall be a non-ending wish for the luxuries.

5. Therefore, one should not always be in rage nor only in a mood to excuse but have to strike a balance and timing when to be in rage and when to excuse.

6. The incidences for adopting the policy of excuse are—

(a) A person, who has been good, if commits some default, he should be excused for one folly.

(b) The folly, committed out of ignorance, should be excused.

(c) The first folly should be excused for any one.

(d) Kaurvas have once been excused. They do not deserve to be excused again for such cheatings.

(e) A man in rage can never decide between good and bad. One should, therefore, not have rage to the extent possible.

(f) One should avoid being in rage, even if the other man is in rage and try to pacify such person. If still he does not behave then he should be reciprocated with rage only.

(g) One, who is able to suppress rage, is a pious man.

(h) One can reach conciliation with another only if rage is not there otherwise rather than conciliation, there would be fighting only to solve the problem.

(i) The tapasvis did not resort to rage as rage killed their tapasya.

(j) Even now Duryodhana shall have to be given a chance to conciliate, otherwise war is imminent.

During the period of exile, Arjuna was advised to go to Indra and ask for arms (sastras) from him. But for going to Indra, one shall have to first come across Shiva while passing through Kailash. So Arjuna had to face and fight with Shiva. Shiva was pleased and gave him very good astras. He then went to Indra. In Indra sabha, he learnt music. Once Urvashi came to him for having relation having been charmed by him. But Arjuna said that he saw his mother Kunti in her and did not agree to sleep with her. She passed on a curse on him that he would look like a eunuch for an year. What has been shown here is the maintenance of protocol as Urvashi had been the mother of Shakuntala, who was a great grand mother of Arjuna. So, how Arjuna could have relations with her although Urvashi told him that all these earthly relations had no relavance in swarga. This is Bhartiya protocol, not available anywhere in the universe. Arjuna got many godly armaments from Indra and other gods.

Sanjaya had known all this and narrated to Dharitrashtra, who was upset on knowing the preparations Pandavas were making to fight with Kaurvas on completion of the period of exile, and thought that on their return and fight, his sons would be no more. Sanjaya had also told that Krishana, Darupada and others had vowed to give a tough fight to Kaurvas. All this information had been received by Sanjaya from his spies. It shows that spy system was very much in vogue in those days.

Similar to the happenings with Yudhisthra, Nala and Damyanti too had faced tough situation. Nala too, a raja, had been sent out in exile after he lost his rajya in gambling. Damyanti too went with him but having not been able to carry Damyanti with him, he left Damyanti in a sarai and went out in search of a job. He got the job of a sarthi with a raja. Damyanti too went through forests and reached the mahal of a raja, where she got a job. Then Damyanti's father's men recognised her and took her to her father's house. They also searched for Nala and could find him. Nala and Damyanti then came together. Nala, having learnt the intricacies of gambling, defeated the raja, who had snatched his rajya and became raja.

Here Damyanti had told Nala that after marriage, the husband cannot live without wife. She said that according to doctors, there is no panacea for man's ailments, except wife, after marriage. In her absence man remains upset :

न च भार्यासमं किंचिद् विद्यते भिषजाम मतं,
औषधं सर्वदुखेषु सत्यममेतद् ब्रवीमि ते। (61/29)

This had been the relation or protocol between husband and wife in Hindus eversince ancient times. Here it has been shown that.

1. One gets consolation after hearing to the happenings severer than to those one has to face. Yudhisthra, while in forests, thought that he had been having the worst time in the universe and after hearing the incidence of Nala and Damyanti, he felt consoled that fate can make the man face worst times.
2. There was the system of love-marriage in those days. Nala and Damyanti had love marriage.
3. After marriage, the wife was prepared to face all good and bad times with the husband.
4. Neither husband nor wife can be in peace if separated after marriage, particularly when the wife had been fully devoted to the husband.
5. Husband is all in all for the wife after marriage.

भर्ता नाम परं भार्या भूषणं भूषणैर्विना
एषा हि रहिता तेन शोभमाना न शोभते। (68/19)

The wife saves herself in bad times from all evil environ and even in bad days she does not have rage or bad feelings for the husband thinking that good or bad days are all in fate and the husband cannot be taken to provide good days only.

Raja Nala has been shown as raja of Jambu Dweep. Jambu Dweep is one of the Six Dweeps (continents) mentioned in Bhagwat. It represents Asia. So Nala is said to be the emperor of Asia and he had many rajas under him, working as vassal states, the concept prevalent in modern international relations. Hearing Nala-Damyanti episode, Yudhisthra felt consoled along with Daropadi. When the stars are not favourable and the efforts go waste, then the great men do not lose heart.

Yudhisthra too then learnt gambling from Brihadsva, who was stated to be the master of gambling in those days so that in case of eventuality, he may face the Kaurvas in gambling too. Then rishis narrated the importance of Pushkar Lake, Kurukshetra and other places around Kurukshetra from religious point of view. Our rishis have attached importance to the places of pilgrimage with a view to imbibe faith in the people for those places and such pilgrimage gives chance to the relations' meeting as also absorption in almighty forgetting the involvements in universe. Similarly, importance of Gangasagar, Ganga, and Prayag was also explained.

In Hindus, the sons have to perform 'shradha' of the dead elders so that their souls may rest in peace. In that context once Agusta muni saw his ancestors being punished by Yamaraja. On enquiry, he came to know that shradha performed by Agusta's son could save them from the punishment inflicted upon them. Agusta then tried to have a capable woman. He came across Lopamudra as the fit lady but she wanted a luxurious life as she had been passing in the house of her father. Agusta being a muni, did not have that much wealth. So he went to raja Shrutarva and demanded wealth. The raja placed his account of receipt and expenditure of the kingdom before the muni. The account did not show any surplus. Agusta muni, therefore, thought that payment of any money from a balanced account would be at the cost of some one else. So he left the mahal without taking anything. He then want to another Raja Bradhanasva. He too presented his kingdom's account which, too was balanced. He, therefore, did not accept any money from him too. Then he went to a rich man Trasadasyu but he too had a balanced account. So leaving his mahal too Agusta muni was told that Ilwal, asura only could spare wealth for him. The muni went to him and he gave the required wealth. Here the writer has desired to bring out that :

1. The munis did not have any wealth and in case of need, they used to go to rajas for wealth.
2. The rajas were, as per 'Rajadharma', required to take 'Rajbhag' out of the products in the kingdom and used to spend out of that collection. The rajas generally had the balanced accounts.
3. The rajas did have a budgeting system like the present day and used to spend commensurate with the income.
4. The raja could give out of his receipts only at the cost of some other item, which had to be dropped.
5. It was obligatory for the munis to accept wealth from the raja

only if there was surplus in receipts and not otherwise.

6. The asura rajas did have a lot of wealth because they used to collect the same from other rajas. They could, therefore, afford to pay to the munis etc. although it was again not desirable to accept money from the asuras as the wealth with them was generally ill-gotten. But since here it was a necessity of the muni, he would have accepted the same—might be after making sure that it was not ill-gotten.

Agusta muni then went to Lopamudra; married her and on birth of a son, performed shradha of the dead ancestors and then again left for tapasya. So the munis could involve in worldly pleasures only out of necessity and as soon as the necessity was fulfilled, they resorted to tapasya again. Similarly, Viswamitra too, resorted to tapasya after Urvashi had left.

Further mention is that of Parshurama. He was the son of Jamadagni rishi, who came in conflict with Raja Sahasrabahu over a cow in possession of the rishi, which raja had taken by force. Parshurama got enraged and killed the raja and brought back the cow. But, although the raja was at fault, the rishi did not approve of the killing of the raja by his son as :-

1. Killing anyone is the job of the raja and not of a brahmin and in case the raja himself was involved, he could be punished either by public or by God.
2. The raja could be punished by public in case of any wrong done by him as Rama had to separate Sita on criticisim by a washerman.
3. The job of the brahmin is only to excuse and not to punish.
4. For having killed the raja, Parshurama had to repent.
5. The brahmins could also adopt the vocation of a kshatriya, if need arose as Parshurama had subsequently killed all kshatriyas as they had left the 'Rajdharma' and got involved in luxuries forgetting the public well-being. In such a case, it was better to kill such rajas.
6. This also proves that the varna institution was not as per birth but it could be changed according to one's interest. Similarly Viswamitra had become a Brahmrishi from an kshatriya. There was, therefore, flexibility in varnasharma institution of Hindus.

Once Parshurama's mother had gone to fetch water for puja. She saw Raja Chituratha and fell in love for him resulting in delay in bringing the water for puja. The rishi could know it and asked his five sons—one by one—to kill their mother for having indulged in bad action but the sons refused. Parshurama killed them for disobeying him. Then Parshurama, the youngest son, agreed and killed his mother. Subsequently, having been very happy, the rishi asked Parshurama for a boon and then Parshurama requested for his mother and all brothers being enlivened. The request was conceded. This way Parshurama obeyed the father and at the same time, made his mother and brothers enlivened. Here the question of protocol arises whether, the position of a father is higher to that of the mother. In Ramayana, the position of mother is shown higher. At the time of Rama going to forests, Kaushalya had asked Rama, if the order for going to forests was that of the father, then she, having greater right over the son, could undo it but if the order was that of Dasratha and Kaikayee, both, then she was helpless. So here protocolically, the mother should have a greater right over Parshurama, If so, then how Parshurama could kill his mother except that the mother had indulged in undesirable action. Also how Jamadagni rishi, who some time back had coached Parshurama that brahmin is there to forgive and the job of awarding punishment is that of the raja, had ordered his sons to kill their mother. This too is unprotocolic. The rishi could have alternatively passed a curse on the wife, as Gautam had done in case of Ahilya.

In this context, on Sahasrabahu having been killed by Parshurama, his sons killed Parshurama's father Jamadagni but then Parshurama killed Sahasrabahu's sons and brought back the head of his father and joined the same with the other part of the body and thus Jamadagni was re-enlivened. This shows that surgery was at its top in those days, when even after murder one could be enlivened after joining head with the body.

There is also mention of the greatness of granting refuge to anyone. Raja Ushinar was a very benevolent person. Once Indra and Agni wanted to test his benevolence. Agni as a pigeon came in the lap of the raja and Indra as an eagle followed asking raja to give the pigeon to him as it was his food and one could not deny anyone taking his food. The eagle said :

आहारात् सर्वभूतानि सम्भवन्ति महीपते,
आहरेण विवर्धन्ते तेन जीवन्ति जन्तवः (131/7)

Everyone is born of food, brought up with food, lives with food and dies for food. Then how he could be denied his livelihood. The raja offerred his flesh equal to that of the pigeon and this was agreed to. Then Raja cut his flesh and gave. Then Indra and Agni came to their actual forms and blessed him. Here the benevolence of the Indian rajas has been shown even for the birds, what to speak of human beings. Also, it is shown that even gods used to test the benevolence of human beings. This also shows the sacrifice for one, who has taken refuge.

In Mahabharata, as in all puranas, the Dharma has been narrated with some incidence. Once, Bhima had been going to bring kamal (lotus) for Daropadi. On the way he found Hanumanji blocking his way. After some dialogue and discussion, Hanuman allowed him to go and told him the way he could get the lotus. At that time Hanuman had told the Dharma of each of the varnas as under :

1. The gods have to be worshipped by everyone and gods become happy soon if properly worshipped by yagya, puja, havan, mantras etc.

2. One should follow the tenets of one's Dharma, i.e., the Dharma of one's varna.

3. Learning and teaching are the jobs of brahmins.

4. Governance and to punish the criminal/enemy are raja's Dharma.

5. Trade and agriculture are vaisha's Dharma.

6. Further, truthfulness, holding yagyas, accepting alms are brahmin's jobs along with getting yagyas performed and teaching vedas and shastras to others, for earning livelihood.

7. Service of the three varnas is the Dharma of a shudra.

8. In respect of kshatriyas, Hanuman further told that protection of life and property is the prime Dharma of kshatriyas. The raja should further :

(a) Respect the learned and elders.

(b) Follow four principles of sam, dam, dand and bhed.

(c) Should keep spies and well-qualified advisors.

(d) Should keep all consuitations secret.

(e) Should not have women, poor, minors, greedy and mean persons as his advisors.

(f) He should appoint religious persons in jobs pertaining to Dharma; economists in economic planning; eunuchs to serve ladies and strong men to deal with criminals.

(g) He should properly analyse the viability before starting any project, and once started, should complete it quickly so that its advantage could be obtained.

(h) He should be benevolent to those seeking refuge under him.

(i) The raja should be thankful to his helpers and should punish the persons, who are ungrateful.

(j) Hanuman promised to help him, when Bhima would fight with his enemies and this could be known by his roar.

While Bhima had gone to collect a lotus, he saw gardens with many flowers. Names of so many flowers have been given indicating the knowledge of botany in those days.

Once Bhima had been caught by a pythone and it did not leave him inspite of his strength. Then Yudhisthra came in search and found the pythone having caught him. He checked up, who the pythone was. The pythone told that he was a raja and had become pythone because of a curse passed on him by brahmins for having harassed them. Now Bhima could be left if he could give correct replies to his questions. Yudhisthra agreed to the same as indicated below :

Question : Who is brahmin and what is that he is desired to know?

Answer : A brahmin is he, who has truthfulness, almsgiving, forgiving, very intelligent, not rude, tapasvi, and benevolent.

Question : Truthfulness, almsgiving, non-raging, non-rude, non-violence are in people of all varnas. Then what is special in brahmins ?

Answer : In fact anyone having above elements is a brahmin and anyone not having these is a shudra.

Question : It means that varna is of no avail, if a person is known by conduct alone.

Answer : It is difficult to distinguish anyone by varna as there is cross-breed in existence. All persons are born from women. Birth, living and death are common in all human beings. A child, when born is shudra and he becomes whatever only after he is educated in a particular vocation of brahmin, kshatriya or vaish.

The python was satisfied with the replies and he left Bhima from his captivity.

Marcandey rishi too had come to meet the Pandavas in the forests. Yudhisthra asked him about the Ishwara-Jeeva relation and the way how one faces the result of good or bad deeds.

1. When a soul leaves the body, then how one faces the good or bad deeds in this universe or the other one?
2. Whether one faces the result of good or bad deeds in this universe or the other and how the account of good or bad deeds is maintained after one dies?

Marcandey told that although Yudhisthra knew all this but he had probably asked this question for the knowledge of the human beings in general. At first Brahma was born. Then he created all species and the dharma-shastras. At that time all people were truth-loving. Then they started the bad deeds and as a result some were born in mean families, some remained ill and some became rakshasas. Their age was fixed according to their deeds. One creates a record of his good or bad deeds in ones' life. Then leaving that form he joins another specie. There is no time gap between leaving one specie and joining the other one. How one gets the next specie. The family in which one is born etc. starts from the birth itself as per deeds of the previous life. This is called 'Swarga' or 'Naraka'. One gets the result of the deeds in previous life in the next one—some results appear immediately and some take time. Some get good results in this universe and some in the other universe and some get good results both in this and the other universe. Then there are some, who neither get good result in this universe nor in the other one but later on. Those, who have lot of wealth, they enjoy the life in this universe satisfying all their lusts but do not enjoy in the next universe.

Those, who are involved in yoga, tapasya, studies and do not fall prey to worldly ambitions, they do not enjoy life in this universe but enjoy later on. But those, who lead their life as per Dharma; earn money honestly; get married and still keep the life involved in Ishwar-bhakti, enjoy life in this universe as also in the next one. Those, who do not study nor perform tapasya etc. but are busy in producing children only, they can neither enjoy this life nor the next one. One should, therefore, enjoy life in this universe as per tenets of Dharma and then leave this univers. In this way he shall lead a contented life in this universe and would get salvation at the end of his life.

Marcandey goes on telling that Krishana is the incarnation of almighty God. He is responsible for creation, maintenance and annihilation of mankind. He knows everyone but he is not known even by vedas. After the destruction of whole world (प्रलय), he created it. At first Satyayug came, in which there was all truthfulness only. It remained for 4000 years. Then came Tretayug, which lasted for 3600 years followed by Duapar for 2400 years and then shall come Kalyug. After Kalyug again there will be destruction and then Satyayug and so on. In Kalyug, tap, jap, alms, yagya etc. shall be in name only. The brahmin shall be doing shudra's jobs and leave jap, tapasya etc. The raja shall be only extractor of money from public and would not care for their well-being. Kshatriyas too shall be doing mean jobs. The cows will not give much milk. The brahmins shall be greedy; the grihasthas shall be cheats; there shall be no rains in time; no crop leading to famines; all shall tell lie and the vaishas shall deceive others to make money by foul means; there shall be violence everywhere; people shall have shorter lives; the ladies shall not have satisfaction with one husband and vice versa. There shall be no trust-worthy person and hunger and poverty shall prevail. Then only there will be the overall destruction and new cycle of yugas shall start after God has eliminated all bad characters. In Satyayug there is all truthfullness; in Treta, three-fourth Dharma; in Duapar, half and in Kalyug only one-fourth and by the end of Kalyug there will be all lies only when no one shall act as per his Dharma and there shall be all anarchy and chaos, when father shall kill the son and vice versa; no affection or love in husband and wife, guru and disciple etc. No one will recognise God as almighty. In a few words there would be all kinds of sins only.

In the context of a person leaving his home and resorting to tapasya in young age, it has been stated that one Kaushika brahmin left his parents, when he was quite young and went to forests for tapasya. After some tapasya, one day he had taken bath, when a bird eased on him. The brahmin looked at him with rage and the bird was burnt. The brahmin became proud of his tapasya and went to the town. At one house, he begged but the house-lady was busy in serving her husband. She took sometime in attending to the brahmin. The brahmin was enraged but the lady told that she was not the bird, who could be burnt by his rage. The brahmin was surprised how she could know it as he had not told the fact of having burnt the bird to anyone. Then the lady directed him to go to a butcher, who shall tell him everything. He went to the butcher, who was selling meat. After he was free, he took bath, attended to his parents and then attended to the brahmin. Ofcourse the butcher begged to be excused for the delay but his first duty was to attend to his daily job of earning the livelihood and then attending to his parents. This he could not give up at any cost. The butcher then told him that he would have been sent by the lady. The brahmin was surprised how he had known this fact.

The brahmin asked him how while doing the mean job of selling meat, he had attained this knowledge. The butcher told him that he was dealing in meat because of some curse passed on him in his previous life but he did not kill animals and had only been selling the meat out of the animals killed by others. This too for earning his livelihood. He told that he treated his parents as gods. After they had taken meals, he took; after they had slept, he slept. He gets up before them in the morning and then attends to their comforts and then goes to the shop etc. He told the brahmin that he too should go to his home and attend to his parents as one can not be comfortable, annoying the parents. The gain by tapasya is momentary and gets finished after one is down in rage or due to other vices whereas the service of parents does not permit one to fall victim to the vices. The brahmin then went to his home; served his parents and thus got salvation. Then the protocol between the husband and wife and the parents and son has been narrated. This is missing in present day life, particularly in the west, where the children have their own ways and after they become major they do not care for the parents, when they need the children most. Such a protocol in Hindus is called the Dharma.

Once Krishana with Satyabhama, his wife, had come to meet the Pandavas in the forests. While Krishana had been busy in talking to Pandavas, Daropadi and Satyabhama were sitting together and talking about thier husbands as usual with the ladies. The difference in the condition of the two was whereas Krishana had many wives, Daropadi had five husbands. Satyabhama asked Daropadi how she had been able to control the five brave Pandavas, as her husbands. Daropadi in reply narrated the entire protocol between husband and wife. At first Daropadi told that to have control over the husband, is for characterless wives. The wives with good character in fact like to be controlled by the husband and that is what she had been doing, i.e., remaining under the control of her five husbands and such a thinking was atleast not apt for the head queen of Krishana to ask for any mantra, herb, power, tap, vrat etc. to control the husband. Indirectly she told that usage of such things only destroys the relation between husband and wife and the husband would start doubting the intentions of the wife. Moreover by serving some herb to husband can also lead to husband falling ill because of its use as someone who wanted to kill a person might give poison to the wife saying it was herb to control the husband and on its being served, husband might die. Therefore, a pious lady should not harm the husband in any way and should :

1. Serve the husband and his other wives without any pride, rage or desire.
2. Serve the husband killing all her ambitions.
3. Be always alert not to speak anything, which may not be assimmilable to the husband.
4. Not talk to any stranger person and should not look like a shameless lady.
5. Treat the husband as the best and above gods and should serve him well.
6. Not divert herself even by seeing gods, or very brave and rich persons etc.
7. Not eat till the husband and her servants had eaten; should not take bath till husband had taken bath and should not sleep till husband had slept.
8. Keep the house, utensils and clothes (of self and of husband) clean.
9. Prepare the meals as are liked by the husband and serve at appropriate time; keeping all the requisites for preparation of meals, in store.
10. Never be lethargy or come in contact with undesirable ladies.
11. Not stand on the door unneccessarily, and should laugh when with husband only.
12. Never be uncontented and should live as the husbands wants her to live.
13. Leave taking eatables, drinkables and other things as are not liked by the husband such as if husband is vegitarian, the wife should not be non-vegetarian.

14. Live as per tenets of Dharma for wife and her varnadharma.
15. Be ready and in the service of the husband since morning and serve the parents, elders, guru etc. as directed by the husband.
16. Serve the husband herself even when servants are there.
17. Keep the accountal of the income and expenditure of the husband and put demands as may be met out of that income.
18. Serve the husband well as it is because of the happy husband only that she gets good clothes, good ornaments etc. and all other things of leisure and pleasure
19. Get pleasure after pleasing husband only.
20. Be in waiting when the husband is likely to come, and then serve him as per his requirements.
21. Be prepared to do a job herself even when the husband entrusts the job to the maid servant to be done.
22. See that the bed has been arranged before the husband enters the bed room.
23. Not leak out anything told by husband in confidence.
24. Use good clothes, ornaments, perfumes etc. to attract the husband towards herself.

Hearing that the Pandavas were happy in the forests and had collected many armaments from gods, Dharitrashtra was upset. Then Duryodhana, Karna and Shakuni made a programme of giving a fighting in the forests and kill them there itself in solitude. They told Dharitrashtra that they were going to forests for hunting etc. and to see the Pandavas living like tapasvis. The mean persons, get pleasure in seeing others unhappy. Even though he did not like the programme, Dharitrashtra gave permission to the Kaurvas for going to forests with the warning not to interfere in the way of living of the Pandavas. They started with a big army and supplies etc. In the forests, Gandharvas were playing. Duryodhana's men asked them to shift from that place as Kaurvas were to stay there. They developed quarrel leading to a big battle between the Gandharvas and Kaurvas. Karna was made unconscious and Duryodhana etc. had been arrested by Gandharvas to be taken to their loka. At that time some sainiks of Kaurvas went and requested Pandavas to help them. Bhima, Daropadi etc. were happy to know that the Kaurvas had already been finished by the Gandharvas without their having to face them. But then a question of protocol arose that the fighting was between the Kaurvas and Pandavas and when Kaurvas were down and arrested by aliens (Gandharvas) then Pandavas should help them and ordered Bhima and Arjuna accordingly.

> प्रियदर्शी महाबाहुर्धार्तराष्ट्रो महाबलः
> गन्धर्वैर्ह्रियतं राजा पार्थस्तमनुधावत (242/11)

Pandavas had been told that Kaurvas had come to destroy them in isolation in forests but they had put themselves to trouble. Inspite of bad intentions of Kaurvas, Yudhisthra said :

> भवन्ति भेदा ज्ञातीनां कलहाश्च वृकोदर,
> प्रसक्तानि च वैराणि कुलधर्मो न नश्यति। (243/2)

Even if there is infighting in brothers, when it comes to the image of the family, then all should unitedly face it.

> परै परिभवे प्राप्ते वयं पंचोत्तरं शतम (243/4)

We are one hundred and five in case an alien attacks us.

Tnis is what Bhartiyata is and we were at the top of the universe, with such thinking only. When we lost such thinking and did not give a united fighting to Muslim invaders, we were subdued and had to face their rule with all attended tyranny for 600 years and further came in the rule of English because they took advantages of the infighting of all rajas and nawabs and became the rulers of India helping one against the other.

During that time Yudhisthra listened to Duryodhana crying for help and told Bhima etc. that there would not be anything more pleasing than to help Duryodhana when he was begging for it. So the Pandavas went and defeating the Gandharvas, got Kaurvas released. But then Duryodhana was so much down with shame that he decided to die and not to return to Hastinapur. Then Karna etc. all pursuaded him not to resort to suicide and face the things in the universe and then Pandavas had only done their duty in helping the Kaurvas as they had been living as subjects of Kaurvas and as subjects it was their duty to fight for their raja. But there was no effect on Duryodhana. Then some Asura rajas came and pursuaded Duryodhana not to finish his life and should for their sake return to Hastinapur. Duryodhana then agreed to return. On return, when Bhishma etc. came to know of what had happened, they praised Pandavas and cursed the Kaurvas. He advised them to come on good terms with Pandavas but then Karna spoke otherwise. Then Karna told Duryodhana that he would go to 'Digvijay' and that shall convince him of his bravery. Karna then proceeded to Panchal and other places and defeated all rajas and took lot of wealth from them as compensation/presents. This was the common practice at that time that after defeating the raja, the rajya was handed over to him or his son after taking some presents and after his having accepted the suzerainty of the victorious raja and was allowed to rule autonomously so that independence of the raja was not crumbled. Karna had won Drupada, the raja of Panchal, and the rajas of North, Anga, Vanga, Kalinga, Mithila, Magadha, Karakkhanda, Nepal, Kerala, Kosala, Tripura, Mohan, Rukmi, and all rajas in south. So in this way, Duryodhana/ Dharitrashtra became the chakravarty ruler of the entire Bharat. On return to Hastinapur, Karna was held in high esteem and was received with great honour by Duryodhana, Dharitrashtra, Dushashana etc. brothers according to normal protocol.

तमागतं महेष्वासं धार्तराष्ट्रो जनाधिपः
प्रत्युद्गम्य महाराज समातृपितृ बान्धवः। (254/23)

But Dhartirashtra (a chakravarty raja) going to receive Karna is not normal protocol. Duryodhana should have been enough but Dhartirashtra might have gone on pursuation by Duryodhana to accord the best possible reception to Karna. Also Karna was not visiting Hastinapur on a normal visit but after conquering the entire Bharat. Therefore, chakravarty raja Dharitrashtra would have gone to receive Karna as he had been made chakravarty by Karna himself by conquering all rajas. After that Duryodhana and Shakuni took it for granted that Karna would defeat the Pandavas and that was the main purpose of Karna to impress and encourage the demoralised Duryodhana by his bravery.

Now one jealousy still remained in the mind of Duryodhana i.e. the holding of Aswamedha yagya, which Yudhisthra had held so that he came at par with him and got recognition from all rajas as was the case with Yudhisthra as seen by Duryodhana. So, Karna, now having held the digvijaya, Duryodhana gave his mind for holding Aswamedha yagya. He called Purohit to work for holding the yagya but the Purohit and other brahmins told him that till Yudhisthra (an elder brother) and Dharitrashtra were alive, he could not hold Aswamedha yagya. But, the Purohit advised, there was another 'Vaishnav' yagya. Which was equally important. That could be held by Duryodhana. So, arrangements were made for holding that yagya in which all rajas, including Pandavas, had been invited. All the rajas had been allotted accommodation for their stay. Lots of presents were received and alms given to brahmins and others. But still some rajas did say that Duryodhana's yagya did not equal that of Yudhisthra's and this, was not even 1/16 th of that yagya. Some, however, prasied Duryodhana for having performed that yagya.

As per protocol, at the start of the yagya, Duryodhana at first touched the feet of his parents; then of Bhishma, Darona, Kripacharya, Vidur etc. respectively and then all elders, brahmins etc. Then the younger brothers paid their respects to Duryodhana. Here as per protocol, guru should have been honoured first but he comes after parents, and Bhishma, which does not appear as per protocol unless it is held that the yagya being conducted by Duryodhana was yagya on behalf of Dharitrashtra, the raja. So he had to be honoured first. Anyway he was on the throne surrounded by his brothers. There, Karna promised to kill Arjuna, who had frightened Kaurvas.

On the other side, Pandavas had already spent eleven years in the forests. They had become very weak. Once Ved Vyasa came there to see his grandsons. He became upset seeing them very weak but then to encourage them he only said that tapasya is a must to have anything marvellous. So sorrows and pleasures visit the people in turn and that makes the life more enjoying.

नातत्तपसो लोके प्राप्नुवन्ति महासुखम्,
सुख दुखे हि पुरुषः पर्यावणो पसेवते। (259/13)

Tapasya only carries the man closer to almighty. Further, truthfulness, non-rage, worshipping gods, respecting guests, control over senses, non-violence, keeping oneself pious—internally and externally — and not finding faults in others is the way of life one should adopt. These are the things our munis have told after their life-long research and living in this way, one would be happy in this universe as also attain salvation—the ultimate aim.

How much jealous of Pandavas, Duryodhana had been, is know from the visit of Durbasha muni. Durbasha muni used to lose temper on very small things and used to pass on curse. He once came to Hastinapur. Duryodhana respected him carefully and having been happy, he asked Duryodhana to ask for some boon. He only asked him to visit Pandavas. Durbasha was with his thousand disciples. So Duryodhana thought that in case he went to Pandavas, they would not be able to serve him and his people in the forests and consequently the muni would pass curse on them. Such a mean mentality towards his brothers, who had saved him from the clutches of Gandharvas is rather unthinkable. So he went to Pandavas and asked them to arrange for meals till they came after taking bath in the river. They were very upset as they had already finished their meals at that time and it was not bhiksha time as well. Then Daropadi remembered Krishana, who came and helped them by arousing a feeling of fulfilment in the muni and his men and they went from the river after taking bath. This way Krishana saved Pandavas from very awkward position, they would have to face.

Once, when all Pandavas had gone for hunting, Jayadratha, brother-in-law of Duryodhana came there while going some - where else and saw Daropadi. He fell in love for her but when he made advances towards her, she told that she was Daropadi, the wife of Pandavas, who would be just coming but then like Duryodhana, he was a bad character. He forcibly kidnapped Daropadi. Then on the way, Pandavas saw him. They defeated him along with the army and arrested him but then acquitted him being the husband of Duryodhana's sister. It only shows that inspite of the other man doing all bad things, one should not lose patience and treat the other man honourably, particularly when one is closely related. Already Bhima had given him a lot of beating and then he was brought before Yudhisthra to decide. Yudhisthra and Daropadi excused him but his head had been shaved so that he could remember the fate of his evil action and was asked to call himself as the servant of Yudhisthra in all gatherings of rajas.

But the incidence of Daropadi's kidnapping left a mark or Yudhisthra. He was very upset as to why Daropadi had been facing all those bad happenings. It is seen that whenever Yudhisthra had been having such feeling and was upset either Ved Vyasa or Krishana or some other rishi would come to console him and boost his morale. This is how God saves his bhaktas in case of difficulty. Here too Markandey Muni came and Yudhisthra asking him why Daropadi had to face all those happenings, he told that still greater trouble had to be faced by Sita in the forests along with Rama and Lakshmana but ultimately Dharma had its way and brought happiness. The muni told that Ravana, an asura raja was Rishi Pulstya's son and Brahma's grandson. He had, by virtue of tapasya, got boons from Brahma that he shall not be defeated by anyone in the battle and shall not be killed by anyone except the human being. He accepted this condition as he thought that human being would never be able to kill him. In this way, Brahma also kept some loophole while awarding the boon so that he could be killed too in case he became a cruel man, as Ravana had been.This, therefore, is the protocol between bhagat and Bhagwana. Then Kumbhkaran asked that he should have sleep for 6 months in a year. This was accepted. Vibhasan asked for Bhagwad bhakti, which again was granted. Then Ravana settled in Lanka and caused terror all around. He would not permit any yagya etc. being performed and would kill rishis etc. This all caused havoc in the universe as a result of which,as usual, God came incarnation as Rama in Ayodhya after all gods complained to Brahma for his having granted such a boon to Ravana as made him an asura. All gods then came as Vanaras etc. to help Rama in battle with Ravana. After education, Rama and other brothers started taking part in rajya job. Then Viswamitra took Rama and Lakshmana to forests to protect him performing yagya, from the asuras. After completion of yagya, the four brothers got married. Then Raja Dasratha thought of handing over rajya to Rama and himself to proceed for vanprastha. He consulted the guru and the council. This indicates that there was democracy at work in a limited way in those days as raja could not take any important decision without having consulted the guru and the council.

मंत्तयामास सचिवैर्धर्मज्ञैश्च पुरोहितैः
अभिषेकाय रामस्य यौवराज्येन भारत। (217/7)

But then Manthra, the maid servant of rani Kaikaye came to know of it. This shows that the queens had their own spying system in the mahal so that they were able to know all that had been happening in the kingdom. Manthra narrated everything she saw to her queen Kaikayee and coached her to manage somehow so that Bharata became the raja. The queen had two boons to ask. Here was the time for that one and as per first Bharata should be raja and for another Rama should go and live in forests for fourteen years. Although Rama had never done anything which could cause any annoyance to Kaikayee, yet her feeling was that he would not care for her after he became raja. This is what we call the step-motherly treatment.

Here the first boon asked was to make Bharata as raja and the second to send Rama to forests. If a little intelligence had been applied, raja Dasratha could have fulfilled the first boon first and since Bharata would not have accepted it as raja himself had thought so too, the fulfilment of the other could have been saved. Further, according to the theory of primogenitor, the eldest son had a right to the throne, unless he was incapable or the father and the council did not like him. Here the father and council were very much in for Rama only to be coronated. Anyway

Ram, Lakshmana and Sita had gone to forests and Dasratha had died and Bharata had been called to Ayodhya. Bharata was very annoyed and rebuked his mother and then proceeded to forests to meet Rama taking many brahmins, Vashistha muni, Vamdeva and other elders from the town so that all may say that Bharata never wished to be the raja and he was not a party to Rama going to forests and Rama should as such return back to Ayodhya. Rama, however, pursuaded Bharata to go back to protect the praja, the primary duty of the raja, and he would fulfil father's will.

"गच्छत तात प्रजा रक्ष्या सत्यं रक्षाम्यतं पितुः" (277/39)

Then in the forests, once Sarupnakha, the sister of Ravana, Khara and Dooshana came and fell in love for Rama/Lakshmana. She proposed herself but was not accepted by them. As she insisted and frightened them, her nose and ears had been cut off, as killing of a lady is prohibited according to tenets of shastras. She complained to Khara and Dooshana, who were also killed with their army by Rama. She then went to Ravana. Ravana made plan and went to Maricha, who because of fear from Rama, had become a tapasvi. After Ravana had settled, Maricha asked him the purpose of his visit. He narrated the plan for his becoming the golden deer, whom Rama would like to kill and in his absence, he would kidnap Sita. Maricha discouraged him and told him that Rama was very brave and should not be antagonised. But Ravana threatened him. So he became golden deer. Rama went to kill him. While dying Maricha said in loud voice 'Hai Lakshmana, Hai Sita'. Sita got frightened that Rama was in trouble and asked Lakshmana to go to help Rama. But Lakshmana was there for her protection. So he did not proceed. Then Sita rebuked him:

नैस कामो भवेन्मूढ़ यं त्वं प्रार्थयसे हृदा (278/27)

Lakshmana was a man of character but had to proceed on Sita having rebuked him. In his absence, Ravana kidnapped Sita. Jatayu (an eagle) tried to protect her but he too was killed. Rama and Lakshmana on not finding Sita in the ashrama, became upset and started searching for Sita. They met Jatayu, who told that Ravana had taken Sita. Rama performed the last rites of Jatayu himself. This shows that all beings are equal to Rama. Rama then met Sugreeva and killed Bali after entering into an agreement with Sugreeva for mutual help.

There was thus a system of entering into international agreements. Sugreeva challenged Bali for battle. Tara had through her spies, known about the arrival of Rama and his friendship with Sugreeva. This shows that even the vanar raja had his spying system. Tara checked Bali but then, as a raja, he could not stay back and fought with Sugreeva, and was killed by Rama. Sugreeva was coronated. Rama passed the period of rainy season but Sugreeva, having been lost in the pleasures of the rajya, forgot Rama's job — the fulfilment of his part of the contract. Rama got annoyed and asked Lakshmana to check up the position and only to frighten Sugreeva and not to develop quarrel with him if he was making efforts to search Sita. Lakshman was in rage but then Sugreeva came forward to receive him and worshipped him. Sugreeva told that he had already sent Vanaras in all directions to find out the whereabouts of Sita. All vanaras returned and Hanuman told of having found Sita in Lanka and also handed over the ornament given by her. This was the protocolic requirement to bring something in writing or otherwise to confirm that he had actually met the desired person. Rama proceeded to Lanka with 60 crore troops. Then the question of crossing the sea arose. Rama told that all could not cross sea and also they could not go by boats etc. as in that case the army would be scattered and the enemy would be able to kill it easily. This was the war strategy, known to the people of that time. Then a bridge was constructed by Nala and Neela vanars. They must be good engineers and the construction of such a bridge is the engineering fete of those days, not so far marvelled. At that time, Vibheeshana came to join Rama. Then doubts were expressed by Sugreeva about his bonafides, being the brother of the ememy but Rama verified his antecdents and only then gave him refuge.One consideration in keeping such a person was that he would tell every secret of the enemy, and Vibheesana proved to be of help to Rama in this respect. Rama entered into an agreement with him for mutual help and in turn to make him the raja of Lanka (Again an international agreement). Ravana sent his spies to see the reaction of Rama on Vibheesana joining him as also to know the strength of Rama's army. But they could be recognised by Vibheesana and were arrested. Then Rama took pity on them and acquitted them.

Before, attacking Lanka, Rama gave one more chance to Lanka's raja to surrender. This is how Indians believe in peace and resort to war only when there is no other alternative left. Lanka was fully protected by a wall, trench etc. and there was sufficient stock of armaments, foodgrains etc. for the army. Also there was sea on all sides and very strong gates to enter. There were radars fixed on all sides to detect any encroachment and missiles and launchers provided. Angada was sent to Lanka. He asked Ravana to surrender to Rama if he did not want war with him. But Ravana did not agree. Rama then attacked Lanka and killed all. There is mention of guns, topkhana, missiles, rockets and other bombs etc. used in the war. This shows the advancement in this direction in India in those days. Subsequently, these appear to have gone out of use after Mahabharata. The war strategy of Shukracharya and Brihaspati was at full play in the battle from both sides. Of course, laws of war were followed viz. One person fighting with one, army fighting with army etc. This shows that there were —

1. Strong forts provided to protect the kingdom from any invasion.
2. Most advanced armaments, guns, topkhana, missiles, rockets etc. were in use besides the traditional weapons.
3. Proper international agreements had been entered into for mutual help between the rajas as was between Rama and Vibheesana.
4. War was resorted to as the last way to settle a dispute and all other ways were tried for a mutual settlement.
5. Civil engineering was also at the top as enabled a bridge having been constructed on the sea.
6. Aeroplanes were also in use showing technological advancement.
7. There was constant dialogue between the persons of the earth and of other stars. Infact all gods had come to witness the battle. After Rama and Lakshmana had become unconscious as a result of some hitting by Meghnatha, Kuber sent some medicines which enlivened them showing the advancement in medical science.
8. The asuras had been fighting with all 'mayavi' way but Rama could undo all these manipulations.

After Ravana was killed, all gods came to praise Rama. Then Vibheesana was coronated. Although Rama should have straightaway brought Sita back but there were protocolic requirements to be fulfilled. This required Vibheeshana to be coronated first as :

1. The kingdom could not be left without a king even for a single day. So the job on top priority was to coronate Vibheeshana.
2. Then the king of Lanka only could release Sita as she was with him for so much time.

Then Vibheeshana brought Sita but she had to establish her piety before she could be accepted by Rama after having stayed in Lanka for so many days. Then all gods from 'Swarga' came and vouched her piety after which only Rama accepted her. Dasratha too had come there. He had not attained salvation as he had died in affection of Rama, so he had not fully detached himself from worldly involvements. Dasratha came there and was not respected by Rama as his father but was treated as his bhakta. Then Dasratha got salvation. Then gods asked for any boon to be given and Rama asked all the vanaras, who had given up their lives for the sake of gods only, should be re-enlivened. This was done. Then Rama bade farewell to all and set for Ayodhya. But here one protocol came up whether Rama should straightaway go to Ayodhya or not. As a precaution, Rama sent Hanumana to Ayodhya incognito to check up about Bharata's intention as to whether he was still waiting for Rama to come, so that he may not have to face an awkward position if situation was different. Also another purpose was to advice Bharata of Rama's arrival in advance so that he was prepared to receive him. After Hanumana's return, Rama reached Ayodhya and he was received with full protocol. Then Bharata, retunred to Rama the rajya of Awadh, which was held by Bharata, as a trustee.

> तस्मै तद् भरतो राज्यभागतायातिसत्कृतम,
> न्यासं निर्यातयामास युक्तः परमया मुदा। (291/65)

This shows that Bharata recognised Rama as the successor to the throne and had been acting as Rama's lieutenant in his absence for fourteen years to govern the kingdom. Then all brahmins, rishi Vasistha, Vamdeva coronated Rama as the king of Awadh. Rama held many Aswamedha yagyas during his reign.

In this way, Marcandey consoled Yudhisthra not to lose heart as good and bad days have to be faced by all.

There is mention about Karna's birth. He was born of Kunti, when she had not been married and so she had left him in the river in a cupboard from where he was picked up by Radha, a Soot's wife and brought up. Once Kunti's father expected some brahmins to visit the king. The Raja entrusted the job of serving the brahmins to Kunti. Kunti looked after their comforts well. On departure, the brahmins gave her a boon that she could call any god, when she wished. After the brahmins had left, she wanted to try the boon and called the Sun. Sun came and got attracted towards her but she could not let herself to the Sun. Then Sun told that he was witness to all that happened in the universe and that by involving herself with him, she would not lose her virginity. She gave in. When

Karna was born, she left him in the river to avoid bad name in the universe for having given birth to a child in virginhood. Karna had born with kundal and kavach on his body, which protected him from any attack. But Arjuna, having been named as the best in use of arrow and bow, Karna had always been feeling jealous of him. So Duryodhana kept him on his side. Kunti had known that Karna, being brought up by Radha, was her son. Yudhisthra, however, always had fear of Karna not being won in battle with kavach and kundal on. Indra too wanted to help Pandavas. So once Indra came and begged for the kavach and kundal. Karna was a great alms-giver donor. He took out the kavach and kundal and gave to Indra. In exchange Indra gave him an 'Amogh Shakti', which, when used certainly killed the targetted person. Karna wanted this to be used against Arjuna, his sole enemy.

Once the Pandavas felt thirsty in the jungle. Then Yudhisthra asked Nakula to climb a tree and see if water was visible. He saw water tank at a distant place. Yudhisthra sent him to bring water. But in the tank there was a Yaksha. He asked Nakula to give reply to his questions first and then only to take water. Nakula did not care for him and took water. He immediately became unconscious. Then Yudhisthra sent another brother to see where Nakula was held up. They all came, one by one, and became unconscious. Then Yudhishtra came there. Yaksha told him too same thing. Yudhisthra gave replies to all questions asked by Yaksha. The Yaksha inter alia asked, who is happy ? What is strangest thing in the universe? Which is the best way to be followed and what is best to be talked about? Yudhisthra replied that the happiest man in the universe is he, who does not have any debt on his head; who is in his house and eats and lives well in the house. Those in the universe, who see the people dying, day in and day out, and still think that they shall never die, is the strangest thing in the universe:

अहन्यहनि भूतानि गच्छन्तीह यमालयम,
शेषाः स्थावरमिच्छन्ति किमाश्चर्यमतः परम (313/116)

Since no two rishis agree on any matter, the best way to be followed is from where many people go :

(महाजनो येन गतः स पन्थाः) (313/117)

The best matter to be talked about is how one is dealt with after death according to one's karma. The Yaksha having satisfied himself with all he wanted to ask, he was ready to release all the Pandavas. Yudhisthra also told the Yaksha that a man who kept himself composed in all bad any good days, is the richest man in the universe and who does not involve himself in worldly involvements, even though living in the universe, is the overall lord of all riches and wealthy people. But then Yaksha told him that at first he would release one whomsoever he wanted. Yudhisthra recommended Nakula to be released. Yaksha questioned why he wanted Nakula to be released when Arjuna and Bhima were more dependable and his own real brothers. Yudhisthra told that his father had two wives—Kunti and Madri—and he wanted sons of both to be alive. So he recommended Nakula to be enlivened. Yudhisthra also told that if one does not care for Dharma, Dharma too leaves caring for him. Therefore, one should continue to act as per Dharma only. Then Yaksha having been pleased, released all the Pandavas. The Yaksha then disclosed that he was his father Dharma only and henceforth he would act as per Dharma only in the universe.

4
Virat Parva

Now the Pandvas had passed twelve years in the forests and were left with one year during which, they should not be recognised by Kaurvas' men. They, therefore, decided within themselves to act differently. Yudhisthra to entertain the raja by playing chauser; Bhima to be incharge of kitchen; Arjuna to coach music to the daughter of the raja; Nakula to look after the astabal; Sehdeva to keep an account of cows and Daropadi to work as maid of the raja's wife and daughter. This shows one should be able to do any work, howsoever mean it might be. Pandavas' Purohit advised the Pandavas to act in Virat-nagar keeping following principles in view :

1. Send for the intention of meeting the raja first through his men if anyone watned to meet the raja.
2. One should take the lowest seat unless some other seat was allotted.
3. One should never think that he was the closest to the raja as there would be many jealous of him and would convey such a feeling to raja and it may then harm him.
4. One should not advise the raja unless called for to do so.
5. One should work quietly and should praise the raja from time to time.
6. One should not tell a lie before the raja as the raja by his means could go into the truth and then the lier shall be caught.
7. One should neither develop any interaction with the queens of the raja nor with the persons whom the raja did not like.
8. One should conduct himself as desired by the raja and not otherwise.

9. One should not come close to raja and should keep distance.
10. One should keep himself on left and right side of the raja as the raja does not want anyone to go in front of him and in the back, the escort follows the raja.
11. Even when provided with all luxuries in Raj Bhawan, one should continue to serve the raja selflessly and without any lethargy.
12. One should always offer oneself for doing any work even when the same was being entrusted to another person.
13. One should never speak ill of the raja.
14. One should wear the clothes and armaments given by the raja, as such usage pleases the raja.
15. One should not take any bribery in doing the job of the raja.
16. One should not try to equate oneself to the raja in eating, wearing clothes or other actions as this would annoy the raja.

Pandavas then kept their armaments on a tree and hanged a dead body there so that everyone would, out of fear from the dead, not search the tree. Then they reached Viratnagar and all got jobs there according to their respective vocations. They started living there and doing their jobs to the satisfaction of their masters.

Once, Keechaka, the brother of queen and commander-in-chief of the raja's army saw Daropadi there. He got attracted and proposed himself but Daropadi declined and told that she was only a maid servant and he was a very highly placed person. Further, she told that she was a married lady having five Gandharva husbands, who always protected her. But Keechaka did not give up. He even told this to his sister, the queen and queen also proposed to Daropadi but she had put the condition, not to be disturbed by anyone, at the time of her appointment itself. So she refrained. But having been forced, queen told Keechaka to hold a party at his house and she would send Daropadi to bring the bottle of liquor and then, he could catch her. They acted on the plan but Daropadi could come out from his clutches. Then she was quite upset and narrated the entire matter to Bhima, who advised her to call Keechaka to a lonely place and there he would kill him. This plan worked and Keechaka was killed by Bhima. All thought that Gandharvas had called him. Subsequently other brothers of Keechaka arrested Daropadi and wanted to burn her but then Bhima went there and killed all brothers.

The news of Keechaka's death reached everywhere. Duryodhana was already in search of the Pandavas but his spies failed to locate anyone of them. Then, the news of Keechaka's death reached Duryodhana. He knew that Keechaka was a brave man and that he could be killed by Bhima only. So they made a plan to attack Viratnagar. In case the Pandavas were there, they would come to help the raja and in case they did not come out openly, then the raja could be defeated easily and Pandavas caught. Darona and Bhishma too agreed to the proposal. It was decided as a matter of strategy that the raja of Trigrat kingdom, Susharmane should attack first from one side and then the Kaurvas would attack from the other side. When raja of Trigrat attacked, the raja of Viratnagar came out to face him. Yudhisthra and Bhima, Nakula and Sehdeva also accompanied him. Fierce fighting took place but the raja of Viratnagar won because of the help of Yudhisthra and Bhima. The raja was thankful to them and even offered them the kingdom to be ruled. But Yudhisthra declined. When raja of Virat was out to fight with Trigrat Raja, Kaurvas attacked on Viratnagar from the other side as planned by them. The son of raja of Virat was pursuaded to fight by Daropadi, who also asked to take Arjuna with him. Although the son was too small a fry before Kaurvas, yet he ultimately agreed. Arjuna at first took his armaments from the tree. The son Uttam Kumar, fled from the battle field out of fear from facing the Kaurvas. Then Arjuna made him agree to work as his sarthi and he would fight with the Kaurvas. He even told him that he in fact was Arjuna. Then Uttam Kumar could have confidence. Fierce fighting took place and Duryodhana recognised Arjuna. He told Bhishma that he had been able to locate Arjuna and so the period of exile be repeated. Then Bhishma told that according to calendar, the period of exile had already been over the day before. Arjuna defeated the Kaurvas and returned. Arjuna had told Uttam Kumar not to disclose the secrecy of Arjuna having fought. He sent word of having defeated the Kaurvas.

This was being celebrated in Viratnager. Yudhisthra was asked to play and during the play, raja had praised the bravery of Uttam Kumar but Yudhisthra had been mentioning about Arjuna. The raja got annoyed and threw the disc on Yudhisthra's face. The face bled but Daropadi, who was seeing it, brought a pale of water and in this way the blood was not allowed to fall on earth, as according to Arjuna's undertaking, he would kill anyone, who was responsible for a drop of blood oozing out from Yudhisthra.

Next day all the Pandavas reached the viratnagar raja's sabha, duly decorated as rajas and occupied the seats meant for rajas. Then Virat Raja asked, who they were. Then Arjuna disclosed who they were. Virat

Raja begged to be excused as demanded by protocol but then Yudhisthra could not be thankless for him as after all the Pandavas had got refuge under him.Then raja desired to marry his daughter with Arjuna but Arjuna declined as she had been her disciple and marrying with the disciple was bad in ethics. Such was the protocol at that time. But he agreed Uttara to be married to his son Abhimanyu. Then Abhimanyu's marriage took place in Viratnagar, where all rajas on the side of Pandavas had also gathered. Krishana gave a lot of money and ornaments as required according to protocol to be given by metarnal uncle. Even today such a tradition continues but it was all out of affection and not by force.

Arjuna, in this way, accepted Uttara as his daughter-in-law for his son Abhimanyu. Arjuna said that there was no difference in daughter and daughter-in-law. Therefore, in accepting Uttara, who was her disciple like a daughter, there was nothing wrong, whereas in case of accepting her as wife, would be like marrying a daughter. So the marriage was performed before fire, where brahmins worshipped all gods and performed havan. The father of the girl gave daughter in marriage to the groom along with a lot of dowry, comprising of many cows, lot of gold and diamonds, costly clothes, beds etc. It show that the tradition of giving dowry to the bride continues from ancient period and it was given by the father of the bride willingly to enable the daughter to set up a new house for herself in case of need and even otherwise she may not immediately, on reaching the in-law's house, have to ask for something being bought for her, which she may feel awkward in asking. In dowry, even the bride's father placed himself at the disposal of the groom's people.

तस्मै सप्त सहस्त्राणि हयानां वातहंसाम्,
द्वे च नागश्ते मुख्ये प्रादाद् बहुधनं तदा।
हुत्वा सम्यक् समिद्धाग्निमर्चयित्वा द्विजन्मनः,
राज्यं बलं च कोशं च सर्वमात्मानमेव च। (72/37)

5
Udyog Parva

As usual, the book starts with worship of God Krishana, his friend Arjuna and Saraswati. All were happy after Abhimanyu's marriage in Virat. Next morning, all the rajas assembled in Virat's Sabha. The Sabha Bhawan was adequately decorated with paintings, jewels and seating arrangement had been made befitting the occasion. In the sabha at first Raja Virat, who was the host, occupied the chair being the oldest and most respected, then Balrama and Krishana sat with their father Vasudeva. Then the other rajas like Drupada, Satyaki, and Yudhisthra and other brothers and their sons, all took their seats. The sabha had been organised by Krishana to decide the further course of action by Pandavas. He also asked the rajas, who had assembled there to find a way out so that Pandavas and Kaurvas could live in peace and cordiality and in accordance with the tenets of Dharma as without Dharma,Yudhisthra would not even accept the kingdom of the gods. The Kaurvas had always been ill-treating the Pandavas, although they were the owners of the entire kingdom of Hastinapur as according to the theory of primogenitor, Pandavas had to succeed Pandu and the coronation of Dharitrashtra was a stop-gap arrangement and he should have coronated Yudhisthra, when he came of age. Instead, he was given half the kingdom but the Pandavas felt contented even with that with a view to maintain harmony in the family. But the Kaurvas, by their deceitful actions, called Yudhisthra for the gambling knowing full well that he was weak at gambling, and then defeating him got their all, and expelled them for thirteen years of exile. Still Pandavas have passed this time although facing great hardships so much so that they had to serve Raja Virat as his menials for one year. Even now if Kaurvas did not return the kingdom, the Pandavas shall have no alternative to fight with them. Krishana advised that as a prelude, a wise man should be sent as the Pandavas' ambassador to convey their feeling to Dharitrashtra. The ambassador was to be such a person as could act patiently and convince Dharitrashtra to part with half the kingdom to Pandavas. The international problems solved peacefully is to the benefit of all and the solution through war is only killing and disastrous. This has been the feeling of the Hindus throughout to avoid war, if possible, and to face it whole-heartedly, if it could not be avoided.

Satyaki and other rajas also spoke in the sabha to express their feelings and all stated that Yudhisthra did not know playing gambling but still by invitation he was forced to agree to the same as he could not dismiss the invitation by Raja Dharitrashtra, whom he respected to the core. He could not expect such cheating when Dharitrashtra, Bhishma, Darona were there. But Duryodhana and Shakuni had their way and no one could prevent the proceedings. All offered to fight with Kaurvas for the sake of restoration of kingdom to Pandavas.

It was also decided in the sabha that simultaneously messages be sent to all rajas to help the Pandavas in case the battle took place as it would be difficult to win them over after they had given a word to help Kaurvas in the battle with Pandavas. So the strategy was to take a word from them all before they could commit to help the Kaurvas. Accordingly, able ambassadors had been sent to all the rajas to apprise them of the situation and to extend help to Pandavas in case of need. In those days, words had meaning and if word had been given to one party for help, it could not be traced back as by deceitful means Duryadhana had lured Raja Shalya to his side when in fact he had come to help Pandavas only and once a word had been given, he could not change side although Pandavas were his nephews—Shalya's sister being mother of Nakula and Sehdeva. There shall be such situation in many other cases as prima-facie all treated Kaurvas and Pandavas equally. Even Krishana told he had good relations with both and it shall be difficult to side one against another in case of war. Accordingly, the kings who had gathered in the sabha, sent invitation for war to all the kings. A Purohit was selected to go to Hastinapur with the message for giving half the kingdom to Pandavas as agreed to before they departed for the thirteen years' exile.

Meantime Kaurvas too having made up their mind not to part with half kingdom to Pandavas, had already started contacting the kings to fight for them. Duryadhana had gone to Dwarka to win over Krishana. He reached there even before Arjuna could reach. Krishana was still sleeping and not thinking it proper to awake him up, Duryodhana waited sitting on the side of his head. Subsequently, Arjun reached there and sat on the side of his legs. When Krishana got up, he saw Arjuna first being in his front and Duryodhana later. Krishana asked Arjuna what he wanted. Then Duryodhana said he had come first. Therefore, he had the first right to demand. Krishana then told that although he had seen Arjuna first yet he shall give a choice to Duryodhana to opt for himself alone without taking up any arm or for his Narayani force. Duryodhana asked for the later. Arjuna was happy to have Krishana alone on his side—Duryodhan could not visualise that Krishana alone was more than the entire universe. Duryodhana then went to Balrama and on his selection of the Narayani force, Balrama told him that for his sake only he had puersuaded Krishana to be neutral but then he selected a wrong thing. Now since Krishana would be on Pandavas' side, he could not fight for Kaurvas and, therefore, would not take part in the war. Balrama accordingly left for pilgrimage during that period. This is how important decisions were taken keeping the protocol, and the Dharma in view.

After Duryodhana had gone back from Dwarka, he heard of the arrival of Raja Shalya. Duryodhana arranged for his marvellous reception. Shalya was happy with the welcome granted in his honour. He could not so far make out who was behind the reception. He thought it was Pandavas and praised Yudhisthra for such an arrangement. Then Duryodhana appeared on the scene and Shalya had to offer his help for him on Duryodhana's askance having accepted his welcome arrangement. Duryodhana also requested him to be a commander of his army, which Shalya accepted. This is how the word had to be honoured in those days. Shalya then told Duryodhana that he wanted to meet Yudhisthra but Duryodhana requested him to return back quickly after meeting Yudhisthra. In Pandavas' camp, Shalya was again welcomed with great warmth but then he told Yudhisthra about his having accepted to help Duryodhana. Yudhisthra took it in right spirit looking into the situation in which Shalya had extended help to Duryodhana but requested him to atleast discourage Karna while fighting with Arjuna as Shalya would certainty be his sarthi in that battle. Shalya committed doing it and also told that he would not rise in arms against Nakula and Sehdeva, who were his nephews. Asking a sarthy to betray his master does not appear protocolically alright but in the context that Duryodhana had betrayed in winning him over to his side when he wanted to be with Pandavas, the small favour asked for by Yudhisthra is negligible.

As a result of the invitation of various kings to help, by Kaurvas and Pandavas, Kaurvas could gather eleven Kshoni troops and Pandavas only seven. This force had gathered from all parts of India and a few countries in east like Cambodia and China.

भगदत्तो महीपालः सेनामक्षौहिणीं ददौ,

तस्य चीनै किरातैश्च काँचनैरिव सवृंतम्। (19/15)

and सुदक्षिणश्च काम्बोजो यवनैश्च शकैस्तथा। (19/21)

Although it has been said that kings of the entire universe had gathered there but it seems they were only from India and a few neighbouring countries.

Drupada's Purohit reported to Raja Dharitrashtra, Bhishma and Vidur, who paid due respect to him as a Purohit and not as a messenger of Raja Drupada. He at first told about the well-being of his people and then enquired about that of Dharitrashtra and his people as per protocol. He then told the sabha that the Pandavas, after forgetting all that had happened in the past, were desirous of having cordial relations with Kaurvas and wanted to have back their portion of the kingdom without any bloodshed and the war. He also told that Duryodhana should not be proud of his eleven kshoni force as Pandavas' seven kshoni force was mightier than his force. He also told that whatever Pandavas had asked was their own, which had deceitfully been taken over by Kaurvas and this too was in accordance with the undertaking held at the time of their exile. Bhishma agreed with the proposal of the Purohit and praised Arjuna, who was enough to defeat the entire force of Kaurvas. He also told that Krishana and Arjuna were the 'Nar' and 'Narayan' of the previous time and there was none on the earth to face them. He told the Purohit that whatever he had said was correct but there was some sharpness in whatever he had said. This might be because he was a brahmin, who could speak with confidence. While Bhishma was amidst his speech, Karna told that Pandavas had gone to forests because of their defeat in gambling and now they wanted half kingdom by force with the help of Raja Drupada and Virat, which would not be possible till they had fought. In fact he stated that Pandavas had been caught before completion of the period of exile and, therefore, they should again live in exile for another thirteen years under the protection of the king of Hastinapur. Bhishma, however, snubbed him as to why he was allured to talk on the family matters of Kaurvas and Pandavas and was thus asked to keep silent. Dharitrashtra thus told the Purohit that he would ponder over the matter and then send Sanjaya with his proposal.

Dharitrashtra then told Sanjaya that the Pandavas had been living as per tenets of Dharma and they were flawless in this regard. He asked Sanjaya to request Yudhisthra not to resort to war but then he did not say anything about passing over half kingdom to him, which Duryodhana did not agree to part with. He told Sanjaya to tell Yudhisthra that he was not afraid of war or Arjuna or Bhima's bravery as much as he feared the rage of Yudhisthra, who was the follower of Dharma through and through.

Sanjaya accordingly went to Pandavas and after asking about their well-being and telling about the well-being of Kaurvas, presented all that Dharitrashtra, had told him. These royal representatives were free to narrate, whatever they had been asked to convey, without any fear as the other king could not harm them according to the then existing protocol and sort of 'ambassadorial immunity' existing even at that time. That is how the Purohit could convey the message to Kaurvas inspite of lot of thrashing against what he was speaking, from the other side. Similarly, Sanjaya could speak fearlessly in the sabha of Pandavas. Yudhisthra, as per protocol, asked whether :

1. Bhishma Pitamaha was well and had affection for Pandavas as he always had?
2. Whether Raja Dharitrashtra was well ?
3. Whether Daronacharya, Kripacharya and other gurus were well with their families ?
4. Whether all the kings of vassal states of Hastinapur were well ?
5. Whether Yuyuts, the son of a Vaish queen of Dharitrashtra was alright and whether Karna, who always kept Duryodhana under his control, was well?
6. Whether all mothers in the mahal and the attendants in the mahal were alright with their families ?
7. Whether Dharitrashtra has been favourably inclined toward brahmins and others respectable in the kingdom.
8. Whether the ministers and others were adequately paid, not giving them a chance to betray ?
9. Whether the Kaurvas had been thinking of passing on the half kingdom to them in the assembly of Dharitrashtra?

This was protocolic requirement of that time when even after the bad relations with Kaurvas, Yudhisthra had enquired about their well-being first. In a way, such enquiry also had a strategic importance in as much as if anyone of the categories indicated above, were not happy in the realm of Dharitrashtra, that would give an indication of the ill-administered state. Sanjaya narrated how Duryodhana, inspite of the best behaviour of Pandavas toward him, had been having a bad feeling against them. Sanjaya then requested to find out a peaceful solution to the problem. Sanjaya also told about the bravery of Bhishma, Darona to create some fear in the minds of Pandavas in case they insisted on war. But immediately Yudhisthra checked him and asked to tell how he had reached the conclusion that Pandavas wanted to resort to war only. He rather told him that Pandavas were in for a peaceful solution. The dialogue continued and in the end Yudhisthra told that there was a thin line between Dharma and Adharma. At some place non-Dharma becomes Dharma itself such as killing anyone is Adharma but killing an enemy in the battle is a Dharma. Sometimes Adharma become Dharma like fighting is a Dharma for Kshatriyas but Adharma for others. Therefore, it is with a lot of prudence that Dharma and Adharma have to be determined. In the present context, war, if it had to be resorted to, would cause millions of deaths but it would be a necessity if Kaurvas did not act according to the ethics of Dharma and they did not part with half the kingdom, which was Pandavas' their own and as had been undertaken before they proceeded to forests. Krishana also advised Sanjaya that he was in for the well-being of both Kaurvas and Pandavas but in case Pandavas were not given their due, then he shall be with Pandavas, and this shall cause the complete annihilation of Kaurvas. He also reminded Sanjaya of what had happened at the time of Pandavas defeat in gambling and how at that time they had been abused by Kaurvas, particularly Dushashana, Karna and Duryodhana. Such actions could not be forgotten and still he said he would visit Hastinapur and persuade Kaurvas if they could arrive at a peaceful settlement without resorting to war, which shall be disastrous.

Sanjaya then begged for their leave and begged to be pardoned if he had said anything not to their liking as a result of discharging his duty as a representative of Dharitrashtra and also in the heat of the moment. This is a protocolic necessity although Sanjaya was aware of ambassadorial immunity, which permitted him to convey whatever he was required to by his master. Yudhisthra too accordingly consoled him that he, being a well-wisher of both Kaurvas and Pandavas, would not say anything which was not in the interest of both. Sanjaya then left for Hastinapur.

On reaching Hastinapur, he sent a word to the king about his arrival and permission to meet him. Dharitrashtra immediately called him in. Sanjaya narrated all that Pandavas told him and advised that Krishana would come there to make a final effort to sort out the matter and try for a peaceful solution before going in for war, the ultimate resort. After listening to what Sanjaya had told, Dharitrashtra had been quite upset as being a shrewd politician and diplomat, he knew that war meant the annihilation of Kaurvas. He, at such a time, called in Vidur, who was the only man, who talked sense. Vidur immediately came and discussed all the pros and cons of war between Kaurvas and Pandavas and he advised the king to leave the affection of his son and strongly come forward to pass on half kingdom to Pandavas as this was the only way to save his family. In other words this shall be the real affection for his sons not to yield to what they wanted but to order the correct thing. Dharitrashtra told that he too was not in favour of war and had in fact persuaded Duryodhana to part with half the kingdom to Pandavas and to live peacefully enjoying the other half but he was not prepared to understand it and was insisting on not giving anything to Pandavas. He, therefore, had decided to leave the things to take shape as in the fate. To have further consolation in the course of action, that had been taking shape, Vidur arranged a meeting of Dharitrashtra with Santsujata Muni. Dharitrashtra asked him, for the benefit of general public, that he had heard that there was nothing like death, then why did even gods try to save themselves from the clutches of death by following 'Brahmcharya'. The muni told that both things were correct — one there is death and one can save oneself from it by his action (Brahmcharya Vrata) and the other is that there is nothing like death, and both the beliefs are correct. Those, who accept there is death, they try to avoid themselves from its clutches by following 'Brahmcharya', which works as 'Amrit' for them and those, who think death is not there, involve themseles in various vices to enjoy life in this universe, but then they come to know of the result of their actions, when they wander through various species but still such people take it that there is nothing like soul which passes from one specie to another as they do not remember the deeds of the previous birth in the next life. The difference only is rebirth and salvation in the two thinkings which persons with each belief have to follow. The muni also explained to the king, the various kinds of yagya, tapa, which help in attainment of salvation but this was possible on restraint, renunciation of worldly vices and non-assumption.

Meantime Sanjaya came to apprise the king about the outcome of his meeting with Pandavas. As per protocol, he waited at the door and sent intimation of his arrival to the king. The king called him in the assembly after everyone in the assembly had taken his respective seat. On arrival, Sanjaya told that he had been to Pandavas, who have sent their good wishes through him. As per protocol, they have conveyed their respects for the elders; their appropriate wishes to the people of their age and their blessings for the younger ones—

> अभिवादयन्ति वद्धांश्च वयस्यांश्च वयस्यवत्,
> यूनश्चाभ्यवदन पार्थाः प्रतिपूज्य यथावयः। (47/16)

Then Sanjaya narrated what had transpired between him, Pandavas and Krishana. Bhishma praised Krishana and Arjuna for observation of Dharma and rebuked Karna for self-assumption and bad behaviour and responsible for creating a wedge between the Kaurvas and Pandavas. In fact it was because of Karna only that Duryodhana had been ready to give a fight to Pandavas otherwise he too thought that there was no match for Arjuna in his army. He cautioned Dharitrashtra that Karna only assumed himself otherwise he was no match for Arjuna. He lost to Gandharvas along with Duryodhana and it was Arjuna only who saved them from the clutches of Gandharvas. Also in the battle with Virat, all, including Bhishma, Karna, Duryodhana, Darona had been defeated by Arjuna, then how shall he now kill Arjuna is anybody's guess, particularly when he has already lost his 'kawach' and 'kundala'. He is, therefore, not even 1/16th of the Pandavas. Sanjaya then explained the bravery of each one of the Pandavas and their associate kings as also of Krishana. Dharitrashtra was upset on thinking of the bravery of Bhima and Arjuna and other Pandavas and impending defeat of Kaurvas and urged Duryodhana to give up his ego and be ready to part with half the kingdom to Pandavas so that the war could be avoided and as a result he too would be able to enjoy the balance half of the kingdom. Duryodhana then explained that he, with the help of Bhishma, Darona, was quite strong in giving a befitting defeat to Pandavas. Ultimately the stage was set for the war between Kaurvas and Pandavas as Duryodhana considered Pandavas rather inferior to them since all were born and brought up together and taught by the same guru and since Pandavas were only five and they were one hundred, they were on a better footing. Dharitrashtra then consulted Vidur, who again advised for a peace treaty with Pandavas and to avoid war otherwise all Kaurvas shall be annihilated. All the elders again persuaded Duryodhana to agree to a peace treaty by handing over their kingdom to the Pandavas but he did not agree. Then Ved Vyasa and Gandhari came to the assembly and they too advised the king to agree to give their kingdom to Pandavas but their persuation also had no effect. In fact it was the weakness of Dharitrashtra for his sons, which did not permit him to agree for the peace treaty with Pandavas. What was required was to assert and, being the king, he should have ignored the feeling of Duryodhana and others of the like-mind and part with half kingdom to Pandavas since he himself was convinced of the right of Pandavas as also the resultant annihilation of all of his sons in case war took place. This non-assertion was, therefore, responsible for the Mahabharata resulting in the death of crores of people. Ved Vyasa himself had also indicated that Krishana was God's incarnation and he alone was sufficient to inflict a defeat on Kaurvas. Krishana keeps everyone indulged in worldly vices through his power 'Maya'. But his efforts also fell flat.

On the other side, after Sanjaya had left and the outcome of his persuation at Hastinapur had been known through his spies, Yudhisthra took all his brothers and the kings, who had collected there to request Krishana to proceed to Hastinapur and make the last effort for a peaceful settlement so that the war and consequent killing of crores of people could be saved. They went to Krishana and requested him to go to Hastinapur explaining the uptodate position and to ascertain the thinking of Kaurvas. Yudhisthra told Krishana that in the situation they had been put, they could not give up their right of ruling their part of kingdom and since a king's Dharma is to fight with another king, who had encroached upon his kingdom, he shall have to resort to fighting in case Kaurvas did not vacate their part of the kingdom atleast, although they are successor to the entire kingdom of Hastinapur. Krishana too told Yudhisthra not to depend on what Kaurvas gave but to snatch whatever is their right as kshatriya is not to beg for anything when he was brave enough to have it perforce and with Kaurvas the main thing was that even after cheating Pandavas and expelling them from the rajya, they never repented over it rather enjoyed the kingdom of the Pandavas and having got used to it, they did not now want to part with it. Krishana told that he would be meeting the Kaurvas to explain Pandavas' point of view; the sufferance they had to undergo in forests as a result of their deceitful action in defeating them in gambling; having enjoyed the kingdom and wealth of Pandavas for thirteen years; the undertaking given by the king for returning the kingdom after completion of thirteen years period of exile in forests and the Pandavas' right to the entire kingdom of Hastinapur as also the force they had and then to ask for entering into a peace treaty and avoid the war, which shall be disastrous. Also the purpose of Krishana's meeting with Kaurvas was to know the war preparations made by them. Similarly, when Rama had sent Hanumana to Lanka in search of Sita, he was asked to check up the security arrangements in Lanka, the power of Lanka, the power of Ravana as also to explain to Ravana to make peace in his own interest. Meantime Krishana saw each one of the Pandavas demoralised in having to face the war with their own brethren for the sake of kingdom only. This is natural after one had lived in forests for such a long period and making livelihood by bhiksha, to pass the remaining life accordingly rather than entering into the complications of war. So Krishana's job was also to boost up the morale of Pandavas and prepare them for the war as Krishana, inspite of the efforts to be made for a peace treaty, knew that war was inevitable. Also at that time after hearing all Pandavas demoralised, it was Daropadi, who, through Krishana reminded the Pandavas of the humiliation faced by them and Daropadi at the hands of Kaurvas. So strategically morale-boosting was necessary in the minds of the warriors before the fighting started. Krishana then started for Hastinapur and as a matter of protocol, all Pandavas and kings followed to see him off. Even today such a protocol is followed. After seeing him off, Pandavas walked around Krishana and returned. This too is a way of offering respects.

On the way, many rishis followed Krishana with a view to watch the proceedings with Krishana in Hastinapur. Duryodhana came to know of Krishana coming. He, as a matter of protocol, made proper arrangements for his stay en-route and Dharitrashtra had consultations with Bhishma, Darona, Vidur as apart from being a representative of Pandavas, Krishana ipso facto was respectable for Kaurvas too and was to be honoured accordingly. Dharitrashtra made all preparations to receive Krishana and for the presents of elephants, chariots, maids, gold, jewels and other things. Banners were displayed on roads, perfumes sprinkled, and ladies were there to receive Krishana. Dharitrashtra himself went to receive Krishana along with Bhishma, Darona, Vidur. This was the normal protocol shown when the king of another country came and same protocol is followed at present too. Vidur told Dharitrashtra to behave properly with Krishana and should not allow any untoward incident taking place in Hastinapur during his stay and his talks with him and others in the capital, as Krishana was the harbinger of peace as also the God incarnate. It is greatness of him that he was himself coming to sort out the matter and now Duryodhana should agree to pass on the Pandavas' territory to them and avoid war as war shall be more of harm to Kaurvas. Duryodhana, however, did not agree to what Vidur had said. He even forbade Dharitrashtra from presenting costly jewels to him as that was not the proper time for offering such presents as Krishana might consider that they had offered all the things out of fear. Further, when the fighting was imminent then there was no use entertaining the representative of the enemy. He rather had the programme of arresting Krishana, when he comes to Hastinapur. This was questioned by all present there and all had told Duryodhana not to resort to such action as it would be against laid down protocol as also arresting Krishana would not be possible for any human being as he is God incarnate. Bhishma then left the assembly rebuking Duryodhana for his plans. Duryodhana even did not go to receive Krishana on his arrival. People were standing on both sides of roads to have a glimpse of Krishana. On arrival in the mahal, Dharitrashtra and others got up from their seats in respect. Krishana paid respect to Bhishma and met all others as per their position. Krishana took a specially provided seat for him in the assembly on askance by Dharitrashtra. This is normal protocol that the guest takes the seat after the host has asked for it.

After accepting the honour extended to him, Krishana met all the kings present at that place. Then he met Darona, Bahalika, Kripacharya and others present there and kept sitting there for some time after which Vidur took him with him and told him the thinking of Kaurvas. Krishana met Kunti at Vidur's house. She had been living there for the last thirteen years. Kunti asked Krishana to tell her sons to rise in fighting against the Kaurvas, who had done such a misbehaviour with them as also with Daropadi. After taking her permission, Krishana went to Duryodhana's house. He stood in his honour along with his ministers. Krishana met them all as per protocol. Krishana sat there on a specially decorated seat. Duryodhana offered a lot of presents and invited him for meals but Krishana declined. Duryodhana asked Krishana, why he did not accept the hospitability offered by him, Krishana replied that an ambassador can accept hospitability after his job had been done. He could, therefore, extend hospitability to him and his ministers after the job was completed. Krishana also told that one takes meals at other's house only out of affection or when one is in trouble. Here Duryodhana had no affection for him and in trouble Krishana was not. Krishana then went to Vidur's house to stay during the night. Bhishma, Darona, Bahalika, Kripacharya and some other Kaurvas also followed him. They all offered their houses full of jewels and diamonds to Krishana. Krishana, however, told them to go to their houses and take it that their hospitability had been duly accepted.

After Kaurvas and others had left, Vidur paid respects to Krishana and served meals. Krishana served the meals to brahmins first and then he too took it. Vidur was, however, not happy over Krishana's arrival at Hastinapur as Duryodhana had given up all ethic. Duryodhana felt that Karna alone could defeat all Pandavas. He would not, therefore, accept any peace talks as the Kaurvas had already decided not to hand over any part of their kingdom to Pandavas. Krishana, however, justified his having come there as it was the duty of a friend to make the brothers reach a cordiality in case of any difference between them and Krishana had come to fulfil that obligation.

Next day after Krishana had got up and was free from daily chores, Duryodhana and Shakuni came there to fetch Krishana to the assembly. They advised that Raja Dharitrashtra and others had come in the Sabha Bhawan and were waiting for him there. Krishana gave away alms to brahmins and left for the assembly along with Vidur followed by Duryodhana and Shakuni on another chariot. All residents of Hastinapur had gathered on both sides of the roads to have a darshan of God Krishana. On arrival at the assembly, the followers of Krishana blew shell with a view to make the kings sitting inside the assembly know the arrival of the honoured guest. Krishana entered the Sabha Bhawan escorted by Duryodhana, Karna and others. The raja, Darona, Bhishma stood from their seats in honour of Krishana, followed by other kings. The Kaurvas paid their respects to Krishana. Narada and many other rishis, and munis had also come there. Krishana asked Bhishma to provide them with appropriate seats after offering respects to them. They were all provided with seats. Duryodhana and Karna sat with Krishana. Krishana then told the assembly that the purpose of his visit was to see if Kaurvas and Pandavas could reach any peaceful settlement as *Kuru dynasty was the only one in the universe, where Dharma was followed.* He told Dharitrashtra that a peaceful settlement could be arrived at by the efforts of Krishana and Dharitrashtra only. Krishana told the king that in case of war, there had to be great disaster and in case of death of either Kaurvas or Pandavas, no one shall be in peace throughout his life. He conveyed that Pandavas had respectfully conveyed that they had a lot of sufferance in forests as per conditions of gambling and that now the other part of handing over the kingdom should be fulfilled. Passing over of the part of kingdom to them is as per tenets of religion. His sons had become extra greedy and, therefore, had to be brought under control and cordiality should be arrived at with Pandavas, who were prepared to serve him as before. Everyone present there welcomed what Krishana had said and no one was prepared to talk against the same.

Narada also spoke and narrated several incidents which went to prove that all was well only in peace and all disaster in war. Bhishma, Darona, Vidur and Dharitrashtra persuaded Duryodhana to leave his ego and greed and pass on the half kingdom to Pandavas and to live peacefully with the remaining half kingdom, which itself was enough for them. They even asked Duryodhana to go to Yudhisthra and settle with him so that war could be avoided. Yudhisthra, being a follower of Dharma would welcome him and in this way a peaceful way could be found. Duryodhana, however, told Krishana that he had unnecessarily been holding him responsible for war if it takes place whereas it is Pandavas, who had been caught during the last year of exile and so as per the terms of agreement, they should again undergo the exile for thirteen years. It was Pandavas, who had themselves agreed for the gambling; it was Yudhisthra, who had chosen to play with Shakuni; it was Yudhisthra, who had lost in gambling and the exile was only the consequence of Yudhisthra's defeat in gambling as settled before the start of gambling. Therefore, the entire suffering of Pandavas was as per their own creation. In fact out of grace only, they had once been excused by Dharitrashtra and his kingdom was returned to them but again Yudhisthra came forward for gambling with the condition of exile for thirteen years. How can then the Kaurvas be held responsible for their sufferings. He also stated that Pandavas were no match for them and even gods could not face Bhishma, Kripacharya, Darona and Karna in the battle field. Even whatever had been given to the Pandavas was wrong and they had no right on the kingdom as Dharitrashtra was eldest and was entitled to be crowned, when Pandu was wrongfully enthroned side-passing Dharitrashtra. The entire kingdom was, therefore, theirs and Pandavas had no right to have any part of it. Hearing this, Krishana got enraged and told Duryodhana that in case of war, all Kaurvas and their helpers would be killed and in that case, Pandavas shall be the rulers of entire universe and he started leaving the assembly, after telling Duryodhana that whatever he had done to Bhima to poison him in the childhood; having thrown him amongst snakes; then having tried to burn them in Lakshagriha and having deceitfully sent them to forests in so called defeat in gambling, was all wrong and that Dharitrashtra, being a blind, was not entitled to be enthroned as per ethics and so the Kaurvas were not entitled to it. Krishana also told Dhairtrashtra to rise to the occasion and after arresting Duryodhana should enter into agreement with Pandavas as for the sake of dynasty and kingdom, it was better to leave the sons if occasion demanded—

त्यजेत् कुलार्थे पुरुषं ग्रामस्यार्थे कुलं त्येजत्,
ग्रामं जनपदस्यार्थे आत्मार्थे पृथिवीं त्यजेत्। (128/49)

Dharitrashtra then called in Gandhari in the assembly and asked her to persuade Duryodhana to come on terms with Pandavas if he wanted to live in peace along with his brothers and others. Duryodhana, who had left the assembly, had again been called in and Gandhari persuaded him to leave his ego and pass on half kingdom to Pandavas as it was due to them and he should be content with the remaining half as it was sufficient for even the most leisurely living by them. Duryodhana, however, decided in consultation with Karna, Shakuni and Dushashana to arrest Krishana before the king could arrest him. This shall demoralise Pandavas, who would give up their demand for the kingdom. Satyaki could know their plan and asked his people to be ready with the force to give a fighting to Duryodhana before he could arrest Krishana. Krishana too came to know of their plan and offered himself for being arrested and challenged the Kaurvas whether he could be arrested or the Kaurvas shall be captivated. This too would be a way to solve the problem. Dharitrashtra then called in Duryodhana and rebuked him for having planned to arrest Krishana, who could not be arrested even by all gods. Vidur too praised Krishana and apprised Duryodhana of his deeds. Krishana then became a very dreadful God and showed to all present there the Pandavas and all gods sitting there with their forces. This put everyone to astonishment and no one could, out of fear, look towards Krishana except the rishis, munis, Bhishma and Darona. Even Dharitrashtra got eyes to see Krishana. Krishana then came in his ownself and went to meet Kunti before departure for Viratnagar.

Kunti again told Krishana to advise Pandavas to give a fighting to Kaurvas to have their kingdom back as now it was clear that Kaurvas would not come to peaceful terms. She told that as per shastras, the brahmins had to live on alms in exchange of educating the people; kshatriyas had to govern; vaishas had to earn money and shudras were there to serve the people of the other three varnas —

ब्राह्मणः प्रचरेद् भैक्षंक्षत्रियः परिपालयेत्,
वैश्यो धनार्जनं कुर्याच्छूद्रः परिचरेच्चतान्। (132/30)

She narrated many incidents how the kings had to fight for getting back their kingdoms and that the Pandavas should remember the humiliation they had to face in the Kaurvas' assembly after gambling and the promises they had made to take revenge for the dishonour meted out to Daropadi and should now come up to fight with Kaurvas as they were quite brave to face the Kaurvas and the Dharma of kshatriyas is to fight for their rights and undoing the wrongs being done by other kings. After hearing Kunti and taking the message for Pandavas, Krishana left Hastinapur and proceeded to Viratnagar. After Krishana had left, Dharitrashtra, Bhishma and Darona again persuaded Duryodhana to come to peaceful terms with Pandavas in his own interest and Krishana, who was with them, alone could destroy the entire universe what to speak of the tiny kingdom of Hastinapur and its force. But Duryodhana would not buzz from his insistence of not parting with the kingdom.

Karna had gone to see Krishana off. On the way Krishana revealed to him that he was the son of Kunti and, therefore, the eldest brother of Pandavas and if he could join Pandavas, they would make him the king of their part of the kingdom. Krishana told him that when he was born Kunti was a virgin and to save her honour, she put him on birth in a box and threw in the river from where Radhey and Adhiratha took him and brought him up like their son. Karna, however, told that he, at that stage, would not give up Radhey and adopt Kunti as his mother, when Radhey had faced all troubles of bringing him up and Kunti had left him in despair. Also Duryodhana had developed the enmity with Pandavas on his trust and he could not leave Duryodhana in the lurch when Duryodhana had bestowed the honour of making him the king of Angadesh when all had left him branding him as a Soot's son. It was ethically not correct for him to now go and join the Pandavas for the sake of becoming the king of Hastinapur, whereas the kingdom of entire universe could not compel him to depart from his present Dharma of continuing to help Duryodhana even at the cost of his life. On Dharitrashtra having asked what transpired between Krishana and Karna, Sanjaya could know and explained the same to the king.

On the other side, Kunti too feared the disastrous results of war after discussion with Vidur. She decided to meet Karna and to ask him to be with Pandavas as they were his brothers. She did not know that Krishana knew this fact and he had already discussed this matter with him. Accordingly Kunti went to Karna and narrated that he was her son and had to be abandoned having born of a virgin mother. Karna, however, did not submit to her will and could not agree to betray her mother Radhe, who had to face all sufferings in bringing him up as her son. However, he assured that in the battle, he would not kill any Pandava, other than Arjuna. So on the death of either Arjuna or Karna, she would still have her five sons. Kunti's narration was also confirmed by Akashwani. Akashwani was always trusted to be true. So Karna accepted her version of being his mother but then he had bound himself with Radhe as mother and Duryodhana as a friend and he could not betray them for the sake of kingdom. Kunti then returned.

On arrival in Viratnagar, Krishana narrated to Pandavas all that had happened in Hastinapur and then secret talks started for conducting the battle and making all preparations for the same. Krishana had told how out of the four fundamental policies of the king—sam, dam, dand and bhed, he had made use of the three and the fourth viz 'dand' had to be used now as he failed to get result out of the usage of other three. He persuaded Kaurvas to accept peaceful talks i.e. 'sam' policy to avoid war. When the 'sam' policy did not work then efforts were made to create division by winning over Karna and by telling the Kaurvas that Pandavas had godly powers and also to create a wedge amongst the kings present there to help Pandavas against Duryodhana. When 'bhed' policy did not work, then Kaurvas were told that by having cordiality with the Pandavas, they would be able to be more wealthy and enjoy this kingdom peacefully. But this 'dam' policy too had failed and now the fourth way that is 'dand' only remained to be tried by resorting to a war.

Then the organisation of the army was taken up. The first thing was to appoint a Commander-in-Chief (Senapati) of the army. Yudhisthra suggested that Senapati should be out of Kings Drupada, Virat, Drishtdumana, Shikhandi, Satyaki, Chekitana and Bhima as they were quite well-versed with monitoring the war efforts and could face Bhishma, who was the Senapati from Kaurvas' side. So all these considerations were laid down for selection of an appropriate Senapati as much depended on Senapati in the war. Sehdeva suggested the name of Raja Drupada, who was the fittest man from the consideration of age, knowledge of usage of armaments, respectable from dynastic and elderly consideration, trained in warfare by Maharishi Bhardwaj, a far-sighted and true to the core person and was also rival of Bhishma and Darona. Arjuna suggested the name of Dristduman, who was having all the specialities of his father besides having godly powers, having born out of yagya, and rival of Darona to kill him having born out of yagya with kawach, dhanush and sword in his hands. Bhima suggested Shikhandi's name for the purpose as he was born to kill Bhishma, who was the Senapati from Kaurvas' side and was well-versed with the tactics of warfare. Having known the opinion of all, Yudhisthra suggested that Krishana knew the capability of all the kings and, therefore, he could suggest the name of the Senapati.

Krishana told that all the persons considered by various kings here are really fit to be Senapati of Pandavas' army as all are brave, well-versed with battle-tactics and monitoring the army as also for facing Bhishma. He suggested Daristdumana to be the Principal Senapati. All approved.him to be the Senapati. Then the entire force was organised. This comprised of seven kshonis. The army followed Bhima, Nakula, Sehdeva, five sons of Daropadi. Daristdumana, Drupada, Abhimanyu started for the war. Daropadi also accompanied Yudhisthra for some distance along with other woman but returned back. Pandavas started after making arrangements for the safety of all ladies and other requirements of the army like food, arms, clothes etc. They gave alms and cows to brahmins. This was considered the usual protocol before starting for any project and for kshatriyas, war was the main project. Pandavas' army reached Kurukshetra in proper formation. There, a place was selected for the stay of the army. The selected place was levelled and had grass for the horses and trees for being used for getting wood for burning and away from the ashramas of rishis, munis, places of pilgrimage and temples so that there was no disturbance in the performance of tapasya by them. Tents/camps were laid for the stay of all kings, and their commanders and troops. These were the requirements laid down in the rules of war existing at that time. A canal was then provided to bring clean water for the force. Stores of food-grains and eatables were provided with arrangement for their adequate recoupment on consumption. On the other side, Duryodhana too selected a place for the stay of his force which was eleven kshonis and made arrangements for their fooding and nominated commanders of elephants, chariots, horses and troops on foot as per requirement and made arrangements for repair of chariots, as chariots were broken in the battle very frequently. Arrangements were also made for arms and armaments, oils, foodgrains, kawach, clothes. Specially trained persons were posted as sarthis (to drive the chariots as such persons had important role in the battle that is why Krishana became the sarthi of Arjuna. Then Bhishma was coronated as the Principal Senapati and the army settled at Kurukshetra. Yaduvanshis along with Balrama also came there but since Balrama did not want to favour either Pandavas or Kaurvas, he prefered to proceed on pilgrimage during the period of war.

Duryodhana, after having settled with his army, sent Ulooka, son of Shakuni, to Pandavas to convey to Yudhisthra that whatever Pandavas had undertaken to do would be able to do now and now Yudhisthra, who had always believed in non-violence, truthfulness and religion, was indulging in disaster of the crores of people including his guru and brethren, and also he had said that he had not completed the condition of exile when Pandavas had been traced during the last year of hidden exile. As per Dharma, he should have gone to forests for thirteen years again. Now the Pandavas shall have to face the lions. Therefore, even now if they had any reservations in fighting with Kaurvas, they could be excused by Duryodhana. Duryodhana also asked Ulooka to tell Krishana that Kaurvas were ready to face the Pandavas and would show that whatever Krishana had said in praise of Pandavas was wrong. He challenged Pandavas to atleast remember the humiliation they had faced and undertaking they had made at the time of Daropadi's 'Chirharan' and should be completed now or revert back in impotency. Duryodhana also asked Ulooka to tell the Pandavas about the extent of his army and the brave people in his army, whom Pandavas would not be able to face even for a day. Ulooka went to Pandavas and apprised them of whatever Duryodhana had desired him to convey. The representatives of the kings having all immunities, could speak anything desired to be conveyed and, as a matter of protocol, no action could be taken against such representatives. Pandavas got enraged on whatever Ulooka had told them on behalf of Duryodhana. Ulooka was told to go back and tell Duryodhana that his message had been well received by Pandavas and his wish of giving him a fighting shall now be fulfilled and that he alongwith his brothers and helping kings should think of getting away from this universe as they would not be able to face the arrows of Arjuna and strength of Bhima. Bhima, Nakula, Sehdeva, also apprised Ulooka of their strength and to tell all on Kaurvas' side to count their days and be prepared to go to Yamloka.

Ulooka went back to Duryodhana's place and apprised him of what Pandavas had told him to be conveyed to Duryodhana. Duryodhana then ordered his army to march on Pandavas.

The Pandavas' army was ordered to march to the battle field under the Senapati Daristdumana. The army was distributed in groups and placed under competent commanders. They were also assigned jobs of fighting with particular persons of Duryodhana's army, according to the capability of each commander.

On the other side, Bhishma undertook to be Senapati of Kaurvas' army and apprised Duryodhana of the duties assigned to various commanders under him along with the army allotted to each. Bhishma also explained the qualifications and capability of each of his commanders to Duryodhana and assured him that his army was fully prepared to give a fighting to Pandavas. Knowledge of each of the commanders and the post and army assigned to him had to be explained to the king by the Senapati. So that job had been done by Bhishma to his king Duryodhana and satisfied him with the arrangements made. Duryodhana too explained to the Senapati the arrangements for recoupment of food, army and armaments made by him so that there was no difficulty on any account to be faced by the fighting army and commanders. Senapati then introduced his commanders—Shakuni, Aswatthama, Darona, Kripacharya, Brihadbal, Karna's son Varikhsen, (Karna was not allowed to fight till Bhishma was there) Bhagdatt, Bahalika, Satyavan, and Asur-raj Alambusha explaining the specialities attained by each of them in the art of warfare. But while introducing Karna, Bhishma told Duryodhana that he wished to fight with Pandavas but he had always been letting him down such as during the campaign of war against Pandavas while in forests, he could not face the Gandharvas and fled away from the field enabling Gandharvas to arrest Duryodhana and other brothers and ladies. Again during the fight with Virat, he fled away from the battle field. Now again he had made tall talks but the net result has been nil. He was good for nothing, particularly, when he had already lost his kawach and kundal. He had developed hate against Pandavas and did not know their strength putting himself equal to Arjuna whereas he was not a part equal to him. Darona also confirmed what Bhishma had said. Hearing all this, Karna got enraged and told Bhishma that although he had never done anything wrong to him but still he had always been rebuking him. He even said that Bhishma had not been doing anything for the Kaurvas but Kaurvas did not know this fact and had been having full faith in him, which is not correct as he shall betray them anytime. In kshatriyas, one is known by his strength and not by the dynasty he belonged to nor by the vast family he owned and from that angle there was none in the universe to face him. Karna told that it was not proper for Bhishma to have said all this at that juncture when the armies had been standing face to face waiting for the command to fight as such actions could cause division in the commanders as also demoralise them. Karna even said that one should listen to what old people said but should not listen to the people, who are very old as in that age they develop childish habits. He said that although he would destroy the whole of Pandavas' army but the credit for it would go to Bhishma, being the Senapati. He would not, therefore, fight with Pandavas till Bhishma was alive and shall fight only after his death.

Bhishma told Karna that he was responsible as a Senapati to monitor the war and would not like him to be in the battle field as by his appearance, he did not want to mar the chances of his victory. He told that he could not be defeated even by Parshurama and there was no kshatriya in the universe to face him in the battle-field. Duryodhana then had to interfere and requested both of them to fight in the battle to the best of their ability as his victory depended on their fighting mainly. Such demoralising thing should not take place in the battle-field but it seems Bhishma was convinced that Karna was a betrayer in the battle field based on his experience at past several times and so did not want him to be present in the field, when he was fighting.

Bhishma then praised before Duryodhana the bravery and skill of Pandavas, Daropadi's sons, Abhimanyu and other kings. Although such talks were not apt for the occasion but it seems that since Bhishma was deadly against the war with Pandavas, as he was dead sure of the defeat of Kaurvas as also he had been finding it difficult to compromise to give a fighting to Pandavas, whom he thought were equal to Kaurvas before him, so he might have thought of giving a chance even at that time to patch up with Pandavas and to avoid war. Bhishma had even told Duryodhana that during war he shall not kill the Pandavas being his grandsons and shall not fight with Shikhandi, being a lady converted to manhood. Duryodhana could know the reason of not killing Pandavas but he could not absorb the idea of not fighting with Shikhandi, who was a commander with Pandavas and asked for the matter being explained to him. It is a matter of great protocol that the kshatriyas did not fight with disabled and women. So Duryodhana had a right to know the reason for not fighting with Shikhandi who was not woman then. The readers would also be inquisitive to know it although it pertains to protocol aspect a little only.

Bhishma was the oldest person in Kaurvas. After his father Shantanu's death, his son Chitrangada had been enthroned but he too died early and then the other son Vichitravirya had been coronated, although he was minor at that time. When he became marriageable, Bhishma started finding a suitable girl for him. He came to know of the swayamber of three daughters of Kashiraj. The condition of the swayamber was that the mightiest king could have them in marriage. Many kings had, therefore, collected. Bhishma defeat them all and brought all the three daughters to be married to Vichitravirya. The eldest of them Amba told Bhishma that she had wooed for Raja Shalvaraja and, therefore, should be allowed to go to her first love. Bhishma agreed to her request and married the other two Ambika and Ambalika with Vichitravirya. Then even Raja Shalva did not accept Amba, having been in possession of Bhishma for sometime. She went to Parshurama for help and narrated his story. Parshurama challenged Bhishma but could not defeat him in the very fierce battle that took place between them. Amba then performed tapasya to take revenge from Bhishma. In the next life she was born as a daughter in Drupada's house. Drupada was told that he would have a daughter but after some time, she would become a boy. Therefore, after the birth, she was brought up as a boy. The fact of her being a girl was known to Raja Drupada and his wife only. She was educated also in all warfare activities as a boy. In course of time, she was married too with the daughter of Raja Hiranya Verma of Dasharnadesh. After sometime, the daughter of Hiranya Verma, told about Shikhandi being a lady and hearing this the king became furious and threatened Drupada to face the consequences of his having cheated him by marrying his daughter as a boy with his daughter. Drupada was afraid of the attack by Hiranya Verma. Shikhandi left the mahal and went to the forest, where he met a yaksha. He narrated his story to the yaksha, who agreed to pass on his manhood to Shikhandi in exchange of his womanhood for some days only. Shikhandi accordingly attained manhood. It shows that in those days, surgery must be at top when even such operations of change of gender could take place. Even today a few cases of sex change have come to light. So Shikhandi came back to his mahal and told the entire happening to his father Drupada, who accordingly apprised Raja Hiranya Verma, who sent a few good looking girls to find out whether Shikhandi was a girl or a boy. When those girls found him a boy, they reported the matter to Hiranya Verma, who came back to his town, duly satisfied.

On the other side, after sometime, Kuber, the king of yakshas came to the ashrama. When he did not see Sthoon Karna, the yaksha, who had changed sex he enquired and was told that he had changed sex, He then met the yaksha and out of rage passed on a curse that he shall continue to be a woman now. So subsequently when Shikhandi went to exchange the sex with the yaksha as promised, it could not be exchanged because of the curse passed on him by Kuber and consequently Shikhandi continued to be a boy. Now since he was a woman converted into a man, he could not fight with him.

Duryodhana then asked about their strength from each of his Senapatis in wiping out the army of Pandavas. Bhishma told that he could finish at the rate of ten thousand persons per day. He also told that this was on the basis of the fight as per rules. If the fight by other party was against the rules, then his party would also follow the same system. According to the special godly arms, the Pandavas' army could be finished within one month at the rate of ten lakhs each day. Daronacharya also told that although he was now an old person yet he too could finish Pandavas' army at the same speed as Bhishma could do. Kripacharya told that he could finish it in two months. Karna told that he could finish the Pandavas' army within five days. Bhishma, however, told that Karna had been boasting of his strength till he faced Krishana and Arjuna. After commencing fighting with Arjuna, he shall fly away.

On the other side, Yudhisthra too called his brothers for secret consultations and told that through his spies, he had come to know that Bhishma could finish Pandavas' army in a month and, Drona and Kripacharya in two months, Karna in five days and Aswatthama in ten days. He wanted to similarly know how many days Arjuna and others shall take in finishing Kaurvas' army. Such a reckoning was necessary with a view to see whether a particular king was in a position to fight on equal footing or not. Arjuna told that whatever Kaurvas had said might be correct as they were all very brave persons, well-versed with use of armaments and war tactics. But since he had desired to know his strength, Arjuna told that with the help of Krishana on chariot, he could finish the entire universe, including Deva Loka and Patal Loka within a moment as he had the arm, which Shiva had used for finishing the entire universe at the time of annihilation of universe but the usage of such godly weapons in the ordinary battle was not advisable. He shall, therefore, use only the traditional arms and methods of fighting. He also told that Shikhandi, Satyaki, Drupada, Daristdumana, all his brothers, Abhimanyu and Virat were not less in strength comapred to Bhishma and Dronacharya.

Next day both sides started for fighting after worshipping their respective gods, paying alms to brahmins, wearing kawach as was customary on such occasions. Duryodhana and Yudhisthra ordered 'march' to their respective armies. The armies comprised of elephants, horses, chariots and on foot, accompanied by the eatables, clothes, extra chariots, and medical arrangements as required during the war.

6

Bhishma Parva

The Pandavas' army was on the left side of the Kaurvas' army facing the Kaurvas' army from the right side. All the countries were left with children and old persons as all youngmen had joined the army of Kaurvas or of Pandavas.

This would indicate that in case of war, al. the people, irrespective of Dharma or varna, they belonged to, took pa.t in the battle and fighting was not left for the Kshatriyas only. This principle had not been followed in the Rajputs' battle with Muslim invaders. At the time although it was called 'Dharamyudha' but was left to be fought by kshatriyas only and in this way three-fourth of the people remained unaffected leading to the defeat of Rajput kings.

शून्या च पृथिवी सर्वा बालवृद्धावशेषिता,
निरश्वपुरुषेवासीद् रथकुंजरवर्जिता। (1/7)

Meaning that the entire universe was left with children and old persons only and all horses, elephants, chariots and young persons had gone to the battle field. Not only this but even ladies went to the battle field probably to look after cooking, serving the wounded soldiers, managing the supplies etc. So, Hindu shastras provide for unity of purpose. In case of war between Kaurvas and Pandavas it had become a war of the entire universe as kings of all countries took part in the war either to help Kaurvas or Pandavas. Such a big war in fact has never been fought in India in which many crores of people died. Although it is said that people of entire universe had taken part in the war in subsequent shaloka it is said that people of Jambu Dweep took part in the war. Jambu Dweep refers to Asia continent —

यावत्तपति सूर्यो हि जम्बूद्वीपस्य मण्डलम्,
तावदेव समायातं बलं पार्थिवसत्तम। (1/8)

Yudhisthra had made arrangements for taking rest during the night as the fighting was during the day only. The troops had been given special dresses and insignias with a view to recognising them. The armies of both the sides started moving and conches were blown from both sides. Then Kaurvas, Pandavas and others made out rules of war, esablishing the 'Yudhadharma'. This would indicate that there were detailed laws of war in those days followed by both the parties to the battle. These continued to be followed even during Rajput period that is why Prithvi Raj allowed Mohammed Gauri to go away when he had been defeated treating this in accordance with the principles of war. But the shastras too permit not to follow the rules of war if the other party did not follow the same:

आर्जवेनैव युद्धेन योद्धष्य इतरो जनः,
मायायुद्धेन मायावी इत्येतद धर्मनिश्चय। (193/10)

So Kaurvas and Pandavas desired to fight the war according to laid down rules mutually agreed to by both.

ततस्ते समयं चक्रुः कुरुपाण्डवसोमकाः,
धर्मान संस्थापया मासुर्यद्धानाम भरतर्षभ। (1/26)

The laws of war drafted by them are as under :

1. The fighting shall be during the day time only and after the day's fighting was over, they shall live cordially without any enmity for anyone. It is very difficult to follow such rules but it did happen in Mahabharata that Kaurvas and Pandavas used to talk cordially during the night ; used to attend the funerals of the close people after the battle for the day was over although the killing was by either of the two parties.

2. Tongue-fighting be reciprocated by tongue-fighting only by the other party.

3. Those, who had gone out of the army, should not be killed.

4. The person on chariot should fight with another person on chariot; one or horse should fight with the other too on horse; one on foot should fight with another on foot; one on elephant should fight with the other too on elephant.

5. One should attack on another after apprising him of the way he wanted to fight and the force with which he wanted to fight.

6. One, who was not attentive or who was nervous because of the war, should not be killed.

7. One commandant should fight with one person. The army should fight with army.

8. One, who had surrendered or was fighting with another person, should not be attacked. Similarly, whose arms had been cut off or whose kawach had been torn, should not be attacked.

9. The horse servers or soots, carriers, arms suppliers, band players should not be harmed in any way.

It is, therefore, farce to say that international laws of war have been made by West only. After making these rules, the Kaurvas and Pandavas looked at each other in a very astonished way. Might be none wanted the war but there was no escape. Then the people of both the parties left their repsective places. They were happy and excited.

Thereafter having seen the armies of Kaurvas and Pandavas standing facing each other, Vyasa went to meet Dharitrashtra and told him that the end of his sons had come. He also mentioned giving the power of seeing the war sitting in Hastinapur, who could then see the same.

This power might have been some appliance like the present day television indicating that the technology was so advanced at that time. He also advised Dharitrashtra to take the deaths as per bad time and not worry for the same. Dharitrashtra told Vyasa that he would not be in a position to see his close relations dying in the battle but at the same time, he desired to know what was happening in the battle field. So Vyasa gave such power to Sanjaya, who after seeing the battle, could narrate the same to the king. Vyasa again repeated not to mind the deaths taking place as it was all destined and the victory was on the side of Dharma. Vyasa told of the disastrous results of the war as he could see all this by his power of knowing the past and future. There shall be rivers of blood; dead bodies spread over everywhere, the sky shall be overcast with eagles to eat the deads. Vyasa also told the good and bad signs with the army, which could indicate the loser and victorious in the war. Dharitrashtra then asked Sanjaya to tell him the countries from where the armies had come and the environ of the universe. Sanjaya then told about the species of beings. He told there were birds, animals and human beings. In the battle-field, crores of people had gathered from various countries of the universe. The beings are made of water, air, fire, earth and space. Then he mentioned about Sudarshana Dweep, which is infested with rivers, mountains, trees etc. In this Dweep there were six mountains, which are spread from east to west, touching sea on both sides. This appears to be nothing but Himalaya with East and West ghats of India. This shows the geological knowledge of the people of that time. Dharitrashtra then desired to know about Bharat-Varsha for which Duryodhana, Pandavas and he himself hankered to rule. Sanjya told that Pandavs did not yearn for entire Bharat-Varsha. It is only Shakuni and Duryodhana, who did not want to part with an inch of it. Bharat-Varsha had been dear to rajas like Prithu, Iksvaku, Yayati, Ambrish, Nahusha, Muchkunda, Shibi, Rishabha, Pururva, Gadhi, Dilip and other chakravarty rajas. It has seven mountains—Himalayas, Vindhyas, East and West Ghats, Aravallis etc and other small hills with many rivers like Ganga, Sindh, Saraswati, Yamuna, Krishana, Irawati, Vedvati, Chitrasena, Chitravaha and habituated by Aryas, Malechhas, and Shankar castes. It has about 80 kingdoms of Panchal, Shalva, Madreya, Sursen, Pulind, Bodh, Mal, Matsya, Kaushal, Kunti, Kanti, Chedi, Kuru, Godha, Kashi, Kukkur, Dasarna, Avanti, Gomant, Vidarbha, Pandurastra, Magadha, Malaja, Vahlika, Virat, Swaraska, Samantra, Bhargava, Sudeshan, Vetdhan, Adhirajya, etc., and the kings of all these kingdoms had gathered armies in help of either Kaurvas or Pandavas at the battle field of Kurukshetra. There had been or shall be four yugas—Satya yug, Treta yug, Duapur yug and yet to come Kal yug. Satya yug was for 4000 years, Treta yug for 3000 years, Duapur for 2000 years and followed by Kal yug, whose life could not be estimated. People were very intelligent, religious-minded, rich and humane in Satyayug. In Treta yug too kshatriyas were courageous, religious, brave and protectors of mankind. In Duapur, people were brave and courageous but thinking of winning other kings. In Kal yug, people shall be lethargy, enraged, greedy and biased. Sanjaya then explained that there were seven continents on the earth plus other lokas. He explained about each loka. So, it is certain that the people of that time had fair knowledge of not only the entire universe but of all planets. The mention of seven continents and seven oceans is correct according to the modern discovery also. Whereas we have been able to reach moon only now with great efforts, our ancestors could reach all planets. So the extent of technological development in those days can be well-imagined.

After the commencement of the battle, Duryodhana made proper arrangements for the protection of Bhishma. In the morning of the first day of battle, both armies with their chiefs had gathered in the battle-field. Both armies were fully equipped with arms and were in good fighting mood. Bhishma had arranged his army and in Pandavas, Yudhisthra had arranged his army. There were eleven kshoni troops in Kaurvas' army and seven kshoni in Pandavas' army but all hoped to be victorious in the war. After seeing the Kaurvas' vast army, Yudhisthra was worried as he could not find the way out to enter the army arranged by Bhishma. Then Arjuna consoled him that the number did not matter in the battle. It was only the bravery and the art of fighting, which mattered. With Krishana being with them, there was no better person knowing the battle tactics at that time. Further, the battle could not be won by number of troops or bravery alone, it is the Dharma which leads to victory and since Dharma was on their side, they shall be victorious.

यत्र धर्मो द्युतिः कान्तिर्यत्र ह्रीः श्रीस्तथा मतिः,
यतो धर्मस्ततः कृष्णो यतः कृष्णस्ततो जयः। (23/28)

Then Pandavas arranged their army to fight with Kaurvas' army. Yudhisthra and other brothers then worshipped God and Goddess Durga and paid alms to brahmins to get their blessings before setting out for fighting. The Goddess appeared and told Arjuna that Pandavas shall win the battle as none could defeat 'Nar' and 'Narayan' or Arjuna and Krishana. Goddess then disappeared and Arjuna became sure of victory.

After seeing both armies standing face to face to start fighting, Arjuna told Krishana to take the chariot in between the two armies with a view to enable him to see the armies on both sides and their commanders.

Krishana then took the chariot in between the two armies and asked Arjuna to watch carefully. After seeing Duryodhana and other brothers, Bhishma, Darona, and Kripacharya, Arjuna told Krishana that he was feeling nervous to see and think that he shall have to fight with his guru, brothers, grandfather and kill them. He said he would rather live without the kingdom than killing those revered persons.

न कांक्षे विजयं कृष्ण न च राज्यं सुखानि च,
किं नो राज्येन गोविन्द किं भोगैर्जीवितेन वा। (25/32)

It is here that Krishana readied Arjuna to fight by narrating his 'Karma' and 'Dharma' theory, which came out to be called 'Bhagwad Gita'. This is a dialogue between Krishana and Arjuna and is repeated by Sanjaya for the information of Dharitrashtra. As it is not possible to extract the entire Bhagwad Gita in the context of this book, it would also be incorrect to ignore it altogether as the theory of 'Karma' and 'Dharma' and the intermingling, inter-relation and interdependence of the two constitute the basis of Indian culture and protocol. Therefore, the more important provisions have been discussed here. On Arjuna surrendering arms as he could not fight with his guru and brethren, Krishana told Arjuna that such thinking at this juncture could neither keep him happy in this universe nor after death. The only way open for him at that time was only to fight. Krishana told that human being is a combination of body and soul. The body without soul has no meaning and is burnt at the earliest even by the very close relations of the dead. As regards soul, it never dies and, therefore, by killing anyone, one only deprives him of this body.

न जायते म्रियते वा कदाचित, न्नायं भूत्वा भविता वा न भूयः।
अजो नित्यः शाश्वतोऽयं पुराणो, न हन्यते हन्यमाने शरीरे।।

(26/20)

The soul neither dies nor has rebirth, it is eternal and does not die with the death of this body. One should not, therefore, think in terms of deaths and births of individual but think of what his job was in a given situation. So far as the body is concerned, the human being could not be seen before birth and would disappear again after death. so it is for a small time in between that he is seen in the universe in a particular position. It is, therefore, not advisable to tie up relation with such a mortal thing at the cost of one's 'Karma' and 'Dharma' as per one's varna and should not develop so much intimacy with the human beings as it takes them only for all his happiness and sorrows. Krishana told that by 'Karma' only one attains 'gyan' leading ultimately to salvation. Arjuna then asked if 'gyan' only leads to salvation, why then should one resort to 'Karma'. Krishana told that as he had already mentioned 'Karma' has to be performed as it is a necessary preliminary to reach 'gyan'. All beings are born of food and brought up by food and food is produced by rains. Rains in turn are caused by yagyas and yagyas are performed by 'Karma'. Therefore, 'Karmas' are the product of vedas and vedas are produced by God. Therefore, it is 'Karma' which ultimately leads to absorption in God. A person, therefore, who does not go according to his respective 'Karma' in this universe, indulges in the satisfaction of senses and thus wastes his life. Even Janaka, although detached from universe and worldly involvements, had to perform his 'Karma' as a king till he died. Therefore, even after having become a king or the owner of all wealth, one cannot afford to give up the 'Karma' relevant to his 'Dharma'. Krishana accordingly told him that—

1. One cannot attain salvation without performing 'Karma'.
2. By giving up 'Karma' one cannot attain 'gyan'.
3. One cannot remain without 'Karma' even for a second.
4. It is farce to go on thinking about the worldly matters and giving them up externally.
5. One should, therefore, perform 'Karma' without any consideration after controlling all senses.
6. It is better to continue performing 'Karma' rather than giving it up.
7. One cannot earn one's livelihood without 'Karma'.
8. The 'Karma' involved in holding 'yagyas' does not hold him in worldly involvements but leads to salvation.
9. One is liked in the universe if one keeps performing 'Karma'.
10. It is farce to feel enjoyment in the satisfaction of worldly passions without discharging one's 'Karma'.
11. By performing 'Karma' and living on what remains after yagyas, one gets relieved of all sins. In other words, one, who follows this system he does not commit sins at all.
12. A man, who does not perform yagyas and eats for the sake of maintaining this body only, is a great sinner.
13. The life of a person is waste if he creates obstacles in the working of others.
14. One attains salvation by performing 'Karma' without indulging in worldly involvements.
15. In ancient period, Janaka had attained salvation through 'Karma' only.
16. The people follow the greatmen. The greatmen, therefore, should perform their respective 'Karmas'.
17. Although the God has nothing to do, yet he is always busy in the well-being of all in the universe.
18. Even though one does not think of attaining any 'gyan', one should go on performing 'Karma' for the people at large.
19. One should, therefore, perform 'Karma' and incite others doing 'Karma' too.

20. A learned person should not discourage the people from performing their 'Karmas'.

Krishana told that attaining 'gyan' and then 'Sanyas' is also a 'Karma' as also the result of the 'Karma' as one cannot reach these stages without indulging in 'Karma'. Therefore, 'karma-yog' and 'karma-sanyas' are interdependent. Rather 'karma-sanyas' is dependent of 'karma-yog' and not the vice versa.

Accordingly although 'karma-sanyas' and 'karma-yog' both lead to salvation, yet 'karma-yog' is better of the two. Therefore, a person who performs without consideration and does not have any ill-will against anyone, that 'karma-yogi' is a 'karma-sanyasi' as well. Also the best 'karma-yogi' is one, who is not very happy on any achievement and not very upset on the happening of some undesirable incident. He is a person of free mind and a person has to be free-minded first before resorting to the actual 'Karma'. Therefore, Krishana advised Arjuna to be 'karma-yogi' as 'karma-sanyas' shall automatically follow.

Next thing Krishana told Arjuna was that a man, who goes on performing 'Karma' without caring for the result, is a 'yogi' or a 'sanyasi'.

अनाश्रितः कर्मफलं कार्यं कर्म करोति यः,
स सन्यासी च योगी च न निरग्निर्न चाक्रियाः। (30/1)

One should, therefore, go on performing, leaving the result on God himself as God is always there everywhere and anyone, who sees God in everything (omnipresent), for him God never disappears nor does he disappear for God and accordingly God decides the result of actions by any individual. It should not, therefore, be thought as to how God shall be watching the minute actions of any individual. The nature, Krishana told, comprises of earth, water, fire, air, space, mind, brain and ego.

Added to these is the soul. The being, therefore, comprises of the above eight plus the soul and God is available in all of these ingredients of the being. Therefore, each 'Karma' of the human being is watched and monitored by God only.

Arjuna further desired to know what is Brahma; what is spirituality, what is 'Karma'; what is 'Adhibhoota', what is Adhideva,: what is yagya and how the even-minded people reach him at the end of their lives? Krishana told that Brahma is the ultimate God ; spiritualism is the relation of man with God; the 'Karma' is the performance in day-to-day activities of the human being; all mortal things are 'Adhibhoota' and a man absorbed in God is 'Adhideva' and the existence of God in this body is the 'Adhiyagya'. A man gets what he thinks at the time of death as he had always been thinking of the same during his life. If a man had been thinking of God only throughout his life, at the end of his life too, he would be thinking of only God and getting absorbed in him only. Therefore, Krishana advised Arjuna to think of God always and continue doing his 'Karmas' which for him, being an kshatriya, is the fighting. Krishana further told that He is omnipresent. He is, therefore, available in yagya, in agni, in battle-field, in every part of the human body and all actions by human beings are dictated by him only. He is God and any bhakti of any god reaches him only. Anyone, who performs bhakti of other gods, although it reaches him, but the person so conducting the bhakti of other gods, does not know the position in fact and so till he realises the factual position i.e. God only is everywhere and in everyone and comprises of all gods, he does not reach him. God is in all beings, no one is dear or non-dear to him but one, who remembers him with love, is absorbed in God and God also is seen by him within himself.

समोऽहं सर्वभूतेषु न मे द्वेष्योऽस्ति न प्रियः,
ये भजन्ति तु मां भक्त्यामयि ते तेषु चाप्यहम। (33/39)

Krishana has further said that it is not only the brahmins or kshatriyas, who reach him, he is available to all and eveyone, whether he is vaish, shudra, woman or chandal, and everyone reaches him if he takes refuge under him and gets absorbed in him. Here Krishana has dismantled the thinking of brahmins that God is not available and bhakti cannot be performed or religious books cannot be read by shudras, women and chandals. So all are one for God. Even in Ramcharitmanas, Rama himself has told Sabri that he recognises only the bhakti and anyone—mortal or immortal— reaches him by performing bhakti. Krishana too repeats the same lure for the benefit of all people though addressing Arjuna :

मां हि पार्थ व्यापाश्रित्य येऽपि स्युः पापयोनयः
स्त्रियो वैश्यास्तथा शुद्रास्तेऽपि यान्ति परांगतिंम्। (33/32)

Inspite of these pronounments, in Kalyug, brahmins restrained shudras and woman from resorting to Bhagwad bhakti. This belief was very much in vogue during Rajput period and Muslim rule in India and is responsible in a lot of Hindus in lower castes resorting to conversion as Mohammedans and subsequently as Christians as there was no distinction in various people in those Dharmas. This forced Tulsidasa to repeat the same thing in Ramcharitmanas in 16th century and subsequently repeated by people of Arya Samaj and some other reformers in Hindus. This has enabled to put a check on such exodus of Hindus to other Dharmas. Krishana told Arjuna that anyone, who has confidence in him, is his devotee. He worships him, has respect for him, surrenders to him, and ultimately attains him. Krishana told that the reasons for his incarnation in the universe are not known even to gods or to rishis and anyone, who had known the same, achieves him. It is God only, who imbibes in the human beings, the firmness, strength, factual knowledge of things, keeping balanced in happiness and sorrows, non-violence feeling, keeping the senses and the mind under control and ultimately the birth and the death and the specie to be granted on next birth. Therefore, nothing is hidden from Him. It is better, therefore, that one should not think of keeping anything into himself and entrust all his doings to Him, which otherwise too reach Him only. Therefore, anyone, who reaches this conclusion and acts on it, is considered to have known Him. Arjuna asked that whereas it is correct that God is in every soul and he directs the people doing everything but then how shall one remember the God. Krishana told that there is no end to the extent of his size as also to the minutest of his form. That is how he is available in the smallest insect and in the biggest animal, an elephant. He is also responsible for the birth, maintenance and annihilation of each being by his three powers in Brahma, Vishnu and Mahesh as also in all gods responsible for awarding one thing or the other to the beings. So much so that he is even available in immortals, what to speak of mortals since he is responsible for creation of beings and the beings are constituted of earth, water, fire, air and space. So he is present in all these ingredients. On Krishana having told that he is available in all mortals and immortals, Arjuna naturally desired to have a darshan of the almighty. He accordingly requested for it. Krishana then presented himself in a Virata form in which, all gods, beings, all lokas, all stars, all universes, mountains, rivers could be seen. Seeing that, Arjuna narrated that he could see everything present in him confirming the conviction that he in turn is available in everything and told that he only is the almighty God, worthy of being known by everyone and on whom everyone could depend. Krishana then told that all the kings and troops present there could be seen in him and their cotinuance depended on his mercy only. Arjuna should, therefore, not think that he would be killing them as by God's wish they are all destined to be dead and if Arjuna does not kill them even then they had to die. Arjuna, therefore, was only a means to kill them in this apparent Mrityu Loka. Therefore, Krishana ordered Arjuna to kill all Darona, Bhishma, Duryodhana, other commanders and troops, who had appeared there as the enemies. Krishana even told that their destiny only had bifurcated the persons into two—one on his side and another on the side of Kaurvas. Those on his side are mostly to survive, whereas those on the side of the Kaurvas, are mostly to die. Arjuna having been convinced of the 'Karma' and 'Dharma', now to be adopted by him, paid respects to Krishana but still trembling was there in his mind as he was not immidiately able to adjust to Krishana's Virata position, having seen Krishana as his friend, brother and co-citizen. Krishana told him that it is he only who had been able to see the Virata form of Krishana and none else had even seen it. He should, therefore, now get up and pick up his arms to enter into the battle-field and now since Arjuna had surrendered himself to God's will, having become his bhakta, it was only proper that he did whatever was required of him by the God.

Arjuna, then, for the benefit of the public at large, asked Krishana about who is better of the two—who remembers him as a God possessing all attributes (Saguna) or the others, who remember him as a God without these attributes. Krishana told that it is very difficult to get absorbed in a God without attributes and those, who submit their everything to the God with attributes is very close to him and gets absorbed in him. If one is not straightaway able to reach him, he should make continuous efforts in that direction and since he looks into each and every action of the people, the efforts made by the persons to reach him, do not go waste even if they are not able to reach him as it is a continuous process for lives. Such a person in course of time starts remaining the same in happiness and sorrow, able to control all his senses and remembers God without any consideration and is then able to get salvation. For this purpose, Krishana told that Brahma and Jeeva are apparently separate but Brahma exists in every Jeeva and only by yoga, one can realise his existence in himself. Once this recognition is made, the Jeeva reaches him and in other words this is called the attainment of 'Gyan' and then through 'Gyan', one reaches the Nirguna Brahma. But, as already stated, realisation of God within self is through yoga, which can be exercised by a few only. Now within the 'Gyan' too, there are various stages. The best 'Gyan' is one, by dint of which, one could attain salvation. After one is born, he is tied with the three gunas—Satoguna, Rajoguna and Tamoguna. Now it is upto the individual to slowly and slowly give up tamoguna and resort only to satoguna and rajoguna. For this purpose, one has to get detached from all worldly involvements and the ambitions for the fulfilment of all senses. After this detachment, one reaches a stage of rajoguna. Then in course of time, one has to put himself in rememberance of God only and through that one passes over rajoguna and reaches the stage of satoguna. Then, in this stage, one starts having a feeling of absorption in almighty God culminating in full attainment of salvation. In this way, tamoguna puts the man into worldly involvements, including the satisfaction of senses. He thus remains lost in these and dies and gets rebirth. In some life, one gives up these fulfilments and then reaches the rajoguna, which is the stage of 'Karma'. After this 'Karma' based on Dharma, one gets into satoguna or the closeness to the almighty.

निर्मानमोहा जित संगदोषा
अध्यात्मनित्या विनिवृत्तकामाः
द्वन्द्वैर्विमुक्ता सुख दुख संज्ञै–
गच्छन्त्यमूढ़ा पदमव्ययं तत्। (39/5)

Those, who have come up above the greed and ambitions and have got completely detached from worldly involvements and have been thinking of God only always and are not attracted by senses, such person are bereft of happiness and sorrow and such persons by dint of such 'gyan' attain salvation.

Arjuna asked that there are persons, who surrender themselves fully to the almighty but do not follow the tenets of shastras in worshipping him, could they be çalled satvik or rajsi? Krishana told that for this purpose one has to know the fundamentals of the three positions—satvik, rajsi and tamsik. The persons have faith in God according to their inner feelings. Accordingly, those, who perform 'tap' but remain involved in worldly ambitions, i.e. do not follow the vedic tenets of complete detachment, are tamsik even though they perform tapasya as their tapsya is also tied with fulfilment of worldly desires.

One, therefore, have to first give up the worldly attachments and then as tapasya is performed, the person is turned into rajsi or satvik stage depending upon the extent of detachment attained. Like the inner feelings of rajo, tamo and sato, one's liking for food is also based on these inner feelings. Satvik persons take their food which is good for health and to their taste. The rajsi persons take bitter, saltish food and the tamsik persons take alcohol, stale non-vegetarian food. So the food effects one's habits and temperaments and classify a person in one of the gunas and accordingly he proceeds further in attainment of salvation too. On Arjuna's asking about the difference in sanyas and detachment, Krishana told that detachment is again satvik, rajsi and tamsik. The

'Karma' of tap, giving alms and performing yagyas is not to be given up. These are must for any human being as these purify the person's inner feelings. Rather such 'Karma' should be resorted to leaving all worldly involvements and having no consideration for the result. If, however, anyone thinks that all 'Karmas' lead to sorrow and, therefore, if one leaves all 'Karmas' so that it does not involve any labour, such person is only rajsi and does not get full result. Since it is not possible to leave performing all bodily jobs involving labour, one should go on doing 'Karma' but have detachment from worldly involvements and fulfilment of senses in which case he shall become satvik.

Accordingly, Krishana told Arjuna that his declining to fight is to avoid the labour by the body and is a rajsi 'Karma'. If, therefore, he desired the best results then only course open for him was to fight which is the 'Karma' as per his Dharma and Dharma only makes the man satvic and leads to attainment of salvation. His 'Karma', in the situation, is, therefore, to fight which is the Dharma of a kshatriya. Such 'Karma' is his worship of God, his self realisation and self fulfilment. After this he should leave the result to God. By 'Karma' as per Dharma, and complete submission before the almighty, one reaches the almighty. Then it is for the almighty to grant him the best results.

सर्वधर्मान परित्यज मामेकं शरणं व्रज,
अहं त्वा सर्वपापेभ्यो मोक्षयिष्यामि मा शुचः। (42/66)

Krishana then asked Arjuna if he had carefully listened to what he had stated and whether after listening to all that, he had been able to give up the affection created by ignorance of the facts and whether he was now prepared to perform his 'Karma' i.e. resorting to fighting, which was the Dharma of the kshatriya. Krishana also, in the end, consoled him by telling him that according to him, with Krishana and Arjuna with his Gandeva Dhanush, rested the victory, the fame and that was the best course of action. Krishana then stopped further narration and Arjuna got up, got hold of his Dhanush and got ready for the action in the battle field. All the sainiks also got ready and blew their conches and band announcing the start of the battle.

When both the armies were now ready to start fighting, Yudhisthra suddenly put off his kawach and threw all his arms. He got down from the chariot and proceeded towards Bhishma with folded hands. This was the protocol in reverence to the respected elders, although they were now on the other side of the battle-field and ready to give a fighting as enemies. Such a protocolic fulfilment can be seen in Hindu culture only and is the climax of any protocolic ethics. Yudhisthra went to Bhishma. He was also followed by all his brothers, Krishana and some important kings. Arjuna asked Yudhisthra as to why leaving them all, he was going to the side of the enemy. Bhima also enquired similarly why he had put his kawach and arms off, when both the armies were ready to start fighting. Nakula too stated that he was worried why his elder brother was going towards the enemy without telling the reason for the same as he had fear that someone could attack him. Sehdeva also asked that it was not safe to go toward the enemy. But Yudhisthra continued without any response. Then Krishana told Pandava brothers that he had known that Yudhisthra had gone to take blessings of Bhishma, Darona, Kripacharya and Shalya before starting the fighting as according to protocol, continuing from vedic period, anyone starting fighting without the blessings of the guru, and elders used to lose his image in their eyes and the one, who fights after taking the blessings of the revered persons, comes out victorious in the battle. The people in Duryodhana's army considered that Yudhisthra had been going to Bhishma to take refuge having been frightened from the battle and so had been cursing him and had been surprised why he had got frightened when he had brave brothers like Bhima and Arjuna. They were all imagining what the reaction of Bhishma would be when Yudhisthra approached him for refuge.

Yudhisthra on reaching near Bhishma, touched his feet and presenting himself along with all brothers asked for his permission for fighting with him as also his requisite blessings for victory in the battle. As if Bhishma had been waiting for Yudhisthra to come to pay respects, he said that if he had not come to him for asking for blessings, he would have passed a curse for being defeated but now since he had come, his blessings would be with him. He also asked Yudhisthra to ask for any boon he desired of him, except for requesting him not to fight on behalf of Kaurvas, for which he was duty bound. He was prepared to give to Yudhisthra anything, he required. Yudhisthra too in the situation requested him to bless him with his guidance, whenever required and he might fight on behalf of Kaurvas. Yudhisthra then asked Bhishma the way he could be defeated. Bhishma told that none could defeat him in the battle and his last time too had not so far come. So he would tell about it sometimes later. Yudhisthra, after paying respects to him, went to guru Darona. After paying him respects, again Yudhisthra requested for guru's permission and blessings for fighting. Guru also said if he had not come to him before the start of the fighting, he would have passed curse on him, but now his blessings were with him and he could ask for any boon except that he could not decline from fighting on behalf of Kaurvas. Yudhisthra asked him to fight on behalf of Kaurvas but continue to guide him during the battle and wish him win the battle. Guru told that Krishana being on his side, he was sure to win.

यतो धर्मस्ततः कृष्णो यतः कृष्णस्ततो जयः
युद्धयुस्व गच्छ कौन्तेय पृच्छमांकिं ब्रवीमि ते। (43/60)

Again Yudhisthra asked him, that he could not normally be defeated by anyone, then how he could be defeated. Guru told him that he could not be defeated till alive. Efforts should, therefore, he made to kill him early. On being asked the way to kill him, guru told him that except at the time when he was unconscious, he could not be killed. Some one should, therefore, kill him when he was unconscious. Yudhisthra then paid respects and went to Kripacharya. Here again Yudhisthra paid respects and requested for his blessings for the victory in the battle. Kripacharya also said that in case he had not come to him, he would have passed curse on him for being defeated but now having come to him, he wished him coming out victorious in the battle and asked for any boon being granted. Yudhisthra asked him to continue guiding him during the battle and had no objection to his fighting on behalf of the Kaurvas as he deemed fit. Yudhisthra then went to Shalya and paid him respects and requested for his blessings. Yudhisthra told that he had no objection to his fighting on behalf of the Kaurvas but at the time of fighting between Karna and Arjuna, he should discourage Karna as his sarthy. Shayla agreed to this request.

After that Krishana went to Karna and asked him that since he was not fighting on behalf of Kaurvas till Bhishma was alive, he could, during that time, fight on behalf of Pandavas and join Duryodhana after Bhishma was no more. Karna, however, replied that he had already vowed to fight on behalf of Duryodhana and, therefore, could not now change his mind. Krishana came back to Pandavas. Then standing amidst the two armies, Yudhisthra asked if anyone from Kaurvas' side wanted to join him, he was welcomed. On this Yuyuts, who was Dharitrashtra's son from a vaish wife, changed his side and joined Pandavas, who welcomed him and gave charge of some army. All appreciated Pandavas' action. Then the bands started playing from both sides. There cannot be another example of such cordiality and frankness in the commanders of the armies of two enemies as is seen in Mahabharata which has been the biggest war, responsible for killing the maximum number of people and asks for the enemy's blessings for victory in the battle and the way how the enemy could be killed and the enemy too waiting for sush a request, grants the required boon for victory of the enemy as also the way he could be defeated/killed. This is the unique protocol in Hindu culture only.

Then the battle started with blowing of conches and bands. At first Pandavas' army attacked the Kaurvas' army. The commanders had been fighting with commanders and the army with the army. One with bow and arrow had been fighting with another with bow and arrow and one with gada with the other with gada; one on chariot with the other on chariot and on foot with another on foot and so on as per laid laws of war. Arjuna and Bhishma, Shalya and Yudhisthra, Dristduman and Darona, Dushashana and Nakula had started fighting with each other.

In the battle, neither father recognised the son nor the guru his disciple or the brother his brother. Everyone was yearning for a victory by killing his opponent. Some chariots had been broken, many sainiks had been killed. Bhishma had the day. As already indicated, he had already killed over 10,000 persons. So their was fear in the Pandavas' army. Duryodhana had been trying to protect Bhishma. So whenever Bhishma became weak, he had been sending other commanders like Durmukha, Kripacharya, Shalya for his help. Bhishma had been fighting with Arjuna and then with Abhimanyu or Bhima. Dharitrashtra had been enquiring about the progress of battle from Sanjaya and since Sanjaya could see the battle with his eyes, he had been narrating it to the king bit by bit. There was fierce fighting between Sweta and son of Raja Virat in which Swet was killed. Dharitrashtra was happy to know the incidents in which Kaurvas had been victorious. The king had special anxiety about the fighting skill of Arjuna. He told Sanjaya that he and all others had made maximum efforts to check the war but failed. Now, however, he had weakness for his sons and wished their victory. Bhishma had been killing the Pandava commanders, one by one. After the sun set, the fighting was stopped. It was a day for Kaurvas to rejoice and for Pandavas to worry. Bhishma and Duryodhana had been happy and Yudhisthra was worried. He along with his brothers and principal kings went to Krishana during the night and told him that Bhishma had killed a lot of his army and many commanders. In such a situation, he had no option but to go to forests closing the battle as there was no use getting the entire army killed by Bhishma. In such a situation, some one had to be there to encourage the demoralised persons. Krishana did this job. He told Yudhisthra not to worry about such incidents as he had very brave brothers and kings on his side. In course of time, Shikhandi shall kill Bhishma and then all shall be well. Dristduman also told Pandavas that he shall kill most of the

Kaurvas' commanders. Therefore, the battle should be continued.

For the next day again the Vyuhchakra was arranged by both the armies and the fighting started after the blowing of conches. On Kaurvas' side, Duryodhana encouraged his people to face Pandavas with bravery, duly protecting Bhishma, the Principle Senapati. Each of them, therefore, took their armies. Bhishma and Arjuna had fierce fighting. The fighting was again one to one and only after one was wounded, became unconscious or his chariot/sarthi damaged, did the other come forward. Daristdumana and Darona too had fierce fighting with bows and arrows.

Bhishma killed Sakradeva, Bhanuman, and Ketumana with many of their sainiks. Bhima also attacked many elephants, who became ferocious and crushed Kaurvas' army. Then there was sun set and both armies stopped fighting. The second day had been the day of victories for Pandavas.

Third day again there was fierce fighting amongst both the armies, which were in so good a formation that neither could be whithered through for a long time. The Pandavas were victorious on the third day and Duryodhana became anxious as his army was on the run because of the attack by Arjuna and Abhimanyu. After Duryodhana had shown his anxiety, Bhishma became serious. Then at one stage, Krishana got ready to kill Bhishma, when Arjuna could not defeat him. But since Krishana had undertaken not to fight in the battle, Arjuna reminded him of his undertaking and told Krishana that he would fight more seriously. Fierce fighting ensued and Arjuna defeated many commanders including Darona, Bhishma, Jayadratha, Bahlika. Then at the sun-set, the fighting stopped and the armies went to their respective sides.

On the fourth day again Bhishma started to fight along with Darona, Duryodhana, Bahlika, Drumanstana, Chitrasena. On the other side Arjuna and other brothers also set out to face them. Abhimanyu also was at his best so much so that Kaurvas started feeling that Abhimanyu had come up as another Arjuna. Daristdumana killed Shaley's son in the battle. Bhima killed several elephants and wounded many, who crushed the enemy's army. After Arjuna had tired, Bhima came to fight with Bhishma. Satyaki fought with Bhurisarva. Ghatotkachha also came on the scene and he along with Bhima, his father, killed several of Duryodhana's brothers. Duryodhana became anxious and requested Bhishma to kill the Pandavas. Bhishma also told that he had been doing his best and had been killing over 10,000 persons of the enemy each day as indicated by him at the beginning of the war. On the fourth day although Pandavas had a better day, they had fear from Bhishma's side, as he had been giving fierce fighting to Pandavas. Bhishma was, however, convinced that Pandavas had to come out victorious as per boon of Brahma passed in their favour. He also told that Dharma was on their side, whereas Kaurvas had always been taking refuge under misdeeds and cheating. Bhishma also told that Krishana was the incarnation of God and Arjuna the 'Nar'. They are 'Nar' and 'Narayan' of the previous time. Bhishma narrated the birth and deeds of Krishana as an incarnation of God. Even at that time, Bhishma asked Duryodhana to come to terms with Pandavas. Then both Bhishma and Duryodhana went to their respective resting places.

On the fifth day again both the armies stood face to face. Bhishma and Yudhisthra formed their armies in proper Vyuhus. Bhishma and Bhima started fighting resulting in many deaths of men and horses and elephants. Similarly, other commanders also fought from both sides like Virata with Bhishma, Aswatthama with Arjuna, Duryodhana with Bhima and Abhimanyu with Laxmana (son of Duryodhana). Bhurisarva killed ten sons of Satyaki. Arjuna killed atleast 25000 troops and commanders. They had all come as per Duryodhana's direction to kill Arjuna but were killed by Arjuna. Then there was sun-set and so the day's fighting was over.

On the sixth day again battle started with new kind of formation of both the armies by Bhishma and Yudhisthra, who were masters of formation. Many of Duryodhana's brothers had been killed. Dharitrashtra was told that their army comprised of very brave persons. There were neither youngers nor old persons but all in their youth and fit to fight duly trained in the use of armaments of various kinds. Even then if the Kaurvas' army commanded by Bhishma, Darona was defeated, it shall be the result of nothing else except the fortune. Bhishma, Darona and Daristdumana were at their best. Bhima killed several of Dharitastra's sons. Then Duryodhana came on the scene and injured Bhima. When Bhima came to senses, he attacked on Duryodhana and defeated him. Abhimanyu and Daropadi's sons fought with the sons of Dharitrashtra and killed several of them. Before the sun-set, thousands of chariots, horses, and elephants had been killed and equal number of troops killed. Duryodhana again got anxiety but again Bhishma assured him of a fierce fighting.

On the seventh day again fighting started after the armies had been put to a new kind of formation. The formations had been broken by Bhishma and Arjuna. There was fighting between Darona and Virata and Aswatthama and Shikhandi and Bhishma and Arjuna. Arjuna killed many of the enemy's troops and several commanders.The rest started fleeing. Dristduman defeated Duryodhana, who fled. Iravin defeated Vind and Anuvind, Ghatotkachha defeated Bhagdutta and Nakula and Sehdeva defeated Shalya. Yudhisthra defeated Shrutayu Chekitana and Kripacharya became unconscious, Abhimanyu defeated Chitrasen, and Susharma fought with Arjuna. Fierce fighting also ensued between Arjuna and Bhishma and Bhishma killed many of Pandavas' sainiks. Bhima also killed many elephants and several sons of Dharitrashtra, Shikhandi and Bhishma also were in the field. Bhishma cut Shikhandi's dhanush. Yudhisthra reminded Shikhandi that he had undertaken to kill Bhishma then why he was now going back from his undertaking and not fighting with Bhishma. Then Shikhandi attacked on Bhishma but was on the way checked by Shalya as commanders on Kaurvas' side knew that Bhishma would not fight with Shikhandi, being a woman converted into manhood. Bhima killed several of Dharitrashtra's sons. Also there was fighting between Bhishma and Yudhisthra. Then Nakula and Sehdeva came to fight with Bhishma but were hurt. This caused anxiety in the mind of Yudhisthra regarding the damage done by Bhishma to his army. In the evening both armies went to their places for night's rest praising each other's army-men. In the evening arrangement existed for removing arrows from the body; treating the wounds, taking bath to refresh and taking their meals. There was at that time no enmity amongst the people of the two armies.

On the eighth day fighting started. Each army had been specially formed. Each commander pondered over breaking the formation of the other army. Bhishma had killed many troops of Pandavas' army. Bhima killed eight sons of Dharitrashtra. Duryodhana again showed his anxiety before Bhishma. Thousands of army-men had been killed on both sides. Duryodhana even alleged Bhishma to be biased in favour of Pandavas although he had been his Senapati. Dharitashtra was anxious that his sons were being killed by Bhima everyday. He cursed his fortune that his sons, although quite brave, were being killed everyday by Bhima. He even remembered what Vidur had told him that Pandavas would kill all his sons if he did not come on terms with Pandavas and parted with half the rajya to them. Similarly, even Bhishma, Darona had advised for a peaceful settlement with Pandavas. Iravana killed several of Shakuni's brothers. Then Duryodhana deputed Alambusha rakshas to kill Iravana. In the fierce fighting, Iravana was killed due to deceitful actions of Alambusha as also many of Kaurvas attacked on Iravana alone although it was against the settled law that one shall fight with one. It is here that Kaurvas had started causing breach of the laws of war in desperation. Arjuna had not known the death of his son. He was busy in fighting with the commanders, who had come to protect Bhishma on order of Duryodhana. Ghatotkachha and Duryodhana too had fierce fighting. Then Darona too came to help Duryodhana. Ghatotkachha had been fighting with both. Then Bhishma sent several other commanders to fight with Ghatotkachha, who thrashed them all. Then Bhima too came to help Ghatotkachha and seeing him, Kaurvas' army fled. Then Duryodhana and Bhishma asked Bhagdutta to give a fighting to Bhima, Ghatotkachha and other Pandavas. Again fierce fighting took place. Arjuna came to know of his son Iravana's death and was shocked. Bhima killed nine of Dharitrashtra's sons. And then the fighting stopped on sun-set and the army went for rest during the night in their respective cantonments.

During the night, Duryodhana had secret meeting with Shakuni, Karna and Dushashana thinking of ways to win the battle. Duryodhana told that Darona, Bhishma, Kripacharya, Shalya and Bhurisarva had not been intentionally harming the Pandavas due to the reasons best known to them only as a result Pandavas had been ruthlessly killing his army-men. Bhima had already killed many of his brothers. Karna suggested that he was not able to fight till Bhishma surrendred arms and then all Pandavas shall be killed by him in the battle field. Duryodhana then went to see Bhishma in his camp and stated that he had not been killing the Pandavas as a result of which they had been overpowering the Kaurvas' army. He had made him Senapati thinking that he would kill all Pandavas. On hearing this, Bhishma became upset but since he was talking to the king of Hastinapur, he did not talk raw before Duryodhana. Bhishma then told that he had been doing his best in the battle field and is even prepared to sacrifice his life but is somehow not able to kill the Pandavas as Arjuna is extra-ordinarily capable of defeating anyone in the battle field, including him. Bhishma also reminded Duryodhana how Arjuna alone had got Duryodhana released when they had been arrested by Gandharvas. At that time, even Karna had fled from the battle field. Subsequently at the time of attacking Virata, Arjuna alone had defeated them all, including Karna. So it was not quite easy to win him over. He reiterated that he shall still try to kill all in the battle field except Shikhandi with whom he shall not fight due to reasons already told. Duryodhana then left for his camp after paying respects to Bhishma. He then briefed all his commanders that their main job would now be to protect Bhishma as he only was capable of killing the Pandavas and had now undertaken to kill them.

Fighting started on the ninth day after both the armies had been put to a new kind of formation. Men from each side attacked the enemy's force. Daropadi's sons and Abhimanyu had fierce fighting with Alambusha rakshas as a result of which Kaurvas' army fled out of fear and Alambusha had been badly hurt. Arjuna had been fighting with Bhishma and Satyaki had been fighting with Darona. Kripacharya, Aswatthama and Darona came to help Bhishma and so started fighting with Arjuna. Both had been fighting as per their respective capability. Darona had not been showing any favour to Arjuna, who was his disciple and so Arjuna had not been averse to killing Darona in the battle field as in the battle field there is no relation of father and son or guru and disciple as per protocol of war ethics.

There was fierce fighting amongst the commanders and the army of both sides. On the other side, Sanjaya had been narrating every bit of the battle proceedings to Dharitrashtra and holding him responsible for all this bloodshed as he could not order his son Duryodhana to resist from fighting and parting with the share or kingdom to Pandavas. Arjuna defeated Trigartis, Abhimanyu defeated Chitrasena, Darona defeated Drupada and Bhima defeated Bahlika, Satyaki had been fighting with Bhishma. Yudhisthra and Nakula and Sehdeva defeated Shakuni's army and then fought with Shalya. Bhishma fought with extra vigour as a result of which Pandavas' army fled. Then having desperated about Arjuna not giving proper fighting to Bhishma, Krishana offered to fight in the situation although he had commited not to fight. Arjuna, however, checked him although Krishana had already called in his 'Sudarshan Chakra' to kill Bhishma. Bhishma, knowing full well that Krishana was incarnation of God, invited him to kill him as he would get salvation if killed by Krishana in the battle-field, while fighting with him. But Arjuna was somehow able to check him from fighting with Bhishma. Arjuna then undertook to kill Bhishma. Bhishma killed many in Pandavas' army. In the evening on sun-set, the fighting for the ninth day came to a stop. There was lot of killing of Pandavas' army. They were fleeing the battle field and were afraid of further attack by Bhishma. In the night the Pandavas had secret meeting along with Krishana to consider further course of action in view of heavy damage to their army by Bhishma. They decided that they should approach Bhishma for his advice how he could be killed so that they could be victorious in the war. They accordingly went to him as already agreed by Bhishma to put forth his advice as may be required by Pandavas. They paid respects to him. Bhishma too welcomed them all and asked what he could do for them except not giving up fighting in the battle. Yudhisthra asked him to tell the way, they could be victorious in the war and get kingdom back.

Bhishma told that he could not be defeated in the war by any one. The only way for Pandavas' victory could be by killing him and he could be killed if he stopped fighting and at that time injured severely by arrows. Such stopping from fighting could be possible if Shikhandi could come and fight with him. Then he shall put down his arms and someone could at that time kill him by multiple arrows and this job could not be done by anyone other than Krishana and Arjuna combined. Therefore, Arjuna should fight with him putting Shikhandi before him and when he put down his arms, Arjuna could kill him. Then Arjuna was in a fix, how he would be able to kill Bhishma, when he had put his arms down. Then Krishana again coached him to fight and kill even the closest in the battle-field.

On the tenth day of battle, again both the armies were ready in a new formation. Shikhandi had been inspired to fight with Bhishma, although he was afraid of Bhishma and not prepared to fight with him. He was reminded of his undertaking to kill Bhishma. He could not be told about what had transpired during the night in the talks with Bhishma. Shikhandi accordingly got ready to face Bhishma.

Arjuna continued fighting, when Shikhandi came in betwen and by Arjuna's arrows Bhishma became unconscious. When he came in senses, he again started fierce fighting. Then Krishana took the chariot in a favourable position and asked Arjuna to now attack on Bhishma, injuring sensitive areas. Arjuna did accordingly keeping Shikhandi with him but all Kaurvas' commanders attacked on Arjuna. Arjuna cut off Bhishma's bow. He took another bow but that too was cut. Like this, he had taken many bows but all were cut by Arjuna. Arjuna continued his attack on Bhishma and many arrows had been thrust in him injuring the sensitive parts and Bhishma fell down from his chariot. He kept lying on the arrows. At that time, sun was not in a favourable position as it was inclined towards South and it was not considered as good time for dying. Since Bhishma had control on death and death would reach him only when he wished for it, rishis came and after Bhishma's darshan asked him when he would like to die. Bhishma told that it could take place when sun was inclined towards the North.

This was to take place after six months. Pandavas were happy but there was shock on Kaurvas' side. All armymen put down their arms as required under protocol on the death of the Senapati. Some such protocol even continues today in one form or the other. Dharitrashtra was worried on Bhishma's death. Seeing Kaurvas put down their arms, Pandavas also stopped fighting on that day. Bhishma was lying on arrows except that there were no arrows to keep his head in straight position. He told all, who had come to see him that his head was not in comfortable position. Kaurvas brought very comfortable pillows but he called Arjuna, who was in tears. He told Arjuna that his head was not in a comfortable position and asked him to provide a suitable pillow. Arjuna then took his dhanush and put three arrows in his head to keep it straight with other body. Bhishma felt satisfied and told Arjuna if he had offered some other kind of pillow, he would have passed a curse on him. After sometime, Bhishma told Arjuna that he was thirsty and could not take water etc. by sitting or standing. Arjuna then struck an arrow in earth and there came a fountain of water from the earth enabling Bhishma to quench his thirst. Duryodhana came with some surgeons to remove the arrows from Bhishma's body and treat his wounds but Bhishma told him that he shall continue lying on the arrows till he died. Next day onward many people came for Bhishma's darshan. Bhishma told Duryodhana that he had seen that Arjuna had been able to provide him cold sweet water, which none in Kaurvas cold do. He also advised Duryodhana that there was still time for his agreeing to his suggestion and handing over their share of kingdom to Pandavas otherwise all Kaurvas shall be perished by Pandavas as Krishana, the incarnation of God, and Arjuna, the incarnation of 'Nar' were with them, whom no one could conquer. But Duryodhana as usual, declined to agree to the suggestion and, therefore, war contined. All the kings went to their camps. Then Karna came there. He saw Bhishma sleeping on the stage of arrows. His eyes were closed. Tears came in his eyes. Karna called on him and told him that before him was Karna, whom he had always been treating in a biased manner. Bhishma, then called Karna close to him and embraced him like a father, and told him that he had always been having rivalry with him, which had biased his mind. He also told that if Karna had not come to meet him he would have passed a curse on him. He told him that he was the son of Kunti and Surya as told by Narada to him and that he was not biased against him but did not like him as he had been speaking against the Pandavas on inspiration by Duryodhana. He had such an evil mind because he was born of virgin Kunti and brought up by a mean caste family. That is why he had rebuked him several times. He was not less than Arjuna and Krishana in bravery and operation of dhanushbana. He had no grudge against him now. He advised him to be on the side of Pandavas, his brothers as this shall bring the war to an end. Karna told that he too was aware of what he had told him and it was all correct as he was actually Kunti's son but Kunti threw him in water and it was Radhe only, who had brought him up. Therefore, protocolically and socially as also ethically, Radhe was his mother. Further, since Duryodhana had saved him from humiliation several times and made him the king of Angadesh, as also he had readied himself for the battle on his strength, he could not cause a breach of his trust in him. As Bhishma could not give up Hastinapur Raja, inspite of his unbearable actions, so Karna could not leave Duryodhana in the lurch. This was the protocolic requirement as a friend and as a vassal king under the suzerainty of Hastinapur raja. He knew Pandavas and Krishana and he only could fight and defeat Pandavas. Since he had already decided to fight on behalf of Duryodhana, he desired his blessings to take part in the war. He also begged to be excused for any wrong done to him. Bhishma told him if he cold not get away from the battle, then he should fight for attaining salvation as a warrior attains salvation if he dies in battle-field. He should fight with Pandavas keeping all laws of war and ethics in view. He wished Karna to attain whatever he wished after being killed by Arjuna in the battle. He should fight without pride and according to kshatriya Dharma and in this way, he would attain the last stage of salvation. Karna then took permission from Bhishma, paid his respects, as per protocol and went to Duryodhana.

7
Darona Parva

In the beginning as per protocol, God is remembered. Then Saraswati, the goddess of knowledge is remembered.

Then the narration is started in the form of one asking some clarification from the other. In Mahabharata, this narration is by Vaisampayanji to Janmejaya. After Bhishma had been killd by Shikhandi, Dharitrashtra became very upset as he had been wishing the victory of his sons and killing of the Senapati Bhishma was a great set-back in his designs. The victory of the army depends on collective efforts of the army and the commanders but it more depends on the commander-in-chief as any wrong decision by him could spoil the entire game. Bhishma having been very capable Senapati, his death caused a vacuum in Kaurvas because a capable senapati had gone and secondly it gave credence to Pandavas for victory over Kaurvas as had been foreseen by Vidur. Duryodhana arranged for the proper care of Bhishma, lying on arrows and set off for the battle field. Bhishma's death led to two decisions being taken—one to appoint a new Senapati and another to bring in Karna in the battle-field. Bhishma had not allowed Karna to come to battle-field till he was alive as he did not like seeing him there. Bhishma did not like the battle to take place but it was because of the wrong advice and trust in Karna, that Duryodhana did not agree for peaceful settlement with Pandavas. Further, Karna had been assuring too much and had let Duryodhana down every time. Bhishma called Kaurvas and asked Duryodhana to still come on peaceful terms with Pandavas as Krishana and Arjuna were 'Narayan' and 'Nar' and could not be won. But Duryodhana did not agree. His confidence, because of Karna, had not shattered. So having decided to continue fighting, Duryodhana appointed Darona as the senapati of his army and also asked Karna to join the army.

Karna came to Kurukshetra and at first met Bhishma to fulfil the protocol—one because he had been the Senapati and did not allow Karna to be in the battle-field and not to join the army, he desired to have his blessings and secondly by now Karna having known that he was Kunti's son, it was appropriate to meet the dying ancestor. Karna also wanted to clarify his position to remove the misunderstanding in Bhishma's mind about him. He paid respects to Bhishma, lying on arrows. Bhishma too welcomed him. He told him that he would have passed curse on him if he had not come. Bhishma told him that he was Pandavas' eldest brother, having born of Kunti before her marriage and should now join Pandavas as this action could bring an end to the fighting as Kaurvas were already worried of Arjuna on Pandavas' side and if Karna too joined them, they would never face Pandavas. Karna told him that he had already known this fact but Radhe having brought him with all troubles, he could not now change his affinity from Radhe to Kunti. Secondly, it is because of him that Duryodhana had developed enmity with Pandavas and now shifting side would mean breach of trust, which he could not afford. Thirdly Kunti never saved him in his life when he faced humiliation because of having been a Soot's son and now declaring him as Kunti's son would not be correct. He, therefore, convinced Bhishma that in the situation, his Dharma was to continue on the side of Kaurvas only. He requested Bhishma to bless him so that he was able to kill Arjuna, as already avowed by him. Bhishma too in the situation, blessed him to continue with his people i.e. Kaurvas and earn name in the battle as he had so far been doing. But Bhishma could not bless Karna to be able to kill Arjuna.

Karna then met Duryodhana, who, after consulting him and others, decided to appoint Darona as Senapati in the place of Bhishma. Senapati had a special position in the army—

न बिना नायकं सेना मुहुर्तमपि तिष्ठति,
आहवेष्वाहवश्रेष्ठ नेतृहीनेव नौर्जले। (5/8)

The army cannot fight without the Senapati even for an hour as the boat cannot exist in water without the boat man. It was considered that King could not be appointed as Senapati as all his kings were great warriors and appointment of one may not be tolerated by others.

In the situation, Darona, who was not a king, well-versed in warfare activities and usage of war as also in the formation of the armymen was the fittest man. He was, therefore, appointed Senapati with all formalities. In ancient times, a special system and formalities were laid down for each occasion. So after fulfilling all protocolic requirements, Darona was coronated as Senapati. This also shows that in old days even kings were not free to take important decisions. An autocrat like Duryodhana too did not suo moto appoint Darona as his Senapati. He took decision after consulting all his advisors. Further, a proper request was made to the person for accepting the command keeping confidence in him for holding the charge.

ध्रुवं युधिष्ठिरं सख्ये सानुबन्धंसबान्धवम्,
जेष्यामि पुरुषव्याघ्र भवान् सेनापतिर्यदि (6/11)

Darona too told Duryodhana that he was well-versed with the warfare and usage of various kind of armaments and would fight with Pandavas as his Senapati as per confidence reposed in him.

So the formation of army was arranged on both sides, and fighting started. Karna was on Kaurvas' side and Arjuna on Pandavas' side. They caused a lot of killings. Simultaneously, Darona too started killing Pandavas' army-men. All feared his attack. He caused many deaths.

Sanjaya had been telling all proceedings of war to Dharitrashtra. Dharitashtra explained that Krishana was infact God incarnate as his actions could not be those, of ordinary persons like killing rakshasas in childhood itself then killing Kansa, Sursen and facing Jarasandha and ultimately killing him; killing Shishupala, Shobhasura, and conquering many kings and then after seeing him in his godly form at the time of his having come for peaceful settlement, he was convinced that the side with Krishana is sure to be victorious. Similarly, Arjuna was another person, very dear to Krishana and fighting as per Krishana's advice. He could not be killed by anyone.

Duryodhana in the battle field, introduced all his commanders to the Senapati Darona. He requested Darona to arrest Yudhisthra and produce him. Then he shall put him to play gambling and after defeating him would send all Pandavas again to forests, never to come again. So Duryodhana had known the weakness of Yudhisthra, having a liking for gambling, putting anything on stake and other brothers accepting to whatever Yudhisthra had done. Darona told him that he would be able to arrest Yudhisthra, if Arjuna did not come forward to protect him as he was unable to defeat Arjuna. Darona's commitment of arresting Yudhisthra, pleased Duryodhana as he was confident of Darona doing whatever he avowed.

This commitment by Darona, could be known by Pandavas too

through their spies and Yudhisthra asked Arjuna to be with him throughout so that he was not arrested by Darona. Arjuna told that as he could not kill his guru so he could not permit Yudhisthra being arrested by him. How much Arjuna was a man of character came be known by what he had said.

He did not remember having ever lied. He also did not remember having been ever defeated in battle and did not remember having ever been unable to fulfil his commitment. So when the battle started, Darona started killing Pandavas' army-men to reach Yudhisthra and Arjuna provided him full protection. Darona fought with Drupada and other commanders also fought with their counterparts. Each warrior fought without any fear of death but to attain salvation or victory. One can fight in correct spirit if enthused with such ideas. So connecting Dharma with discharge of duty is the fundamental in imbibing the duty as per Dharma in Hindus. Darona killed many persons, who stood in his way for capturing Yudhisthra and thus reached him. But then Arjuna reached there and repulsed Darona. Then came the sun-set and the fighting was over, and the army went to their respective cantonments. Duryodhana questioned Darona in not having been successful in arresting Yudhisthra. He explained that, as already indicated, he could not arrest Yudhisthra since Arjuna had come to protect him. Then Duryodhana paid respects to many brahmins and gave alms and asked for their blessing to kill Arjuna. Yudhisthra too came to know of all happenings through his spies and alerted his brothers. Arjuna next day entrusted the job of protecting Yudhisthra to Satyajit and himself went to fight with Sansaptik army. Arjuna had pity on them that they all were very happy in the battle field but would all be killed by him. Fierce battle then took place. Kaurvas threw arrows of various kinds on Arjuna, so much so that even Krishana could not see Arjuna. Arjuna then removed the effect of those arrows. These arrows must at that time be of various kinds of bombs—chemical, or atomic of the present day. This shows the technological development in this direction in ancient days. These would have been destroyed in course of time after Mahabharata was over as in Mahabharata more than 166 crore people had been killed. There would not, therefore, have been any war till about 1000 B.C. when again India was divided into many small kingdoms. Arjuna killed many persons and parts of bodies were lost in cases of many others. At that time, Darona arranged a special kind of formation of his army and attacked on Yudhisthra. Yudhisthra got frightened but then Daristdumana assured him full safety. Fighting took place between Darona and Daristdumana. Then Satyajit took arms against

Darona, followed by Shatnik, Dridhsena, Vasudana and others, and in this way, they were able to protect Yudhisthra from being arrested. The fighting was going on between horse-men, elephants, chariots men, on foot and one to one commanders. Bhima and Bhagdutta had been involved in fierce fighting. In between Duryodhana too came and went away after a thrashing by Bhima. Bhima killed several of Kaurvas' eommanders.

Arjuna had been fighting with the army of Sansaptakas and had killed many of their army-men. So much so that even Kaurvas told Arjuna that the killing effected by him could not have been done even by gods. After getting released from Sansaptakas' army, Arjuna came to fight with Bhagdutta, who had already injured Bhima and had attacked on Yudhisthra. Fierce fighting ensued between them. Arjuna cut off Bhagdutta's bow and killed the people of his family and continued fighting with him. Bhagdutta threw Vaishnavastra on Arjuna. Such an arm does not go waste and kills the person aimed at. Krishana could know the arrow thrown by Bhagdutta and he knew that it shall kill Arjuna. So Krishana came forward and took the attack on him and thus saved Arjuna. Since Krishana was incarnate of Vishnu himself, it could not harm him. But then Arjuna felt it and asked Krishana that he had undertaken not to take part in fighting then how was he involving himself in the fighting like that to save him. He also told that till Arjuna had his Gandeeva dhanush in his hands, no arrow, howsoever strong it might be, could harm him. Krishana then told him that he protects the entire universe in his four forms—one is in Badrika Ashrama; the second keeps a watch on the good and bad doings of the people in the universe; the third in which he himself works is for the well-being of the people in this universe as a human being and the fourth is one in which continues to stay underwater. Once when the Prithvi went to see him in the fourth form, she asked for the Vishnu astra as a boon for his son Narkasur. Vishnu gave it to her but instructed that it should continue to be held by Narkasur only. That astra was passed on to Bhagdutta. None in the universe could get rid of the attack of that astra not even the gods. So he had saved Arjuna from the effect of that astra. Now he could kill Bhagdutta rakshas. Arjuna then killed Bhagdutta during fighting. In this way Krishana had been helping the Pandavas in the battle although he had undertaken not to take up arms in the battle from Pandavas' side.

Arjuna was busy in fighting with Sansapatakas and other commanders of Kaurvas' army had been killing the armymen of Pandavas. Bhima cold not tolerate all this killing. He came to fight with Darona and Karna. Fierce fighting ensued between them. Bhima was badly injured by their arrows. Then Yudhisthra came to his rescue and sent Satyaki, Nakula and Sehdeva to fight with Darona and Karna. Again fierce fighting took place. Many men were killed, many fell from horses and elephant and chariots of many had been destroyed. The elephants too had been taking part in the battle. They had been crushing horses, chariots and armymen on foot. Daristduman also joined the Pandavas and on the other side Kripacharya, Jayadratha, Vinda and Anuvinda joined Darona and Karna and Aswatthama. Strong men were there on both sides and, therefore, none could be victorious over the others. Then Arjuna too saw this fierce fighting taking place and came there. Many of Kaurvas' armymen having been killed, others started fleeing from battle field. Karna could check the fleeing with great difficulty and a dual fighting between Karna and Arjuna started. Both had been injured in the battle. Daristdumana too joined them and Karna then left the field.

After the sun-set, the armies stopped fighting and went to their respective places. Duryodhana was not satisfied with the war proceedings. He was anxiously waiting for the arrest of Yudhisthra. He complained to Darona for not having been successful in Yudhisthra's arrest. Rather so many of his commanders, including several of his brothers, had been killed by Pandavas. He even said that Darona was in league with Pandavas that is why he did not arrest him, when he had reached quite close to him. Duryodhana was so much after Yudhisthra that he did not even spare the guru from allegation of bias in favour of the Pandavas. In war ethics, such allegations are not considered advisable particularly when Darona had been trying his best to arrest Yudhisthra. On the other hand, Duryodhana was confident that whatever Darona wanted to do was not impossible for him to attain. Darona, therefore, told him that he had been trying his best to arrest Yudhisthra but no one in the universe could face Arjuna—not even gods. He assured that he would arrange such a formation of army that even gods shall not be able to break it except Arjuna. So Arjuna should be taken away by challenging him as he would not turn down any challenge.

Accordingly, Sansaptakas took Arjuna away during fighting next day too. There was a very fierce fighting and except for Arjuna, none else could have faced it. On the other hand, Yudhisthra saw to it that none could break the new formation of Kaurvas' army, other than Arjuna. Since Arjuna was not available, Yudhisthra permitted Abhimanyu to break the formation assuring him that all Pandavas would follow him after he had broken the formation and in this way there would be no difficulty for him to come out of it. But after Abhimanyu had entered the army of

Kaurvas after breaking the formation, he could not be followed by other Pandavas as they had been checked from proceeding further by Jayadratha, who had obtained a boon from Shiva that except for Arjuna, none would be able to defeat him in battle. So Jayadratha checked the Pandavas from following Abhimanyu and in this way Abhimanyu was left alone in enemy's army. Still Abhimanyu defeated them all individually, including Darona, Karna, Duryodhana etc. But when the Kaurvas found him a hard nut to crack, he was surrounded by Kaurvas' chiefs, including Darona, Aswatthama, Kripacharya, Krit Verma, Shakuni, Brihadbal, Shalya, Bhurisarva, Paurva and Vrikhsen and was attacked by them all. Still Abhimanyu was able to face them and kept them all at bay. It was too much for all Kaurvas' commanders to digest. They, therefore, broke Abhimanyu's chariot, killed his sarthi, cut his bow and before he could take another, he was killed by all the commanders jointly. It is here that the laws of war laid down jointly by Kaurvas and Pandavas at the beginning of the war, had been broken by Kaurvas e.g.

(1) Abhimanyu was alone and he was attacked by many Kaurvas' chiefs, his sarthi too having been killed.

(2) When his chariot had been broken and his dhanush had been broken too, he was not allowed time to change the same.

(3) Abhimanyu was killed by several Kaurvas' chiefs on orders of Duryodhana, when he was without an arm and one was not to be attacked without arm as per laws of war.

So this would indicate that although there were laid down detailed laws of war, their breach had started here by Kaurvas as Abhimanyu had defeated them all individually and even killed many Kaurvas' commanders, including Raja Shalya's brothers, many armymen on horses, elephants and chariots and so the Kaurvas had no alternative except to jointly kill him when he was without arm. Even Dharitrashtra had accepted Abhimanyu bravery and appreciated it.

द्वैधी भवति मे चित्तम् ह्रिया तुष्टया च संजय,
मम पुत्रस्य यत् सैन्यं सौभद्र समवारयत्। (39/1)

Meaning that the fact that Abhimanyu had checked Kaurvas' army from proceeding further, gave him pleasure as also shame. Pleasure to know of such brave youths in his family and shame because a single body had defeated all Kaurvas.

Darona accepted that Abhimanyu alone could defeat all Kaurvas, if he liked. Duryodhana, as usual, was not happy on hearing the appreciation of Abhimanyu and blamed Darona for not killing Abhimanyu jointly when, he had defeated them all individually. It was only then that Abhimanyu was jointly killed by Kaurvas as in heart of heart, Karna, Darona, Shakuni, Duryodhana had all been feeling ashamed of having been defeated by Abhimanyu alone. Abhimanyu had even killed Kaurvas' brothers and many commanders of Kaurvas' army and armymen in Chaturanganisena. As already indicated, Jayadratha did not permit other Pandavas to reach in help of Abhimanyu by use of godly weapons granted to him by Shiva as boon. Abhimanyu had also killed in the expedition, Satyasarva, Kaikaye, Kalikeya, Vasati, Brihadbala, Aswaketu, Bhoj, Karna's son, mantri Rukmaratha and his friends, Lakshman (Duryodhana's son) Kratha's son with six commanders and hundreds of princes and had defeated Darona, Karna, Duryodhana, Dushyanta, Shakuni. Then, when his bow had been broken and till he got another one, Darona asked his men to kill him at that stage as with another bow, he would not allow anyone to conquer him. It is rather a shameful action that Darona himself, who knew all canons of shastras ordered Abhimanyu being killed jointly when he was not having any arm. Everyone accepted that the killing of Abhimanyu in that condition was against the war ethics.

After the sun-set, the fighting for the day ended. Then came the news of Abhimanyu having been killed by Kaurvas and Yudhisthra was quite upset on hearing this news and the situation in which Abhimanyu had been killed, worried him more. He now had no wish even for the kingdom of the entire universe. Then Vyasa Muni came there. It had been a protocolic requirement in ancient period that whenever there was much to worry about, some rishi came to console the worried man. Vashistha had consoled Bharata on Dasratha's death and Rama's exile. So here Vyasa Muni came and consoled Yudhisthra that it was the principle of nature that one, who is born has to die on the specified day. Yudhisthra, after paying respects to the muni, asked him how so many persons together killed Abhimanyu, Vyasa told that persons knowing vedas and shastras like him do not feel sorry during bad times, and that death takes place as destined. He told that initially when Brahma created mankind, he did not provide for their annihilation. So, in course of time, there were so many beings that the earth could not accommodate them. It was in such a situation only that the principle of annihilation was carved out and Shiva (Rudra) was made incharge—God of annihilation. It was at that time considered that there should be some reason for the decay of mankind. Then greed, rage, jealousy, enmity, love, shame had been created to cause decay of the mortals. With the death, all senses of the being, get absorbed in Parloka and then reappear on being's rebirth. In this way, all mankind visit the Parloka on death and after staying there for some time come back in other species as per their doings in the previous life. In this way the birth and death are the creation of Brahma himself. Muni, therefore, advised Yudhisthra that the human beings have to perform in this universe as per their respective Dharma, which for kshatriyas is to fight at that time. They should, therefore, get ready to continue fighting as, inspite of all the worries, the killed being cannot return.

त्यजं शोकं महाराज वैकूलग्यं त्यज बुर्दिमन्,
न मृतः शोचतो जीवेन्मुह्यतो वा जनाधिप। (55/35)

Narada had also come there and he too tried to pacify the Pandavas over the death of Abhimanyu. He even cited the case of Rama, who was to be coronated but instead had to go to forests for fourteen years and had all the sufferings of Sita having been kidnapped, war with Ravana, Lakshman's unconsciousness and on return to Ayodhya again separation from Sita. So even he had to suffer a lot in this universe. Subsequently, even after establishing a state, where all were happy, all got long life, but then Rama too had to die. The phenomena of death has, therefore, always been there and will continue as such in all times to come as birth and death have to continue and one could not be without the other. In this way, the rishi coached the entire theme of birth and death to Pandavas to console them and prepare themselves to continue fighting, which was their Dharma. He also indicated many other instances to console them like that of Raja Bhagiratha, Dilip, Mandhata, Yayati, Parushurama. After that, Narada and Vyasa munis went to their respective abodes.

When Arjuna came to his camp in the evening after finishing his fighting with Sansaptakas, he fell in grief after knowing the death of Abhimanyu in his absence. He enquired the cause of death and having known that Jayadratha was responsible for the death, he undertook to kill Jayadratha by evening, the next day.

The undertaking of Arjuna could be known by Kaurvas too through their spies. Jayadratha was greatly worried and showed his keenness to go to his kingdom in Sind and disappear so that he was not available to Arjuna on the next day and, in this way, could save himself from his clutches. But Darona, Duryodhana, Karna assured him full protection being provided by them all and Arjuna would fail to kill him and ultimately kill himself, having not fulfilled the undertaking and in this way, the war would come to an end. So this way Duryodhana was rather happy on Arjuna's undertaking. Kaurvas, therefore, made all arrangements for Jayadratha's protection. Krishana told Arjuna of the arrangements made for the protection of Jayadratha. He even told Arjuna that without consulting his brothers and others, he had adopted the severe undertaking, which could not be fulfilled normally, and this was not correct and prudent. He did not even consult Krishana before such a vow was undertaken whose non-fulfilment shall only make a mockery in the universe. The Kaurvas too were happy on knowing his pledge as they thought that Arjuna shall not be able to fulfil it and shall lead to his death and they had made full arrangements for the protection of Jayadratha. Even Darona had given him the assurance. In such a situation, how did Arjuna hope of killing Jayadratha by evening ? In the battle, Karna, Aswatthama, Durjaya, Vrikhsena, Kripacharya and Shalya were on his protection and Darona was to hold up Arjuna from entering into Kaurvas' army. Arjuna was confident of his victory. He told that the above six chiefs were not equal to half his strength and as such shall not be able to check him.

Next day there were bad omens in Kaurvas. On the other side Krishana went to Arjuna's camp, where Subhadra was down with the shock of Abhimanyu's death. Krishana consoled her telling her that her son had the best death, a kshatriya could have viz. the death in the battle-field fighting with many chiefs. Subhadra, however, continued crying for her son saying that the whole world appeared nothing to her in the absence of Abhimanyu.

Also Abhimanyu's wife was under great shock on her husband's death. Next day morning Krishana arranged for the worship of Shiva to be performed by himself and Arjuna before proceeding for the battle to accomplish their pledge. This is the normal protocol in Hindus, as also in other Dharmas, to attribute all achievements due to special grace of the almighty. So Arjuna too worshipped Shiva appropriately. Arjuna also told Krishana that he had remained quite upset about the fulfilment of his vow during the night, when Shiva had come in his dream and assured him of his victory the next day in the battle field. Krishana too, during the night, told Daruka, his sarthi that Duryodhana would put all his army and Darona and other chiefs for the protection of Jayadratha and it would not be possible even to reach Jayadratha. He told he did not have as much love for anyone of his wives, friends, family members and others as for

Arjuna. He, therefore, shall have to be helped tomorrow in the fulfilment of his pledge. He even said that anyone having enmity with Arjuna, is his enemy and who loves Arjuna is loved by him too. In fact Arjuna was half of Krishana himself.

यस्तं द्वेष्टि स मां द्वेष्टि यस्तं चानु स मामनु,
इति सकल्प्यतां बुद्धया शरीरार्ध ममार्जुनः। (79/33)

After worshipping Shiva next day, Krishana and Arjuna started for the battle-field. Yudhisthra too in the morning gave away alms to brahmins. After seeing Krishana, he asked him if he had a peaceful night yesterday and whether he was all happy. Krishana too enquired about Yudhisthra's health. Then after Yudhisthra's permission, Virata, Bhima, Daristdumana, Yuyutsa, Subahu and Daropadi's five sons came to Yudhisthra, who then stated that on that day they had dependance on Krishana only and he would save them from all sufferings. Krishana assured him that there was none, even amongst gods, who could equal Arjuna in operating dhanush. He would, therefore, come out victorious defeating all Kaurvas. Then Arjuna too came there and Yudhisthra blessed him with success. Krishana and Arjuna and others then started for the battle-field. There were good omens for Arjuna on the way. The omens— good or bad—used to indicate what was in store for the incumbent.

Dharitrashtra was worried about the well-being of Kaurvas after having killed Abhimanyu and having earned the rage of Pandavas on that account. Sanjaya told him that although Kaurvas had made all arrangements for the protection of Jayadratha, yet Pandavas' under the guidance of Krishana would succeed and Kaurvas under the burden of their own sins, would not be able to succeed. Darona had encouraged all in his army and had provided a special formation to his army (Chakrasaka-vyuh), whose entry was very difficult. Whereas the Kaurvas' army was eager to fight with Arjuna, Arjuna blew his conch and entered Kaurvas' army. Then Arjuna like Yamraja, Indra, Antaka, Death, Rudra, Varuna, Agni entered the Kaurvas' army in rage. He had his vow to be fulfilled on that day. He started killing everyone, who appeared before him and the enemy's army fled. Dushashana came to fight with Arjuna but fled away. Then Darona came forward and started fighting with Arjuna but Arjuna paid him respects as guru and asked for his permission to bye-pass him. He, however, did not permit and fighting ensued. Arjuna had been firing in Darona's feet out of respect and then tried to bye-pass him. Arjuna said that he was not his enemy but a guru and there was none in the universe, who could defeat Darona, so he could not fight with him and wanted a pass as his pupil only. Still he could pass after giving him a fighting. Then Arjuna fought with Kritverma and defeated him after fierce fighting. Then there was Raja Shrutayudha, who too was killed. Then Kamboja raja was killed and then Arjuna had to face a large army. In the army, two lakhs were killed and the remaining fled away. Arjuna also killed Shrutayu, Achutayu, Niyutayu, Raja of Angdesh, defeated Bahlika, Shaka, Parada and Yavana rajas. Arjuna then killed six thousand horsemen, three thousand on elephants, many on chariots and lakhs on foot. He then killed rakshas Ambustha. Then Duryodhana complained to Darona about the victorious Arjuna. Darona then blessed him with a kawach and sent to fight with Arjuna. Daristdumana came forward and engaged Darona in fighting and Duryodhana followed Arjuna. Fierce fighting took place between the two pairs. Then Chitrasena, Vikarna and Vivinsati attacked on Bhima, who was also joined by Ghatotkachha. There was also duet fighting between many chiefs from both sides. After Daristdumana got av ay from Darona, Satyaki came forward and fought with Darona. Both were equally equipped with godly weapons. Therefore, it was a battle with such weapons only. Here godly weapons might be meaning special types of missiles owned by various warriors.

After whole day's fierce fighting, the sun was going to set. Krishana and Arjuna had been proceeding to reach Jayadratha, killing everyone, who checked them on their way. He killed Anuvinda, and Vinda, who were on the side of Jayadratha protecting him. Then Arjuna asked Krishana to let the horses take water and relax as they would have been tired and in the meantime Arjuna kept the Kaurvas' army checked. His specialisation in warfare was quite evident at that time, how he could check such a big army. Krishana could not find water for the horses. Then Arjuna by an arrow could bring water for the horses, by making out a lake of water there. Such was the technological skill of the warriors in those days. After the horses were ready, Arjuna proceeded towards Jayadratha in the last spell of the day's fighting. All the kings, responsible for protecting Jayadratha, attacked on Arjuna, but Arjuna crossed them all and made their attack ineffective. The sun was just to set for the day. So Arjuna was moving like wind crossing all kings and army-men on the way. All army-men of Kaurvas fled from the field. Then Duryodhana appeared on the scene with the kawach put on him by Darona. Under the guise of the protection of kawach, Duryodhana challenged Arjuna for fighting. Krishana inspired Arjuna to defeat Duryodhana as he was the root cause of Mahabharata. Arjuna then proceeded where Duryodhana was much in rage after remembering how he had humiliated Pandavas after defeating them in gambling and how he had insulted Daropadi. All thought now Duryodhana shall be killed.

Fierce fighting ensued. Arjuna's arrows were not having any effect on Duryodhana because of the kawach. Krishana could know that he was wearing the kawach, which even gods could not break. Arjuna had known the way of breaking the kawach from Indra. But before Arjuna could throw the arrow on Duryodhana, it was cut by Aswatthama on the way. Now that arrow could not be used again. Then Arjuna killed the sarthi and the horses of Duryodhana and attacked on the nails, which were not covered by the kawach and with the injured nails, Duryodhana became unconscious and fled from the field. Then many commanders surrounded Arjuna and checked him from proceeding further. Arjuna, however, faced them all and fierce fighting continued. At one time, Arjuna alone had been fighting with nine commanders, including Aswatthama, Shalya, Vrikhsena, Jayadratha, Bhurisarva, and Duryodhana but Arjuna could fight with them all and got his way cleared. On the other hand, Dharitrashtra was worried about the fierceness of the battle and bravery of Arjuna. Sanjaya told him that since entire battle was because of his not having agreed for peaceful settlement with Pandavas, he could not now worry for the outcome of the war. Sanjaya even told that when Krishana had come for the peace talks, he found that—

1. Dharitrashtra was not having even ordinary prudence.
2. He was biased in favour of his sons.
3. He was confused about what Dharma stated in the situation.
4. He was jealous of Pandavas' achievements.
5. He had been making crooked plans against Pandavas.
6. He had been making unnecessary talks of sorrowness and at the same time wishing for the war between Kaurvas and Pandavas so that he did not have to part with the kingdom's part to Pandavas.

Karna came several times and fled from the battle field, having not been able to stand Bhima's attack and in his presence many of Dharitrashtra's sons had been killed. Dharitrashtra stated that he considered fate only mightier than bravery as Karna equipped with all the specialisation of warfare has been defeated by Bhima again and again although he considered Karna capable of winning the entire universe. Then Dharitrashtra's five sons had been killed, one by one, as they came for fighting with Bhima. Seeing this, Dharitrashtra remembered Bhima's commitment of killing Duryodhana and all his brothers. He had already killed about fifty of them. Seeing the bravery of Bhima, all Dharitrashtra's sons were baffled and Karna was upset.

Then seven more sons of Dharitrashtra came to help Karna, whose fighting again started after Karna came back and attacked on Bhima with rage but Bhima made all his arrows ineffective. This was appreciated even by the kings on Kaurvas' side. Duryodhana then sent his seven brothers to help Karna. They attacked on Bhima, who was happy having seen them as Bhima considered them having come to be killed by him. During the fighting all the seven were killed by Bhima. In those, now killed was Vikarna too, whom Bhima did not want to kill as he had been sympathetic to Pandavas at the time of gambling but since he had come along with his brothers and all attacked on Bhima, Bhima was sorry to have killed him too. In this way, Bhima had killed 32 of Dharitrashtra's son on that day itself. Then Duryodhana remembered what Vidur had said that all the sons of Dharitrashtras shall by killed by Bhima if war took place. At the time of Daropadi's insult, Karna had said in the assembly to Daropadi that all Pandavas had already gone to hell and, therefore, she should have another husband. At that time Bhima had vowed to kill all Kaurvas and this was the result of that dialogue. Everyone of the Kaurvas' sons, who came before Bhima, had been killed. Sanjaya told Dharitrashtra that his killing was the result of the humiliation caused to Pandavas by his sons and Karna and subsequently not agreeing to the peaceful settlement with Pandavas even on the most modest terms of five village asked for by them despite best efforts made by Krishana. Dharitrashtra accepted that he was responsible for all this butchering as he had been unjust to Pandavas. The battle field was full of dead bodies of army-men, horses, elephants, chariots, kawach, and ornaments and costly clothes and eagles had the feasting time. Bhima had caused huge killings in Kaurvas' army.

Karna again came to fight with Bhima. Bhima challenged him as to why he had been coming again and again having been repeatedly defeated by him. On the other hand, Karna considered himself invincible by any of the Pandavas so he could not sit quietly after having been defeated by Bhima. Also he was the only person with Duryodhana to check Bhima from reaching Arjuna, who was already after Jayadratha, as all the brothers, he had sent to fight with Bhima, had been killed by him. So now again he came and while the fighting was going on, Arjuna too reached there and on Arjun's attack, Karna fled away from the field.

Satyaki fell from the chariot on attack by Bhurisarva. Bhurisarva caught hold of his hairs and wanted to assasinate him by cutting him from neek, when Krishana apprised Arjuna of the position. Arjuna immediately cut Bhurisarva's arm with an arrow. Satyaki was thus saved. Bhurisarva, leaving Satyaki aside, told Arjuna that he had not done correct thing as per ethics of war as he had cut his arm by throwing an arrow from a distant place when he was not attentive in that regard and was not fighting with Arjuna. According to the laws of war, one can throw arrow on the other person, when the two were fighting in the battle field and not on a man, who was busy in fighting with another. Before throwing arm on any person, therefore, one had to engage him in fighting. Would he be able to defend himself before Dharmaraja Yudhisthra, he asked. Further, he himself knew all the rules of warfare then how he could justify his action. He even said that such an action could not be of his own accord but by instigation by Krishana as Krishana could indulge in such actions and not the Pandavas. Apparently, it was an unprotocolic action if seen in the light of the laws of war laid down by them. Arjuna, however, told him that whatever he had said was not correct. He said that he was well-versed with the laws of war and could not take any action against ethics. Still he had abused him of unethic action. He told that in all battles, father, son, brothers and friends fight with the enemy. Satyaki was his pupil and a relation. He had been fighting for him, putting his life at stake. How, then could he see Satyaki being killed by Bhurisarva. He had seen Bhurisarva draging Satyaki and so Satyaki was incapable of any action. In the battle, one does not save himself only but is responsible for saving all, who had been fighting on one's behalf. Similarly, such protected persons too had a duty to save their king. If he had not saved Satyaki from being killed, he would have earned the sin of having not protected him. Arjuna further stated that so far as the allegation that Bhurisarva was busy in fighting with another person and at that time Arjuna had cut his arm, if conceded, it should be known that he himself had boarded the chariot and developed fighting with all present in the battle field. So when the fighting was amongst the people on elephants, horses, chariots and on foot combinedly then it could not be called a fighting between Satyaki and Bhurisarva but by all with all in the battle field. Further, Satyaki had fought with many commanders and had defeated them. Now he and his horses had tired. It is in this situation that he attacked on Satyaki, an unwilling warrior and claimed to be superior to Satyaki and wanted to cut his head. How in the battle field could anyone, on the side of Satyaki, allow him such a course of action. Arjuna told that rather than blaming Arjuna for such an action, he should curse himself that he was not attentive in the battle field and had been only after cutting Satyaki from the neck.

Bhurisarva did not have any reply to what Arjuna had stated and sat in the battle-field not to get up till he died. Bhurisarva then gave up his life through 'Paranayama' and 'Yoga'. Cutting of his arm when he was going to cut Satyaki's head, depriving him of life, was not wrong. Arjuna also stated that the way in which Abhimanyu was killed when he was without chariot, without arm and without kawach, was actually condemnable by all. Therefore, the killing of Bhurisarva, who was assisting Duryodhana, a mean person not observing the ethics of war, was not unethical. It was rather his duty to protect his men, who were being slain by the enemy in a brutal way. Arjuna, however, cursed the kshatriya Dharma where people had to give up their lives in that way, and had he not already proclaimed for providing protection to all fighting for him within the reach of the arrow, he would not have acted that way in killing Bhurisarva. Arjuna even told Bhurisarva that he had the same affection for him as he had for Yudhisthra, Bhima and other brothers. He along with Krishana prayed for his attaining salvation after death. Krishana too confirmed what Arjuna had stated that he would go to the best Loka, where even gods had no access. The incidence of the death of Bhurisarva is a classical example of the following of the laws of war in India in ancient times and the claim that international laws, including laws of war, are a modern concept, is farce. It also shows that in ancient India, it is not only that the battles were fought according to the ethics of war but also one had to justify one's action, if challenged to be unethical. Further, when Bhurisarva had sat to give up his life, Satyaki wanted to kill him, but he was refrained from doing so by Krishana and others but still Satyaki killed him. Satyaki justified his action by telling that it was his undertaking that anyone, who would kick him, when he was alive, would be killed by him even if it was a rishi, engrossed in samadhi after kicking him. So he had to act according to his undertaking since Bhurisarva had dragged him and kicked him in the battle-field after he had given up arms. So, he stated, Arjuna had fulfilled his commitment in protecting him by cutting the arm of Bhurisarva and he had done his part of fulfilment of commitment by killing Bhurisarva even though he had sat to die himself. He stated that in Rama period even Balmika had stated that vanar, to your allegation that women should not be killed, my reply is that for an active person, the proper action is which annoys the enemy—

सर्वकालं मनुष्येण व्यवसायवता सदा,
पीडा कर ममित्राणां यत् स्यात् कर्तव्यमेव तत्। (143/68)

Arjuna then asked Krishana to take him where, Jayadratha was as sun-set was near and he had to be killed before sun-set as per his undertaking. On the other side, Duryodhana, Karna, Vrikhsena, Shalya, Aswatthama, Kripacharya and Jayadratha prepared themselves to fight against Arjuna to save Jayadratha till sun-set. Duryodhana told Karna that Arjuna was going towards Jayadratha so it was time to check Arjuna from reaching Jayadratha as if Arjuna was detained for the remaining part of the day, their purpose would be served as if Jayadratha could be saved upto sun-set, then Arjuna shall kill himself and that shall bring an end to the war and Kaurvas shall be able to enjoy the entire universe. Kaurvas were happy that Arjuna had made such a promise as will decide the war in their favour. Duryodhana told that he, Shalya, Aswatthama and Kripacharva shall also be at his disposal. Karna told that he had been badly injured by Bhima but still he shall give a fighting to Arjuna at this juncture as he had avowed even to give his life for his sake. Arjuna proceeded further and killed many persons in Kauravas' army and attacked on Jayadratha. Arjuna was, however, surrounded from all sides by Karna, Kripacharya, Shalya, and Vrikhasen. They all put Jayadratha behind them and started waiting for the sun-set. They all jointly attacked on Arjuna although it was a breach of laws but Arjuna faced them all and after crossing them, attacked on Jayadratha. Satyaki and Bhima also came for his help but Karna was able to check them all from proceeding further. Karna and Arjuna had been fighting to kill each other. Duryodhana directed all to help Karna.

Arjuna was throwing arrows from Gandiva dhanush so rapidly that one could not make out when the arrow was taken, put on bow and thrown and those who came forward were either defeated and fled or killed. Arjuna thus had the field. Arjuna thus crossed all commanders and army-men to enable him to reach Jayadratha. He was ulitmately able to reach and attack on Jayadratha. Arjuna injured Jayadratha with many arrows and all other commanders retired from the battle field after having been injured by Arjuna. Jayadratha also threw many arrows on Arjuna but were all made ineffective by Arjuna. Krishana thought and told Arjuna that sun was going to set and it was not possible to kill Jayadratha without first defeating all the other commanders, who were there to protect him. Krishana told that, in the situation, he would act on a strategy to cover sun so that Jayadratha alone would see it as set and shall happily start dancing. At that time, Arjuna should kill Jayadratha without considering that sun had set. Arjuna accepted the proposal. Then Yogeshwar Bhagwan Krishana created darkness over the sun. All Kaurvas became very happy seeing the sun-set. Jayadratha had at that time been closely watching the sun-set and the others were not watching the same. Krishana alerted Arjuna telling him that Jayadratha was watching towards sun-set and shall shortly start dancing. He should at that time kill him, and fulfil his undertaking. Arjuna then started throwing arrows aiming at Karna, Kripacharya, Duryodhana, Vrikhshena, and Jayadratha and others. All commandants then ran away out of fear, leaving Jayadratha alone in the field. Krishana also told Arjuna that Jayadratha's father had obtained a boon from astrologers that Jayadratha would be a great warrior, respected by all brave people but at the end of his life his head would be cut by an kshatriya fighting against him in the battle field. His father was, therefore, worried and passed a curse that anyone, who shall cut and throw Jayadratha's head on earth shall also have his head broken into many pieces. Krishana, therefore, told Arjuna that Jayadratha's father was in samadhi in Samantpanchak area and he should, therefore, cut Jayadratha's head by his arrow and throw it in such a way that it fell in the lap of his father and not on earth and he told Arjuna that he could do it. Accordingly, Arjuna threw an arrow from his Gandiva, which cut Jayadratha's head and placed it in the lap of his father. His father was awakened from tapasya and seeing the head in his lap threw it down on the earth without seeing that it was his son's head and as per his own saying, his head broke into pieces since he himself had thrown the head on the earth. Then Krishana removed the darkness artificially created by him and everyone could see the sun not yet set. In this way, Kaurvas' eight kshoni army had been wiped out and Jayadratha killed, fulfilling Arjuna's undertaking. Then Bhima, Krishana, Arjuna and others blew their respective conches. Yudhisthra could make out that Jayadratha had been killed and was very happy. Pandavas became very happy and all set to attack on Daronacharya. But Kripacharya got enraged and attacked on Arjuna. Aswatthama too joined him. Arjuna was upset with arrows coming from two sides and then one was guru and another guru's son, whom Arjuna did not want to kill. He, therefore, protected himself only and threw only mild arrows on them. Still Kripacharya was injured and became unconscious. Aswatthama too left Arjuna. Arjuna was uncomfortable having seen Kripacharya unconscious. At the birth of Duryodhana, Vidur had told that he would be a means to destroy all Kaurvas. Because of Duryodhana only, Kripacharya was wounded by arrows. Cursed be the kshatriya

Dharma ! Arjuna said. After attaining education from guru, who, give them their desired things, people go to swarga and those, who injure them go to hell. His action would, put him to hell. It is in this context that Dharma of each varna worked. If gurus, who were brahmins, had not taken to arms, which was the job of kshatriyas, this situation would not have come where guru and pupil had to fight with each other. At that time, having seen Jayadratha killed, Karna was going toward Satyaki. Arjuna asked that he too may be taken there. But Krishana told that Satyaki was enough to tackle Karna and he should not fight with him as Karna was having a shakti given by Indra and it would not be possible to face that. Karna had kept that for Arjuna only and would not use on Satyaki so Arjuna should avoid facing Karna till that shakti had been used. On the other side, Sanjaya told Dharitrashtra that Krishana had known that. Bhurisarva would defeat Satyaki and, therefore, he remained close to him. There was none in the universe, who could equal Krishana as he was almighty God himself. Krishana had already alerted Daruka to keep a chariot ready to be used by Satyaki. Since now after Bhurisarva's death, Satyaki was without a chariot, Krishana blew his conch and Daruka appeared with the chariot to be used by Satyaki. This was the war strategy, which could be managed in those days. Udhamanyu and Uttamoja also joined Satyaki to attack on Karna. Fierce battle took place. Karna was furious on death of Jayadratha and Bhurisarva and wanted to reach Arjuna to kill him with the Indra's shakti. So he wanted to get rid of Satyaki. But Satyaki injured him and he fell down from the chariot. Dushashana came for his help but he was also made without chariot. Satyaki could have killed them both but avoided it as Karna was to be killed by Arjuna and Dushashana by Bhima only. So he spared their lives. Karna however, tried his utmost to kill Satyaki but could not. Then a special chariot was brought for Karna and the fighting with Satyaki continued. Bhima asked Arjuna that although he had vowed to kill Karna yet he had rebuked him too and, therefore, he be allowed to kill him. Arjuna then came to Karna and told him that he could only boast and do nothing. Arjuna told that the warriors in the battle field have either to face victory or defeat. Bhima had defeated him several times but had never rebuked him as he had, since he was from a mean caste of Soot. Arjuna warned Karna that he should do whatever he wanted to do in this life as his end was quite near now by his hands. Arjuna told that he was without brain that is why he unneccessarily uttered nonsense. Bhima had made him without chariot several times and spared his life although he could have killed him as he was to be killed by Arjuna only and Karna started abusing Bhima when only once he made him without chariot. He cut the dhanush of Abhimanyu and he was killed by six Kaurvas' chiefs, when he was unarmed. Still Karna boasted of being a brave warrior.He should feel ashamed. Arjuna told that he shall kill him and his son in the battle field shortly. At that time there was sun-set.

Krishana then praised Arjuna for having fulfilled his undertaking but Arjuna attributed this achievement to Krishana only. This is what protocol requires for mutual appreciation and recognition of the achievement in the battle field so that everyone is kept in good humour. Arjuna said that whomsoever Krishana had protected, had to be victorious in the battle. Krishana then took Arjuna in the battle-field and told Arjuna that so many commanders and army-men had been killed by him in the battle field. Their clothes, ornaments and arms were spread there and chariots, horses, elephants smashed by him were scattered. All these deaths, Krishana told, were for the sake of kingdom only. The battle-field was full of corpses which one could not imagine. After showing the battle-field, Krishana blew his conch and took Arjuna to Yudhisthra and told him that Jayadratha had been killed. Conch was blown in those days with a view to advise the arrival of the raja from the battle-field. Krishana bowed before Yudhisthra and told him that his enemy had been killed. Yudhisthara deboarded from his chariot and embraced Krishana and Arjuna. Yudhisthra, as usual, praised Krishana that all victories were because of his help only and would further achieve conquest on enemy because of him only. Yudhisthra told that eversince he had come to know of the godly job done by him since childhood, he was confident that he could not be defeated when Krishana was with him. This is the blind faith one have to have in the almighty God, then only God fulfills the wishes of the bhakta, the normal protocol between the Bhagwan and the bhakta. Yudhisthra told Krishana that he only was the incarnate of God, almighty and because of his grace only Jayadratha could be killed crossing the entire army of Duryodhana. All in the Kaurvas' army had been killed and shall be killed by his help only. Then Bhima and Satyaki too came there and paid respects to Yudhisthra. Yudhisthra was happy to see them back from the battle-field as victorious and embraced them.

Seeing Jayadratha dead, Duryodhana was quite upset and had lost hope of victory in view of how Pandavas had been able to defeat them all and was of the view that Arjuna was supreme in the battle-field and none else could face him. He then went to Guru Darona and told him that all his rajas and chiefs had been killed fighting along with the seven kshoni army. Duryodhana said that he was responsible for so many deaths and now he too shall embrace death owning responsibility for so many people having died because of and for him.

Darona told Duryodhana that he was always of the view that none could face Arjuna in the battle field and after Bhishma's death he was convinced that no one could defeat Pandavas in the battle field. Darona attributed this all to Duryodhana only as he and his men humiliated Pandavas in gambling, cheating them and then insulting Daropadi in the sabha. As if this was not enough, he did not agree for the peaceful settlement as requested by Krishana and on the contrary tried to arrest Krishana. How then could Kaurvas now be victorious over Pandavas, he told. So far as the blame of Jayadratha was concerned, Darona told that he, Aswatthama, Karna, Shalya and Kripacharya were all there to protect Jayadratha. Then how, in the face of all, Arjuna was able to kill Jayadratha defeating them all. How could Darona alone be responsible for such defeat, he asked. If Jayadratha could not be protected by him and Duryodhana then they too should not have hopes of remaining alive in this war. Darona further alerted Duryodhana that fighting would continue during the night too and if he was able, he should protect his army. Then Duryodhana again made up his mind to continue fighting. He went to Karna and told him that breaking the formation of Kaurvas' army, which could not even be done by god, Arjuna defeated them all and was able to kill Jayadratha and seven kshoni army, was something unimaginable. Darona assured safety to Jayadratha and still allowed Arjuna to enter the army, was something, they could not understand and he was also helplessly witnessing Jayadratha being killed. Darona however, told that he could not be blamed as he had been fighting for Kaurvas even at the cost of his life and if Arjuna entered the army crossing Darona, he could not be blamed for it. It was rather a befitting achievement of Arjuna. Karna further told that he was of the firm conviction that no one could change what is in the fate as inspite of their best efforts to protect Jayadratha, he had been killed. It was all in fate and none could be blamed for it. Man should, therefore, do his best and leave the result to almighty God only. Karna told that they had always been unjust to Pandavas. At first, poison was served to Bhima; then the Pandavas were designed to be killed in Lakshagriha; then defeated in gambling and as a diplomatic tactics sent Pandavas to forests; then proposal to kill them in forests—all their efforts had been ineffective because the Pandavas had the better part of fate with them. Therefore, everything depended on the wish of God, who is active even when all human beings were asleep.

दैवं प्रमाणं सर्वस्या सुवृतस्येतरस्य वा,
अनन्यकर्म दैवं हि जार्गार्त स्वपतामपि।। (152/32)

Then fighting started. The army-men were fighting with army-men, elephants with elephants (showing that even the animals abided by the law of war) and horsemen with horsemen. The commanders had been fighting on chariots. Then Duryodhana entered the army and came in front of the Pandavas and fierce fighting ensued inspite of Darona, Kripacharya and Karna having asked him not to enter in Pandavas' army alone. He injured many Panchalis. Then Bhima came to their rescue. Duryodhana then fought with Bhima, Shikhandi, Drupada, Yudhisthra and Daroapdi's sons—one after the other. Then Yudhisthra attacked on Duryodhana. He cut Duryodhana's dhanush and injured him. Duryodhana fell unconscious and hid himself behind the chariot.

In the night, the battle continued. Although in the laws of war, drafted at the beginning of war, no fighting was to continue during the night but after the death of Jayadratha, Kaurvas' army continued fighting in breach of the law and, therefore, Pandavas too had to resume. Darona, Karna and Aswatthama, many Kaurvas' chiefs were defeated and huge army had been killed by Pandavas. Duryodhana was upset bacause of this defeat and he blamed Darona and Karna for such a situation. Darona and Karna then fought more vigorously and Pandavas' army started fleeing. Bhima, however, then came in the field and checked the fleeing army, and with the help of Arjuna attacked on Kaurvas.

Yudhisthra became upset and Arjuna then set for fighting with Karna but Krishana checked him saying that Karna wanted to kill him by the shakti given to him by Indra. Although Arjuna was not afraid of Karna, yet he agreed with Krishana's suggestion. Then they remembered Ghatotkachha, who immediately appeared in the battle-field. Krishana told him that Karna had become a problem for them and he should harass him. At that time Krishana proclaimed a policy statement that father gave birth and brought up the son in his self-interest so that the son could provide protection to him in this universe and help him go to 'Parloka' in peace. This is the basis of Hindu philosophy of transmigration of soul and father-son relation not relevant to this universe only but also after death. Krishana sent Satyaki too for his help. Ghatotkachha assured killing Karna with his army in that day's fighting. Then Alambusha rakshas came to help Karna. But Ghatotkachha killed him in a prolonged fighting. Then Ghatotkachha told Duryodhana that his friend Alambusha had been killed and he should wait to see Karna too being killed by him. Ghatotkachha then went to Karna and attacked on him. Both were brave and had injured each other. Then Ghatotkachha managed his rakshashi maya as a result of which many army-men of Duryodhana were killed and rest fled. Karna's all godly weapons had been made ineffective and then Ghatotkachha challenged Karna and attacked on him but Karna made it ineffective. Then Ghatotkachha came to have duel fighting with Karna. Then another rakshas Alayudha appeared in the field but Bhima came forward to fight with him. Darona, Kripacharya, Kritverma and Aswatthama were all afraid of facing Ghatotkachha and thought that he would finish their entire army. In the battle of Bhima and Alayudha, the latter had the field. Yudhamanyu, Uttamauja and Daropadi's sons were sent to attack on Karna to provide relief to Ghatotkachha. Then Krishana sent Ghatotkachha to help Bhima. Fierce fighting took place between Ghatotkachha and Alayudha. Ghatotkachha killed Alayudha and sent his head towards Duryodhana, who was upset as Alayudha had undertaken to kill Bhima and Duryodhana had been depending on him but on his having been killed, he thought that now he would surely be killed by Bhima. Then fierce fighting took place between Karna and Ghatotkachha. Ghatotkachha had been covered by arrows of Karna. Then Ghatotkachha managed rain of fire. All Kaurvas were afraid and fled for refuge. Ghatotkachha still continued firing his astras on Kaurvas' army. He killed all the four horses of Karna's chariot. Karna was then confused, and all Kaurvas asked Karna to kill Ghatotkachha with the Shakti given to him by Indra, otherwise he would finish the entire army of Kaurvas. Then Karna had to decide to fire the shakti on Ghatotkachha, having seen the smashed condition of his chiefs and army and accordingly after killing Ghatotkachha, that shakti went to Indra. Even after death, Ghatotkachha killed many in Kaurvas' army when he fell on ground. Then all the Pandavas were sorry for Ghatotkachha's death but Krishana was happy. On Arjuna enquiring about the reason for Krishana being happy, he told that Karna was invincible in the war but now he was not so without his kawach and amogh shakti. This shakti had been kept by Karna to be used on Arjuna but now this shakti had also been wasted out. So it was now safe to fight with Karna and kill him. Even now Karna being very brave, could be killed only when the wheel of his chariot sank into earth and Karna got upset because of that. So they shall have to be on the look out for such a chance and kill him. Therefore, Ghatotkachha had been got killed only to save Arjuna from being killed by Karna. Krishana told Arjuna that his purpose of incarnation in the universe was to annihilate all rakshasas and save the rishis etc. Already Kansa, Jarasandha, Shishupala and many other rakshasas had been killed by him and many had been killed in Mahabharata. So Mahabharata had necessarily to take place not only to enable Pandavas to get their kingdom back but also to annihilate rakshasas. Now Ghatotkachha had been killed otherwise he would have to manage his killing in some other way. Similarly, Alambusha, Alayudha and lacs of other rakshasas had been killed in Mahabharata. Sanjaya told Dharitrashtra that Krishana was 'Narayan' and Arjuna his bhakta 'Nar'. 'Nar' cannot survive without 'Narayana' for a minute. So Arjuna was always under the protection of Krishana. Duryodhana, Shakuni etc. had always been telling Karna to throw the shakti on Arjuna only but a situation had been created in which Karna was forced to throw it on Ghatotkachha. This is how Krishana without resorting to arms in the war, had been helping Pandavas to make them victorious.

Dharitrashtra was worried for the use of the shakti on Ghatotkachha when Kaurvas knew that the shakti could be used on one person only.This should have already been used on Arjuna as it would have brought the war to an end with the death of Arjuna. Sanjaya told that Kaurvas had every night been planning to use the shakti on Arjuna but this idea was dismantled by God in one way or the other. It was, therefore, fate only that saved Arjuna from being killed by that shakti. Dharitrashtra also agreed that Krishana had got the shakti destroyed on Ghatotkachha and now he was sure that Kaurvas shall all be killed by Pandavas. Although with the death of Ghatotkachha, Kaurvas were happy and Pandavas were upset, yet the factual position was known to Krishana only. Yudhisthra too was sorry on Ghatotkachha's death but Krishana consoled him. Arjuna then proposed that the armies of both the sides were tired. They should, therefore, stop fighting during the remaining part of the night. His proposal was accepted by all. Such was the understanding amongst the warriors in the battle in those days which can never be seen in enemies.

Next day battle again started. Yudhisthra ordered his men to kill Darona and Duryodhana's men attacked on Pandavas to save Darona. Darona divided his army in two parts. One under Darona and Duryodhana attacked on Pandavas and Panchalis and the other was to tackle other Pandavas' army. Arjuna bye-passed Karna and Darona and attacked on enemy's army. Then Duryodhana, Karna and Shakuni attacked on Arjuna. Arjuna defeated them all. Then Drupada and Virata attacked on Darona. Darona killed three grand-sons of Drupada and then killed Drupada and Virata in a ferocious fighting. Seeing them dead, Daristdumana avowed to kill Darona and then attacked on Darona and fierce fighting started. Nakula came to fight with Darona but was checked by Duryodhana. Nakula, however, defeated Duryodhana, who fled from the field. Karna was fighting with Bhima and Arjuna with Darona. Gods, Rishis, and Gandharvas had come to see the fighting of Arjuna and Darona. Both were superior to each other in fighting and, therefore, neither could defeat the other.

Krishana told Arjuna that no one could conquer Darona till he had arms in his hands. A chance had, therefore, to be found that he is to be attacked, when he had no arms and then only he could be killed. They should leave the feeling that guru is not to be killed and if guru had himself come with arms to fight with kshatriyas, then kshatriya Dharma is to kill such a guru or brahmin. Here the question of protocol comes in to play. Normally the brahmins have to teach others, including kshatriyas and the job of fighting is that of kshatriyas. It must have been with a view to save such a situation, where guru and pupil, both may have to fight. Here guru had taken arms with a view to be victorious in the war. Krishana also told that he believed that Darona would give up arms only after Aswatthama was dead. Someone should, therefore, tell him that Aswatthama had died. Arjuna did not like this strategy although others approved of it. Then Bhima killed one elephant named Aswatthama and proclaimed Aswatthama is killed. Hearing Bhima saying this, Darona became upset but he doubted the bonafides of this pronouncement and Darona continued killing Pandavas' army-men. Darona killed fifty commanders of Matsyadesh; six thousand sainiks of Sarinjay Dynasty; ten thousand elephants and ten thousand men on horses. Seeing Darona killing so many kshatriyas, God and rishis Viswamitra, Jamadagni, Bhardwaj, Gautama, Vasistha, Kashyap and Atri came there along with Agni to take him to Brahmloka. They asked Darona to put-down his arms. They told that he had been fighting against the ethics of varna-dharma and now the time of his death had come. So, he should stop this war. Since he was well-versed with vedas and shastras, fighting did not behove his position. As already indicated, a brahmin fighting in battle with kshatriyas was not as per canons of vedas. It was wrong on his part to have used Brahmastra and killed people, who did not have knowledge about Brahmastra. He should now give up fighting and never to fight in future. Darona was already, confused. He, therefore, left the confirmation of Aswatthyama's death to Yudhisthra as he knew that Yudhisthra would never tell a lie. At that time, Darona wanted to kill all on Pandavas' side. Krishana then told Yudhisthra that in case Darona continued fighting for half day more, then entire Pandavas' army shall be smashed. Therefore, with a view to save themselves, even telling a lie was more important than sticking to truth. Krishana also told that in case one had to tell a lie to save someone's life then such person is not called a 'sinner'.

स भवांस्त्रातु नो द्रोणात् सत्याज्यायोऽनृतं वचः,
अनृतं जीवितस्यार्थे वदन्न स्पृश्यतेऽनृतैः। (190/47)

Krishana told that in case Yudhisthra confirmed the death of Aswatthama, Darona would stop fighting believing him as he was known for his truthfulness. Yudhisthra was double-minded—one he did not tell a lie ever and the other he wished to be victorious. So he loudly said 'Aswatthama had been killed' and mildly said the elephant had been killed.

तमतथ्यभये मग्नो जये सक्तो युधिष्ठिरः,
(अश्वत्थामा हत इति शब्दमुच्चैश्चारह)
अव्यक्तमब्रवीद राजन् हतः कुजर इत्युत। (190/55)

Before saying this Yudhisthra's chariot used to ply four inches above the earth but on telling lie, from that day, the chariot started plying touching the earth. Hearing this from Yudhisthra, Darona could not fight in his usual spirit even seeing Daristdumana before him. Seeing Darona in that state, Daristdumana attacked on him. Then having been under the shock of son's death, he could not use his godly weapons although he continued fighting with Daristdumana and killed his horses. Then Daristdumana climbed on Darona's chariot with a sword in his hand. Darona had in his possession, Vaitistic arrows which were available only with Arjuna, Kripacharya, Karna, Pradyumana, Satyaki and Abhimanyu and were equal to a small Bitti (बित्ती). But this arrow was cut by Satyaki and so he saved the life of Daristdumana. Duryodhana became enraged and surrounded Satyaki from all sides. Bhima, Yudhisthra, Nakula, Sehdeva too came for Satyaki's help and attacked on Darona jointly. Then Darona's arms started burning and he became blunt. He was upset seeing Daristdumana before him as he was his killer. The Panchalis had already killed Basati, Shibi, Bahlika, who were there to protect Darona. Darona cut the bow of Daristdumana and injured him. Bhima then told Darona that in case the 'brahmins having not felt contented with their varna-dharma and resorted to war, the kshatriyas would not have been harmed as in the battle, ahinsa was the best Dharma for brahmins and if brahmins, for the sake of their wives, sons and wealth, resorted to killing kshatriyas and others, as he had done for the sake of the livelihood of his son, they would ultimately feel ashamed for their such action. On Bhima having said so, Darona threw his bow and all astra-sastras and asked Karna, Kripacharya and Duryodhana to themselves make efforts to win the battle. Saying this, he put down all his arms and sat in the back portion of the chariot in Samadhi thinking of Vishnu and got merged with Brahma. Arjuna, Kripacharya, Krishana and Yudhisthra only could see him going to Brahmloka. Daristdumana then cut his head and threw towards Duryodhana. Then Duryodhana's army fled from the field. When Aswatthama asked why the Kaurvas' army had been fleeing, Kripacharya narrated all about Darona's death. Even Karna. Ulooka, Dushashana, Vrikhsena, Susharma, Kritvarma, Kripacharya, Shalya and other commanders and army-men fled from the battle-field having known the death of Darona. Aswatthama got enraged hearing how his father had been killed.

Dhritarashtra asked Sanjaya what happened after Aswatthama came to know about the death of his father against all canons as in his son, Daron had imbibed all his specialities.

एकमेव हि लोथेऽस्मिन्नात्मनो गुणवत्तरम्,
इच्छन्ति पुरुषाः पुत्रं लोके नान्यं कथंचन। (194/5)

The acharyas have many specialities, which they pass on either to their sons or to the best pupil.

Having known that Daristdumana had killed his father deceitfully, Aswatthama got enraged and avowed to kill Daristdumana by fair or foul means. He also rebuked Yudhisthra, who claimed to be Dharmputra, saying how low he could go to win the battle. He further said that father gives birth to the son so that he is protected by him in this universe and after death too but he became the cause of his father's death. This was not assimmilable to him as his father had been slain after catching him by hairs. Aswatthama told that the best astrà of Narayani had been acquired by his father, which he had given to Arjuna and to him. So by that Narayani Astra, he would burn the entire Pandavas' army. Aswatthama, therefore, came to the battle-field at the head of his army and blew conch. Arjuna told Yudhisthra about Aswatthama having got enraged on Guru Darona's death. Arjuna told that on birth itself, he had roared like a horse and, therefore, he had been named as Aswatthama. He is the helper and revenge-taker of the killing of his father. Arjuna also castigated Yudhisthra for having told a lie for the sake of attaining rajya, resulting in the death of the guru. This shall cause his infamy in the universe as he knew that Aswatthama elephant had been killed and he said Aswatthama is dead and further Daristdumana caused insult to the guru by catching him by the hairs and cutting his head and throwing towards Kaurvas on earth. He cannot now be saved from Aswatthama. It is a pity, he said, that at this end of their lives, they had done such unethical actions. Arjuna was sorry that against the impression of his guru that he would sacrifice his parents, sons, brothers, for his sake, he had allowed him to be killed for the sake of kingdom only. The action of his having been killed is wrong as—

1. He was a brahmin.
2. He was an old man.
3. He was their guru.
4. He had put down his arms.
5. He was sitting like a man.
6. The killing was simply to attain kingship and that too by telling a lie.

Hearing Arjuna, Bhima got enraged and said that the job of an kshatriya is—

1. To protect himself and others from any trouble.
2. Killing the enemy in the battle.
3. Being kind to women and gentlemen.
4. Protection of kingdom, Dharma, image and wealth of the rajya.

Although Arjuna knew, all this yet he had condoned the omissions on the part of the enemy, who had snatched their rajya deceitfully, insulted Daropadi in the sabha, put them to exile for thirteen years, and tried to kill them while in forests. But he could not excuse them and remembering all these acts of Kaurvas, he would alone kill them all even if Arjuna did not help him. Daristdumana also said that the jobs of the brahmins are—

1. Performance of yagya themselves and by others.
2. Reading and coaching of vedas and shastras.
3. Giving and taking alms.

But Darona had resorted to the job of kshatriyas forgetting his Dharma. Therefore, a brahmin, if causes harm to others for accomplishing his worldly desires, he is stated to be doing a non-brahmin work. In such a situation, it is not a sin to have killed such a brahmin and if Aswatthama had got enraged, then it could not be helped. Further, the charge of his having killed the guru is also wrong as he had born out of yagya only to kill Darona. He, therefore, had done his destined job and Darona knew it. He was, therefore, not to be blamed for it. Also since Darona had killed his father and brothers, he had not committed a sin in having cut his head. His job was to kill the enemy or get killed. Daristdumana told Arjuna that he had tolerated whatever he had said against him because of his sister, her sons and his relation with him. This shows the affinity and tolerance the sister's brother is supposed to have with his sister's husband. Therefore, neither Yudhisthra was liar nor was he adharmik. On the contrary, it was Darona, who was adharmik and fought against his pupil. He, therefore, rightly deserved to be killed. Dharitrashtra condemned what Daristdumana had said against Darona, who was a true brahmin. In fact Dhritrashtra was wrong in having defended Darona, who had resorted to kshatriya's job, which had even been not liked by the rishis and God, who were present in the battle-field and had asked Darona to put down his arms and not to resort to killing of kshatriyas. Satyaki was not convinced of the justification put forth by Daristdumana in having killed Darona and rubuked him. They both got enraged against each other on this account. Then Bhima, Nakula, Sehdeva and Yudhisthra pacified them.

Next day Aswatthama threw the Narayani Astra on Pandavas and their army. This Astra produced thousands of arrows, artillery guns, (showing that in those days artillery guns did exist and these are not the invention of modern time only), gadas and with the use of arms against the arms produced by the Narayani Astra, its effect went on increasing. The entire Pandavas' army started fleeing for safety. Yudhisthra told Daristdumana to go away with his army and Satyaki to go away with his army in trenches. Let Arjuna have his final say, he said, and be happy on all getting killed. Krishana too, who saved Arjuna in fulfilling his vow of killing Jayadratha, would do his best to save them. Then Krishana raising his arms said—

1. All should put down their arms and get down from their vehicles.
2. All should get down from elephants, and horses too and come on earth.
3. The Narayani Astra shall not harm them on earth without arms otherwise the Kaurvas shall become braver if Pandavas used the arms.
4. They should not oppose Narayani Astra even by heart otherwise it shall kill them.

Krishana, being incarnation of God Vishnu himself, knew how to save oneself from the effect of Narayani Astra. Narayani or atomic bomb, which, when exploded, spread in a large area and keeping other arms would appear to show that these arms might get blasted coming in contact with the flames/splinters of the Narayani Astra. Coming on earth means, getting into the trenches where even now the bombs have no effect. This would only confirm that in those days, India had all kinds of chemical and atomic bombs and they knew the ways of protecting themselves from the effect of such bombs. The knowledge of our ancestors, therefore, far excelled to what it is to-day. Krishana further said that he shall try to make the astra ineffective (as it was his astra only). Bhima did not accept Krishana's suggestion and stated that he shall make the astra ineffective. Then Arjuna, who too knew the effect and remedy from that astra, advised Bhima not to develop fighting against the Narayani Astra and he too put down his Gandeeva dhanush. Bhima still did not agree and attacked on Aswatthama but then he had to suffer because of the effect of Narayani Astra. Then Krishana asked Bhima to get down from the chariot and made the Astra ineffective. Duryodhana asked for reuse of the Astra but Aswatthama showed his inability in the reuse of that Astra. Aswatthama then attacked on Daristdumana and defeated him. Satyaki fought with Duryodhana, Kripacharya, Kritvarma, Karna and Vrikhsen and defeated them all. Aswatthama killed the rajas of Malwa, Paurava, and Yuvaraj of Chedi Desh. Then there was fierce battle between Aswatthama and Bhima and the Pandavas' army fled in fear. Aswatthama then used Agneya Astra and killed one Kshoni army of Pandavas. This Astra, however, did not have any effect on Arjuna and Krishana. This made Aswatthama upset. Then Vyasa Muni came and told Aswatthama the exaltation of Krishana and Shiva and told that water, fire, sun, earth, moon, air etc. are all the formations of Krishana and Shiva only. They shall not, therefore, have any effect on them unless they wished for it and so the bombs/arrows obtained from them too would not have any effect on them. Arjuna having the protection of Shiva was, therefore, not effected by Agneya Astra. Similarly, Shiva and Krishana are the Gods of each other and, therefore, above all effects of Astras. Then the armies of Kaurvas and Pandavas went to their respective places. Then Vyasa Muni met Arjuna too, and explained to him the kindness of Shiva on him. When Arjuna enquired that when he had gone to kill Jayadratha as also after Darona had been killed, some light had been going in front of him, but he could not make out what it was. Then Vyasa Muni told him that it was Shiva himself, who was showing and clearing his way to reach the destination. Vyasa Muni also told that Aswatthama, Karna and Kripacharya are great fighters and only Shiva could undo their actions. He, therefore, advised Arjuna to always worship Shiva, who had been helping him in the battle against the enemies.

8
Karna Parva

After Daronacharya's death, Duryodhana etc. Kaurvas had been quite upset. They came to Aswatthama but he too was wasted out on death of his father. So it was decided to appoint Karna as the Senapati of Kaurvas' army. Karna was accordingly coronated as the Senapati observing all protocolic formalities. Then fighting took place in Kaurvas' and Pandavas' armies and during two days' fighting Karna was killed by Arjuna. Sanjaya, who had seen the entire fighting returned to Hastinapur and explained to Dharitrashtra that Karna had been killed. Sanjaya told that Bhishma had been killed after he had killed ten crore persons of Pandavas' army in ten days. Similarly, Darona had been killed after he had smashed entire Panchali army, Half of the Pandavas' army remaining after Bhishma and Darona had been killed, was eliminated by Karna before his death. Dushashana's son had been killed by Daropadi's son. Bhagdutta too had been killed in fighting with Arjuna. Dushashana had been killed by Bhima. Karna's son Vrikhsena had been killed by Arjuna. Bahalika was killed by Bhima. 31 sons of Dharitrashtra had been killed by Bhima. Lacs of Samsaptakas had been killed by Arjuna. Ghatotkachha killed Rakshas Alambusha. Karna and his brother Kaikaye were killed by Arjuna. Many other commanders and chiefs had been killed by Arjuna. Kaurvas had killed many chiefs. Bhishma had killed all from Kuntibhoja Desh and hundreds of brave persons called Narayan Balbhadras. Satyajita was killed by Darona along with many Panchalis. Abhimanyu was killed by six Kaurvas. Lakshamana had killed son of Ambustha. Brihanta was killed by Dushashana. Maniman and Dand-dhara were killed by Darona. Chitrasena and his son were killed by Samudrasena. Two Rochmans were killed by Darona. Purujita and Kuntibhoja were killed by Darona. Many other Pandavas' chiefs and commanders too had been killed by Karna, Aswatthama and Darona. Dharitrashtra was then told about all those on Kaurvas' and Pandavas' side still alive. To know that most of the leaders of Kaurvas had been killed, Dharitrashtra started crying in sorrowness and said that now all his remaining sons shall also be killed and Pandavas shall be the rajas not only of Hastinapur but the entire universe as all rajas of all countries of the universe shall now be killed.

After Karna had been appointed as Senapati, he arranged Kaurvas' army and Pandavas' army was arranged by Yudhisthra. Both armies started fighting furiously. Bhimsena killed Kshemdhurti after he had entered Kaurvas' army. Satyaki killed Vinda and Anuvinda. Daropadi's sons Shrutkarma and Prativindhya killed Chitrasena and Chitra. Kaurvas' army fled in despair. Aswatthama then attacked on Bhima. Both had fought with bravery and skill and were injured and fell unconscious.

Arjuna had fierce fighting with Sansaptakas. They were in crores and were very ferocious. Arjuna had already killed many of them during the last over one week. Although they were in large number, Arjuna had alone faced them and killed them. Then Arjuna left the Sansaptakas and came to Aswatthama. Very serious battle took place between them. Both had been injured by the arrows. Krishana too got injured. Then Arjuna fired an arrow which seriously injured Aswatthama and again went to Sansaptakas' army and killed many troops and commanders in that army. Then Aswatthama again came to Arjuna and they both got engaged in fierce fighting. Krishana asked Arjuna to kill him as he would continue doing mischiefs, if spared and not killed. Arjuna then injured Aswatthama again and he went away from the battle- field and in fact left his ambition of fighting with Arjuna as he had by now known that it was not possible to win Arjuna.

Arjuna again entered Sansaptakas' army and killed many more out of the remaining army-men and commanders. Krishana asked Arjuna to finish all Sansaptakas and then proceed to kill Karna. Arjuna quietly killed Sansaptakas and Krishana told him that so many killings could neither be done by him nor by Indra himself. On the other side, Aswatthama and Pandey Naresh had been fighting in which Pandey Naresh had been killed after he had killed many army-men in the Kaurvas' army.

Next day Kaurvas' and Pandavas' armies again set for fighting. Meantime Arjuna had completed his training in warfare by Shiva and Shiva had blessed him to be successful in the war. Then Krishana told Arjuna that he was not able to see Yudhisthra. Arjuna then asked Krishana to take him to Yudhisthra. Karna had killed many Panchalis. Then Daristdumana, Daropadi's sons, Nakula, Sehdeva and Satyaki attacked on

Karna. Fierce fighting started in which many people had been killed on both sides. Then many elephants attacked on Pandavas' army. Daristdumana, however, killed most of them. Then Pandavas could reach Karna. Sehdeva and Dushashana started fighting too and Sehdeva injured Dushashana, who fled from the battle field.

Nakula and Karna had been seriously fighting. Nakula told Karna that he was the root cause of all the killings. Now he shall have to face him. Karna invited him to attack on him with all his force. Then Karna too injured Nakula. Then the fighting with godly astras started from both sides. Each was cutting the other's astras. Karna then cutting Nakula's dhanush, killed his sarthi and horses and smashed his chariot. Nakula got down from the chariot with a spear in his hand. Nakula left the battle-field. Nakula could be killed by Karna but he remembered the undertaking given to Kunti not to kill the Pandavas other than Arjuna. He, therefore, spared him. Shatanik and Dharitrashtra's son Shrutkarma had been fighting and in the battle of Sutsoma and Shakuni, Shakuni killed many in Pandavas' army.

Daristdumana had attacked on Kaurvas' army but was checked by Kripacharya. Kripacharya injured Daristdumana. He then went to Bhima.

Duryodhana came to Yudhisthra and started fighting. Duryodhana cut Yudhisthra's bow. Yudhisthra took another bow and injured Duryodhana, who fell unconscious. Yudhisthra could kill him but then Bhima told that Duryodhana was to be killed by him only and so Yudhisthra spared him. Satyaki and Karna had been fighting and Arjuna was smashing entire army. At the close of the day, Kaurvas' and Pandavas' armies went to their respective places.

In the night Kaurvas started consultations. Karna told Duryodhana that Arjuna was a clever, firm and intelligent warrior and Krishana had been advising him what to do and when and how to do. Therefore, they had lost during the day but next day he shall shatter all their designs. In the night all rajas rested. Dharitrashtra was, however, not satisfied on Duryodhana believing on Karna's assurances, since Karna had not so far been able to defeat Pandavas. This was nothing but fortune. Sanjaya too told that having known that Pandavas were very powerful, he did not agree to peaceful settlement as brought by Krishana.

Next day morning, Karna came to Duryodhana and told him that now he shall fight with Arjuna and either of the two shall be killed. Karna told that so many interventions having come, the two could not fight together and once the duel fight took place, Arjuna shall be killed. Karna told that he had the dhanush given by Parshurama and it was stronger than Arjuan's Gandeeva Dhanush. With that dhanush, Parshurama had annihilated kshatriyas from the earth twenty-one times. After Arjuna's death, Duryodhana shall rule the entire universe. Karna, however, told Duryodhana that in the fighting, the role of the sarthi was rather important. He, therefore, desired to have Raja Shalya as his sarthi as he was a very able chariot driver equal to Krishana. Duryodhana requested Shalya to become Karna's sarthi. He, however, straight-away refused saying that he was a senior raja then how could he be the sarthi of a Soot's son. It was rather humiliating for him. In such a situation, he would withdraw his support from Duryodhana and go to his kingdom. Then Duryodhana told him that Krishana was Arjuna's sarthi. Therefore, to make a sarthi was not to humiliate him but it was an elevated position. Then Shalya accepted to become Karna's sarthi on the condition that he shall be free to talk to Karna whatever he deemed fit to talk to him and he shall have no objection to the same. His condition had been accepted by Duryodhana. Here the question of protocol comes in as to whether the fighter is superior to the sarthi or vice versa as also whether sarthi's job is a mean job or not compared to that of a raja. Raja Shalya did not accept the job initially in view of the fact that—

1. He was a raja and had been used to fight when his chariot was driven by another person under him called sarthi. So the sarthi is supposed to be an employee of the warrior raja and he has to drive that chariot as per raja's order. Therefore, a raja is superior to the sarthi.

2. Karna was a Soot's son and to work as sarthi for Karna (a Soot's son) was rather humiliation for him.

3. At the time of Daropadi's swayamber, Karna desired to contest but Daropadi refused to marry with a Soot's son, who was obviously considered to be a menial to the kshatriyas.

4. Duryodhana had been praising Karna as a good warrior but Raja Shalya considered himself to be a better warrior. How then could he become the sarthi of a person, who was worse than him as a warrior.

5. Manu had prescribed the Dharma of persons of various varnas. Brahmin is to be educated and to teach others; kshatriya is to protect the life and property of his subjects from external

aggression and internal crimes; the vaisha is to be a trader, agriculturist and industrialist and a shudra is to serve the persons of the other three varnas. How then kshatriya could serve a sooi, who is a shudra, rather the soots had always been serving the kshatriyas and living on their mercy only.

6. Shalya, therefore, told Duryodhana that with the humiliation faced by him in asking him to work as sarthi, he shall not stay in the battle-field any more.

Duryodhana then adopted another strategy of praising him.He told that his name was 'Shalya' meaning a 'Thorn' that is he was a thorn for the enemies in the battle-field. So that way he was superior to anyone in the battle-field. Further, since Krishana was the sarthi of Arjuna and Karna was better skilled in battle, he has to have a sarthi better than Krishana and it was he only who could fill up that gap. Then Shalya agreed to work as Karna's sarthi but, as already indicated, on the condition that Karna shall have to hear whatever he told him. Here we have to remember that Yudhisthra had requested Shalya, when he indicated how he had to support Kaurvas army, to atleast praise Arjuna before Karna, when he became his sarthi. It shows how Yudhisthra could calculate in advance that Shalya shall have to work as Karna's sarthi, when even Kaurvas did not know it. Shalya also undertook that in case Karna was killed while he worked as sarthi, he shall fight for Kaurvas and kill all Pandavas. He told Karna too that he shall work as his sarthi.

Next day Karna started for the battle-field. He, out of protocol, worshipped the chariot and had a round of the chariot in respect.Then he boarded the chariot along with Shalya, as his sarthi. Shalya then started praising Pandavas, particularly Arjuna, before him saying that Arjuna was invincible even by gods and that Karna's end was near now. All Kaurvas were happy when Karna started for the battle-field as they thought that Karna would now kill Arjuna and that shall bring an end to the battle as without Arjuna, Pandavas would not be able to fight. But there were bad omens in Karna's camp indicating that Karna's end was near now. We have already seen that omens—good or bad—were the correct indication of what was to come in future. Karna, however, did not care for the same and started self-praising. Shalya checked him from assuming so much and boasting so much when he did not stand in comparison to Arjuna at all as not even Indra could challenge the God Vishnu much less Shiva, and it was Arjuna, who could challenge Shiva. Arjuna had also defeated yakshas, rakshasas, gods, asuras, nagas, and even Agni. Shalya reminded

Karna of the incidence when Karna had been defeated by Gandharvas and Duryodhana had been arrested by them. Then it was Arjuna only who could defeat Gandharvas and got Duryodhana released from their captivity. Still Duryodhana had the teeth to quarrel with Arjuna. Similarly, in Virat Nagar, Arjuna alone had defeated all Kaurvas including Bhishma, Darona, Karna and Duryodhana. This made Karna enraged and asked Shalya, not to talk about Arjuna so much since now battle was on head with him. Karna could not see Arjuna in the battle field. He declared lot of prizes to anyone, who could tell the whereabouts of Arjuna as Arjuna shall himself not come to fight with him. This only shows the over-anxiety of Karna for fighting with Arjuna, which is not desirable. Shalya again started praising Arjuna with a view to demoralise Karna. It is a well-known strategy of warfare to demoralise the enemy as fighting with a demoralised enemy is half victory already. Karna told that only an intelligent person could understand the intelligence in another person and not anyone else. He rebuked Shalya a lot and showered his praise on himself. Karna told that he was Duryodhana's friend. Therefore, all his wealth and even his life was at the disposal of Duryodhana. Karna started doubting the bonafides of Shalya and even said so that he appeared to be a spy of Pandavas with Duryodhana. Such person's bonafides could be suspected, as are relatives of enemy and were assuming to be with another party, particularly when one started praising the enemy and demoralising his own men. But Karna said he would not be demoralised by thousands of persons of his like and that he shall definitely kill Arjuna in the battle-field in the presence of all in the field. Shalya told that he was the well-wisher of Duryodhana and had agreed to work as sarthi for him only on Duryodhana's request. He told that he knew the job of the sarthi well. He told that a sarthi should—

1. be able to take a decision in favourable and unfavourable conditions.
2. know the weaknesses of the warrior on the chariot and drive the chariot in such a way that the weaknesses are covered and not exposed to the enemy.
3. know the condition of horses—when they could be put to hardwork and when allowed to relax.
4. see that sufficient stock of all kinds of arms was available on the chariot.
5. have knowledge of the operation of various kinds of armaments.

6. understand the voice of the birds and animals around the battle field as they convey the result of the battle.
7. know surgery to provide first aid for the injuries caused during the battle.

Shalya told that the sarthi was the member of the family of a complete chariot. He knew the art of driving the chariot well and there was hardly anyone in the universe, who could act better than him as a sarthi—not even Krishana. Shalya then told what various birds had been talking about in the battle-field. This shows the specialisation of the people in knowing the voice of birds and animals even. Ultimately Karna accepted the specialisation of Arjuna and Krishana in fighting but he was no less in the vocation of fighting. When they both had been speaking and counter-speaking for long time, Duryodhana stopped them and asked them to be in a very cordial way as both had been there to look into the interest of Kaurvas.

After studying the efficient formation of Pandavas' army, Karna proudly entered the enemy's army and killing many and injuring Yudhisthra, he proceeded futher. Then Yudhisthra asked Arjuna to check Karna from causing the devastation of the army. He also planned that Bhima shall fight with Duryodhana; Nakula with Vrikhsena; Sehdeva with Shakuni, Shatanik with Dushasan; Satyaki with Kritvarma, Daristdumana with Aswatthama and he himself shall fight with Kripacharya. This is how the matches were selected and there was fight of one with one as per laws of war. All accepted Yudhisthra's directions and proceeded to the battle-field after worshipping their respective gods. Again to demoralise Karna, Shalya told about the bad omens happening on their side and good omens on Pandavas' side. This showed that thousands of commanders and lakhs of troops shall be killed on that day. Shalya then introduced all the commanders on Pandavas' side and indicated the bravery so far shown by each of them. At that time both the armies started fighting. Arjuna and Karna had been fighting to the best of their abilities. Sansapatakas too came to fight with Arjuna, but Arjuna started killing Kaurvas' army left and right. Here is an indication that people of all varnas, brahmin, kshatriya, vaish and shudra, were fighting in the armies of both sides and many on them had been killed —

लेषामन्तकरं युं देह पाप्मासुनाशनम्,
क्षत्रविट्शुद्रवीराणां श्म्यें स्वर्ग्यं यशस्करम!। (47/18)

So, although there was distribution of jobs on functional basis, in case of battles with other countries, people of all varnas used to join hand in fighting with the enemy. This aspect had been given up during Rajput period, when fighting was meant for the kshatriyas only and in this way three-fourth of the population did not participate in fighting. This not only deprived the army of 3/4th of the population but also kept those people indifferent at the time of invasions by Muslims resulting in lot of wealth having been taken by Mahmud Ghazni and establishment of Muslim rule in India by Mohammed Ghori.

Karna attacked on Daristdumana and killed many army-men. He also killed Panchali commanders Bhanu Deva, Chitrasena, Senavindu, Tapara and Soorsena. Karna attacked on Yudhisthra. Initially Yudhisthra injured Karna, who fell unconscious. But subsequently Karna got enraged and defeated Yudhisthra. On Karna rebuking Yudhisthra, he said he should face Arjuna and see the result. Karna was able to kill Yudhisthra but to keep the word given to Kunti, he did not kill him. Simultaneously Shalya also advised Karna not to touch Yudhisthra, otherwise the Dharma's son Yudhisthra would kill him. Karna laughed and asked Yudhisthra tauntingly that he was born in kshatriya varna. Then how could he flee from the battle-field. He asked him that he was good at performing yagyas etc. and should not come to battle-field. He should now go home and take refuge under Krishana. Saying this he spared Yudhisthra. Yudhisthra went away from the battle-field. While going from battle-field, Yudhisthra asked Bhima to attack on Duryodhana. Fierce fighting took place between Bhima and Duryodhana. Many horses, elephants and troops were killed and chariots smashed. Then Karna came to fight with Bhima after Duryodhana and his brother fled. Shakuni also came there. Fierce fighting took place. Bhima entrusted the protection of Yudhisthra to Daristdumana and said either he shall kill Karna or die himself. Shalya alerted Karna saying that it was difficult to defeat Bhima as he was in rage and wanted to kill him. But he was injured by Karna and fell unconscious. Then he again got up and attacked on Karna, who fell unconscious and went to the back of the chariot. Bhima could have killed Karna but then he remembered that Arjuna had avowed to kill him. So he spared him. In this way the word or commitment undertaken had great importance even during the war. Because of the word given to Kunti, Karna did not kill Yudhisthra and similarly Bhima did not kill Karna as he was to be killed by Arjuna only. Bhima then killed many army-men of Kaurvas' army. Then Duryodhana ordered his brothers and other chiefs, including Shrutarva, Durdhava, Kratha, Vivitsu, Vikata, Sama, Nisangi, Kavachi,

Nanda, Upanda, Duspradhrasha, Subahu, Vatvega, Suvarcha, Dhanurgraha, Durmada, Jalasandha, Shala and Saha to come and attack on Bhima but Bhima killed them all and then injured Karna, who attacked on him. Then having seen Karna attacking on Yudhisthra, Bhima attacked on Karna and fierce fighting took place. Arjuna was again involved in fighting with Sansaptakas' army from Kaushal and Narayani army and killed lakhs of them, Krishana showed all dead bodies to Arjuna and told that they had all been killed by him.

Having not seen Yudhisthra for a along time, Arjuna asked Krishana to take him to Yudhisthra. Krishana showed to Arjuna the Pandavas' army fleeing due to fear of Karna, who had been killing them, but Arjuna insisted on once seeing his brother and then only to resume fighting. Krishana also showed many dead because of Duryodhana. There were parts of the bodies, armaments, ornaments and clothes spread throughout the battle-field. Daristdumana had attacked on Karna along with some other Pandava chiefs. Karna injured Daristdumana. Then Satyaki came for his rescue and fighting started between Karna and Satyaki. Aswatthama told him that he shall be killed if Arjuna did not come to his rescue. Fierce fighting ensued between them. Daristdumana's chariot had been smashed; his dhanush had been broken; he had been badly injured but still he did not leave the battle-field. Then Krishana told Arjuna to save him from the clutches of Aswatthama. While Aswatthama had been dragging Daristdumana, Arjuna attacked on him, and injured him and he became unconscious and sat in the back of the chariot. Krishana then took Arjuna to Sansaptakas and asked him to finish the remaining Sansaptakas. Krishana then narrated the bravery of Karna and Duryodhana to Arjuna with a view to prepare him to kill Karna. At that time Pandavas' army was fleeing because of the fear of Karna and Duryodhana. Yudhisthra was already fighting for life due to injuries caused to him by Karna, when Satyaki, Shikhandi, Nakula, Sehdeva and Bhima were there. Krishana told him that after defeating Pandavas, Panchalis and Srijeyans, Karna was now looking forward to kill Arjuna too. Krishana, therefore, told Arjuna that he should now take necessary action against Yudhisthra's enemy Karna by attacking on him. At the same time Kaurvas army was going to attack on him along with Aswatthama. So they too had to be finished first. Krishana told Arjuna that since Bhima had been coming, Yudhisthara should be alright. Bhima had been giving a fighting to Duryodhana. Then Kripacharya and Karna came to help Duryodhana. Karna defeated Shikhandi. Daristdumana and Dushashana had been fighting. Bhima defeated Duryodhana and killed many elephants and Kaurvas' army fled.

At that time, Duryodhana came and attacked on Yudhisthra, when he was not being protected by anyone. He injured Yudhisthra. Yudhisthra too injured Duryodhana. Then Karna came there and again injured Yudhisthra. Fighting ensued between them. Both had been injured. Then Duryodhana and some other Kaurvas came there and surrounded Yudhisthra. Then Bhima also reached there. But Karna defeated Yudhisthra, Nakula and Sehdeva and Yudhisthra was taken to the base camp to rest and recover from the injuries caused in the battle-field.

Arjuna defeated Aswatthama in a serious fighting. Then Karnas' army fled from the battle-field. Duryodhana inspired Karna to use Bhargavastra and smash the Panchali army. With Karna's Bhargvastra, many troops in Pandavas' army had been killed. Arjuna too could not help it. Then, Krishana told Arjuna that Yudhisthra had been seriously injured by Karna. So he had to be taken care of first and after that only Karna should be killed. This indicates that time is fixed for everything and Krishana knew it. That is why he had been taking Arjun to various places at appropriate times.Arjuna had already defeated Aswatthama and could not find Yudhisthra anywhere in the battle-field. Arjuna entrusted holding of the battle-field to Bhima and went to meet Yudhisthra in the base camp. They went to Yudhisthra and paid respects. Seeing them in the base camp, Yudhisthra thought that Karna must have been killed. But when Arjuna told that he was still alive, Yudhisthra, who had been badly injured by Karna, could not stand that he was still alive and in rage asked Arjuna to throw away Gandeeva Dhanush if he had so far not been able to kill Karna inspite of his having killed so many persons in Pandavas' army. Arjuna had taken a vow that any one, who asked him to throw Gandeeva Dhanush, shall be killed by him. So to fulfil that bow, Arjuna took out the sword to kill Yudhisthra. Then Krishana asked him the reason for taking out the sword in the camp. Arjuna told him about his vow. Krishana then pacified him and asked him not to be in so much rage now. If he could suppress his rage for the sake of Yudhisthra, when they had been humiliated in the sabha by Kaurvas and Daropadi had been insulted, then why this rage now. Arjuna then rebuked Yudhisthra that because of him they had been humiliated by defeat in gambling; because of him they had to live in forests and because of him now they had to face this battle. Krishana told that he had already abused Yudhisthra so much which was more than killing him. Arjuna then got prepared to kill himself for having insulted his elder brother Yudhisthra. Krishana then further pacified him and prepared him to go to the battle-field and consoled Yudhisthra by telling that Karna shall now be killed. From this incident, it appears that Arjuna had to be inspired and prepared for killing any great man. This happened when Bhishma had to be killed; this happened by death of Abhimanyu and enraging Arjuna on that account leading to the death of Darona and this happened for defeating guru's son Aswatthama. Now for killing Karna, there was need for enraging Arjuna. But why should Arjuna need to be enraged to show good result in the battle-field ? This is where the role of Krishana came in. It is he, who had to arrange everything in a set manner, which Krishana only knew, others were his tools only and this is what is happening to the universe today. Everything is pre-arranged by Krishana alone. Krishana then asked Arjuna that he would not be able to do marvels in the battle-field unless he had pleased his brother first and got his blessings. Then Arjuna fell in the feet of Yudhisthra and begged to be excused. Yudhisthra picked him up and embraced him. They both kept weeping for sometime and then Yudhisthra asked Arjuna to go to the battle-field and kill Karna so that the battle was over. Arjuna undertook to kill Karna that day.

Krishana and Arjuna prepared for the battle-field. Good omens could be seen on the way indicating Arjuna's victory. Yudhisthra and Arjuna worshipped the chariot and Yudhisthra blessed Arjuna to be victorious. They then proceeded towards Karna. Krishana alerted Arjuna that he should not take Karna lightly and should use his best tactics to kill Karna, who was very brave and had the blessings of Parshurama. He could be killed when he was without arms. Therefore, such occasion had to be found. Krishana then praised Arjuna too and reminding him of the doings of Karna and Duryodhana in the past, adequately enraged Arjuna to be prepared to fight with all valour to kill Karna. This is the war strategy in which Arjuna had to be told about the strength of the enemy so that he did not take him lightly and at the same time to praise Arjuna so that he was not demoralised. Krishana told that Karna was the root cause of the gambling and humiliation caused to Pandavas and then Daropadi's insult and the battle in forests to kill Pandavas and then battle at Virat Nagar and finally now Mahabharata. If Karna was not there, Duryodhana would not have taken up arms against Pandavas. It is on his reassurance only, time and again, that Duryodhana could not reach any peaceful settlement with Pandavas. Arjuna then undertook to kill Karna.

Next day both armies started fighting. From Pandavas' side Uttamoja fought with Karna's son Sukhena and after prolonged fighting killed him. Nakula's son injured Karna's another son Vrikhsena. Daristdumana attacked on Karna. Bhima killed many in Kaurvas' army and many fled away. Simultaneously, the Kaurvas' army was fleeing because of the injuries caused to them by Arjuna. Then sarthi of Bhima told that Arjuna was quite close in the battle-field. Bhima was happy to know Arjuna's arrival in the field and gave a huge reward to his sarthi for giving such a good news. Awarding the warriors, particularly the sarthis, is an acknowledged world strategy to boost their morale. Arjuna then started fighting with Kaurvas' army and killed many. Karna then entered Pandavas' army and killed many army-men causing fleeing in the army. He killed many Panchalis. Arjuna too killed crores of people in Kaurvas' army and there were deads and their parts in the entire battle-field. Arjuna then asked Krishana to take him to Karna. Seeing Krishana and Arjuna coming, Shalya told Karna that Arjuna, for whom he had been waiting, was now coming there himself. Shalya praised Arjuna before Karna and demoralised him. He mentioned how Arjuna had defeated Kaurvas in forests and inVirat Nagar and already killed Bhishma, Darona etc. Further, Arjuna was in great rage because of the injuries caused by Karna to Yudhisthra, whom Arjuna respected very much. Further, Krishana was with him as sarthi. Krishana himself was the incarnation of God and a good guide for Pandavas in the battle. Arjuna was then on the way surrounded by Kaurvas' army. Arjuna annihilated many of them and the rest fled away. Arjuna also killed many Kaurvas' chiefs. Arjuna and Bhima then got the news that Yudhisthra had since recovered from his injuries. Dushashana and Bhima also got engaged in fighting. Then Duryodhana, Kripacharya, Kritvarma and Karna attacked on Satyaki, who alone managed them all in the battle. Dushashana again came and started fighting with Bhima. Dushashana cut off Bhima's bow and injured him. Then Bhima took a gada in his hand and threw on Dushashana. Dushashana was injured. He fell on the earth. Mahesh and other Prajapatis had come to witness the battle. Surya (Sun) was in favour of Karna, being his father. Gods had even put stakes on the victory or defeat of either side. Asuras were also on Karna's side. Brahma and Mahadeva told Indra that asuras being on Karna's side, Arjuna should come out victorious as it shall be in the interest of gods too. Brahma, however, told Indra that Karna should attain best Loka on death. Indra agreed and passed on these orders to his people. This shows that—

1. Even gods had interest in the battle of Arjuna and Karna.
2. Gods were divided in siding Karna or Arjuna.
3. Looking into their interest, gods desired Arjuna to be victorious.
4. Gods had put stakes on victory or defeat of either.
5. Brahma asked Indra to allot the best Loka to Karna on death.

This shows that there was division of work in the God's realm also as, although Brahma could have himself allotted the Loka of his desire to Karna after death, but since that department was looked after by Indra, Brahma asked Indra only to do the needful.

6. There is hierarchy in gods. Brahma asked Indra (his subordinate) to allot best Loka to Karna and obeying him, Indra passed on those orders to his subordinates for compliance. This shows the hierarchy existing in gods like the present day system in Government and also division of labour.

All then praised Krishna and Arjuna in reverence. Shalya told Karna that in case Arjuna killed him then he shall kill Krishana and Arjuna alone from the same chariot. On the other side, Krishana assured Arjuna of his victory and in case he was killed then Krishana shall destroy the entire universe and kill Shalya and Karna himself. Arjuna told Krishana that after Karna's death, he would be able to give this good news to Abhimanyu's mother Subhadra and his aunt Kunti.

Arjuna then started fighting and killed many in Kaurvas' army. Then Aswatthama caught hold of Duryodhana's hand and told him to come on peaceful terms with Pandavas as there was no use in continuing fighting. Even his guru (Darona) had been killed in the battle. Same happened to Bhishma too. He told that he and his uncle Kripacharya could not be killed. Hence they were still alive. He shall rule along with Pandavas and he shall make Pandavas agree to such settlement. For the sake of Dharitrashtra and Gandhari, Yudhisthra would agree to such a settlement, and since other Pandavas and Krishana would do as directed by Yudhisthra, they too would agree to such a settlement. Such a proposal, Aswatthama told, was in the greater interest of Kaurvas, Pandavas and other people of the universe. He also told that Karna would not be able to kill Arjuna and then their defeat was sure. It was, therefore, still better to come to settlement. Duryodhana then told Aswatthama that whatever he said was correct but his difficulty was that on Dushashana's death whatever Bhima had said is known to everyone, then how could he think of stopping the war. Further Arjuna was already tired in the battle, fighting with others and, therefore, Karna would easily kill him. There was, therefore, no scope for a settlement.

It would be seen that eversince Pandavas came back from forests, there had been constant endeavor for a peaceful settlement:-

1. By sending a Purohit to request for the return of their share of kingdom to Pandavas as already agreed to at the time of departure

for forests, but Kaurvas did not agree.

2. Krishana went himself and even put the demand on behalf of Pandavas for five villages only but even this demand was not accepted and on the contrary Duryodhana tried to captivate Krishana.

3. Inspite of Krishana having shown his Godly form, Kaurvas, did not agree to come to terms with Pandavas.

4. Bhishma, Darona, Vyasa, Dharitrashtra, Gandhari, Vidur etc. all persuaded Duryodhana to come to peaceful settlement with Pandavas otherwise there shall be disaster. Still Duryodhana did not agree.

5. After Bhishma fell in battle, he asked Kaurvas to stop fighting and come to a peaceful settlement. But Duryodhana did not agree.

6. Now again Aswatthama requested for a peaceful settlement but Duryodhana could not agree.

This shows that Indians are, by and large, in for peaceful living and try their utmost to avoid war. They resort to war when it is a must. Even after independence, war had been enforced on India by China first and then by Pakistan two times. So Arjuna and Karna proceeded for fighting and started throwing arrows on each other. Karna killed many Panchalis in the battle. All Arjuna's arrows had been cut by Karna. Krishana showing surprise, inspired Arjuna to fight with more vigour, and kill Karna. Krishana even offered his Sudarshan Chakra for being used by Arjuna but Arjuna told that he shall devise a ferocious arrow to kill Karna if permitted by him, Brahma and Mahesh and other gods. He then devised that Brahmastra but Karna cut that astra too. Arjuna had already killed all the chief commanders of Kaurvas' army. Karna then injured Krishana, Arjuna and Bhima. Arjuna then injured Shalya and Karna and killed Rajkumar Sabhapati and many army-men. Army-men started crying for help. Yudhisthra too having since recovered from his injuries, came to the battle- field. Arjuna again injured Karna, Shalya and other Kaurvas by his arrows. Karna threw arrows but were cut by Arjuna. Then Arjuna fired a special enemy-killing astra but was made ineffective by Karna. There were greetings by gods to Karna and Arjuna. At that time, one Naga (Aswasena), who had to take revenge from Arjuna, entered Karna's arrow which was to be fired by Karna on Arjuna. But then, Shalya told that his aim was not alright. He should again aim at Arjuna so that it hit his neck.

But Karna told that he did not aim twice. When Krishna saw that astra coming, he pressed the chariot in earth. So the astra went without hurting. This is how the sarthi had to be alert and he could save the warrior on chariot by his manipulations. The Naga again asked Karna to aim properly and then fire on Arjuna so that she was able to cut Arjuna's head. Naga told that she wanted to take revenge from Arjuna as he had killed all his family members and she wanted to kill Arjuna. But Karna told that (1) He did not want to win by using others, and (2) He did not aim one astra twice. Then Naga herself attacked on Arjuna. Arjuna killed her on advice from Krishana.

Arjuna then broke the kawach of Karna and injured him. Karna was upset and fell unconscious. Although Arjuna did not want to kill Karna at that time thinking it against the rules to attack when enemy was in trouble, yet Krishana told him not to miss the chance and it was as per law of war to kill the enemy, when he was in trouble. Arjuna kept firing arrows on Karna. Karna too continued firing on enemy. This shows that Krishana's advice was correct as Karna was still fighting and had not surrendered even when he was in trouble. Then Karna's death-time had come. As per Parshurama's curse, Karna could not remember of firing the Bhargava Astra on Arjuna and the wheel of his chariot got thrust in the mud. Karna tried to take it out but could not. Arjuna fired many arrows but were made ineffective by Karna. Then on Krishana's advice, he fired Brahmastra, and continued firing arrows on Karna and Karna in turn cut eleven ropes of his bow, one after the other. Arjuna went on changing the ropes. Then Karna wanted to take the wheel of his chariot out from the mud and Arjuna wanted to spare him at that time but Krishana again alerted Arjuna to go on firing arrows on Karna although Karna requested Arjuna to wait till he picked up chariot's wheel. Krishana told that the laws of war provided that one should not attack when—

1. One opens hairs and stands in battle-field without arms.
2. One has already given up fighting.
3. One has already surrendered.
4. One begs to be excused to save his life.
5. Whose arrow, kawach and other appliance had been broken.

People observing Dharma do not attack the person in one of the above conditions. He knew the Dharma and the law of war but such Dharma had to be observed, when the other party had been observing the same. Karna had not followed Dharma, when he was a party to Pandavas' defeat in gambling in a deceitful manner; when he insulted Daropadi in the sabha; when he again arranged for gambling resulting in Pandavas' being sent to forests on exile; when he alongwith Duryodhana had gone to forests to kill Pandavas in loneliness; when rajya had not been returned to Pandavas on return from exile and lastly when six of Kaurvas, including Karna had killed Abhimanyu, when he was in the same situation without the chariot and arms. So that was the time not to think of Dharma but to kill the enemy. Arjuna, however, bowed his head in shame after hearing what Krishana told and also Krishana asking him to kill Karna by a special arrow. Arjuna fired the Brahmastra but Karna still made it ineffective and fired one astra on Arjuna and it got thrust in Arjuna's chest and then tried to pick out the wheel of the chariot. Meantime Arjuna came in senses and, on the advice of Krishana, Arjun fired a special arrow cutting Karna's head from the body and thus Karna was killed. Pandavas celebrated Karna's death and Kaurvas fled from the field. Shalya consoled Duryodhana saying it was all written in fate. This is how Hindus console themselves. Other religions too attribute such actions to fate only. This is what Gita tells too to go on acting leaving the result to God (or fate). Pandavas continued fighting. Bhima and Arjuna killed many in Kaurvas' army, smashed all chariot-riders' army resulting in Kaurvas' army fleeing. Duryodhana too could not check the fleeing army. The remaining Kaurvas' army went to the camp base.

After Karna had been killed, Krishana embraced Arjuna and told that like Indra, who had killed Vritrasura in ancient times, Arjuna had killed Karna and this shall be remembered by the people ever. Krishana told Yudhisthra that Karna had been killed and all Pandavas were still safe. This was rather fortunate. Now they should think of completing the remaining job that is the killing of Duryodhana. As per protocol, Yudhisthra thanked Krishana and attributed the success to him only. In fact that was all possible under his guidance only. On the other side, Dharitrashtra was very upset on knowing of Karna's death. Gandhari too started crying. Kurukul ladies then picked up Gandhari and consoled her.

9

Shalya Parva

Initially God is worshipped and then Saraswati is worshipped before starting the Parva. All in Kaurvas' had been crying on the death of Karna. Dharitrashtra then asked about what happened in the battle-field after Karna's death. Sanjaya told that after Karna's death and killing of Kaurvas' army by Bhima, a small number was left, which fled from the battle field. Duryodhana somehow made them agree to fight with Pandavas. After seeing many dead in battle-field, Kripacharya took pity on remaining persons. He asked Duryodhana to listen to what he wanted to say. He said that fighting is the only Dharma of kshatriyas and the best thing for them is to kill or get killed in the battle-field. But one does not fight with braver persons. Arjuna and Bhima were still there. They had already killed Bhishma, Darona, Karna and the entire army. Now there was no use continuing fighting. It was like throwing oneself to the burning furnace. In such a situation one has to reassess one's capability. Now, therefore, it was time to still reach on peaceful terms with Pandavas. Yudhisthra was a kind-hearted person. He shall still make Duryodhana raja for a part of the kingdom. Krishana too might agree to such a settlement. Duryodhana told that he was thankful for his fighting in the battle-field for his sake and for the nice advice now given and he had liked it but still he was not agreeable for a peaceful settlement in view of the fact that—

1. Kaurvas had cheated Pandavas in gambling and then sent them to forests for thirteen years.
2. They insulted Daropadi in the sabha of the rajas, which was not tolerated by Krishana but since it all happened in his absence, he could not do anything then. He remembered Pandavas'

promises at that time.

3. Abhimanyu was killed by six Kaurvas against the law of war and Pandavas and Krishana were upset on it.

4. Bhima had undertaken to kill all Dharitrashtra's sons. He will die but not leave his undertaking unfulfilled.

5. He had already enjoyed the rajya of the entire universe and it was not possible for him now to rule at the mercy of Pandavas

6. Having been the leader of all the rajas, it was not possible for him now to walk behind Yudhisthra.

Duryodhana, therefore, reiterated his thinking of continuing the battle, as he could not now beg for a peaceful settlement, which shall only be asking for mercy only at this juncture. He had, he said, lived with honour and shall now die with honour only, otherwise he would be answerable to all, who had given up their lives for his sake on his not having agreed for a peaceful settlement with Pandavas at the beginning of the war.

Then the question arose about the appointment of next Senapati. Duryodhana asked all his remaining chiefs. Aswatthama proposed Shalya for this position as he was a big raja, a great warrior and a man of bonafides as he joined Kaurvas even leaving his Pandava nephews. All others too agreed to this proposal. This shows the democracy at work in a limited way. Even Duryodhana, who was so much an autocrat, had to consult other rajas for appointment of Senapati. Shalya was accordingly coronated as Senapati of Kaurvas' army. Raja Shalya too on his part accepting the post of Senapati, indicated that his rajya, his life and all his wealth was at Duryodhana's disposal and he shall discharge his duty faithfully. Shalya then indicated that irrespective of what they are, he shall kill all Pandavas and their army.

On the other side, Krishana narrated the bravery of Shalya and prepared Yudhisthra for his being killed in fighting. Yudhisthra told Krishana that Kaurvas had fixed Shalya as their Senapati. Shalya was brave like Bhishma, Karna etc. Krishana said that although Bhima, Satyaki, Dristdumana were all quite brave but he considered Yudhisthra as the best to face Shalya. He indicated that Yudhisthra shall be honoured on defeating Shalya in the battle. Krishna then went to his camp.

Next morning Duryodhana prepared all his troops for the battle. Kaurvas made a policy that all Kaurvas' chiefs shall fight together with

Pandavas as individually they shall not be able to face them. Kaurvas were again sure of their victory. Shalya put the army in a strange formation, with Kritverma on the left, Duryodhana in the middle, Kripacharya on the south-end and Aswatthama in the back. Similarly, Pandavas too formed their army in a specific way. Dristduman, Shikhandi and Satyaki attacked on Shalya's army; Yudhisthra attacked on Shalya; Arjuna attacked on Kritvarma; Bhima attacked on Kripacharya; Nakula and Sehdeva faced Shakuni and Ulooka. On Dharitrashtra having enquired about the remaining force, Sanjaya told him that in Kaurvas' army, there were now eleven thousand chariots, ten thousand one hundred elephants, two lakh horses and three crore on foot. Pandavas had six thousand chariots, six thousand elephants; ten thousand horses and two crores on foot. It means even then Kaurvas were in larger number. This also indicates that there must be some computer in those days, which could tell the correct number of army of various categories at any given time and that way our technology was supreme in those days in computerization. Fierce fighting took place between the two armies and Kaurvas' forces had been defeated and fled. Nakula killed three sons of Karna in a fierce fighting. All chiefs on Kaurvas' side were with Shalya and on Pandavas' side Yudhisthra, Bhima, Nakula, Sehdeva and Satyaki were there. Many persons were killed on both sides. Yudhisthra injured Shalya. Then Shakuni etc. came to help Shalya. Kripacharya injured Dristdumana and Duryodhana attacked on Arjuna. Bhima killed horses of Shalya and smashed his chariot too and injured his sarthi. Shalya then fled from the battle-field. He at first attacked and injured Yudhisthra but was himself injured by Bhima and Satyaki. Yudhisthra was again upset lest Shalya should kill Pandavas' army. Arjuna had been fighting with Aswatthama and Arjuna was injured. Then Arjuna also injured Aswatthama. Bhima defeated Duryodhana and Yudhisthra defeated Shalya. Bhima then killed the sarthi and horses of Shalya and Yudhisthra killed Shalya and his brother in a fierce fighting. Kritvarma too had been defeated in the battle by Yudhisthra. The other commanders and army-men of Shalya had also been killed and Kaurvas' army then fled from the field. Then Duryodhana came in the battle-field and injured all those, who came to fight with him. Shakuni injured Yudhisthra. Then Yudhisthra injured Kripacharya and killed Kritvarma's horses. Aswatthama took away Kritvarma. Arjuna had been smashing Kaurvas' army, left and right. He told Krishana that in case Duryodhana had come to peaceful settlement after the death of Bhishma then all this killing could have been avoided. But he did not agree inspite of repeated persuation by all. The Pandits had said on the birth of Duryodhana that he shall destroy all kshatriyas on earth. Duryodhana fled from the battle-field and went into a hiding. Kaurvas' army fled and Satyaki caught Sanjaya in the battle-field but he was later on acquitted. Bhima killed eleven sons of Dharitrashtra in the fierce fighting and most of the Chaturangani army. Duryodhana kept in hiding and was not traceable. Arjuna further killed Satyakarma, Satyeshu, Susharma and their 45 sons and Bhima killed Dharitrashtra's son Sudarshan. Now Dharitrashtra's only son Duryodhana was left. He had gone and hidden himself in a lake under the water. Sehdeva had killed Shakuni and Ulooka. The remaining army of Kaurvas had been wiped out too. On Kaurvas' side Duryodhana, Aswatthama, Kripacharya and Kritvarma were left alive.

While Pandavas had been searching for Duryodhana, Aswatthama, Kritvarma and Kripacharya could locate him in the lake. They talked to him for continuing the battle. Duryodhana told that he shall take rest for the night in the lake and shall be ready to fight the next day. Some hunters saw Duryodhana hiding in the lake. They had heard the talks of Duryodhana and others and could make out that Pandavas had been searching for him and if they told his whereabouts to Pandavas, they would pay a lot of wealth as prize. They did accordingly and got prize for giving the information to Pandavas. Pandavas came to the lake and were able to locate Duryodhana there. Kritvarma, Aswatthama and Kripacharya went away from there listening of the Pandavas' army coming there. Yudhisthra fcund that Duryodhana had hidden himself in the lake and had checked the flow of water by his 'maya' (skill). Krishana then told Yudhisthra to make Duryodhana's maya ineffective by his maya as maya could be made ineffective by maya only.

मायाविन इमां मायां मायया जहि भारत्,
मायावी मायया वध्वाः सत्यमेतद् युधिष्ठिर। (31/6)

Krishana told Yudhisthra that he was capable of making Duryodhana's maya ineffective and then should kill him. Yudhisthra then asked Duryodhana as to why he was hiding in the lake after getting so many people killed. He should come out and fight with them like a kshatriya as not fighting or fleeing from fighting is cursed by shastras. Duryodhana told that he had not been hiding there because of any fear but because he was neither having any army nor any chariot nor sarthi. Then how could he come out to fight with mighty Pandavas and that after taking rest for some time, he would come out and then fight with them. Yudhisthra told that they wished fighting to take place then and there itself. Duryodhana told that he agreed to give to them the entire universe to rule as he was not left with any of his brothers to rule now. Yudhisthra told that he had already lost in fighting and, therefore, there was no question of his giving the universe, and even if he were in a position to give, Yudhisthra would not have accepted like that but only by fighting. Such was the 'Rajdharma' in those days that kshatriyas did not live on alms but on the rajya conquered by them. Yudhisthra said that before the war, Duryodhana was not prepared to part with the smallest piece of land (equal to the point of a needle) and now he was parting with entire universe because it did not belong to him now. Yudhisthra reminded Duryodhana of all the evil designs of killing Bhima by poisoning him; then burning Pandavas in Lakshagriha; then defeated in gambling by cheating them; sent to forests in exile; went there to kill them and ultimately not fulfilling their promise of returning their rajya on return from forests. Duryodhana then offered to fight with a gada, one by one, with them. Yudhisthra then offered to Duryodhana that he could select any one of the Pandavas and if he was able to kill him, then he shall hand over the entire rajya to him. Duryodhana then came out and asked for anyone to come and fight with him with gada. Yudhisthra asked him to fight with him or anyone else and if he was able to defeat him, the entire rajya would belong to him. Yudhisthra repeated it several times, Krishana then scolded Yudhisthra and asked him if Duryodhana chose to fight with him or with Arjuna or Nakula or Sehdeva, then what would happen. Except for Bhima, none could face Duryodhana. If Duryodhana chose anyone, other than Bhima, then Duryodhana was sure to be victorious and in that case the rajya shall have to be handed over to him and Pandavas shall again live on 'bhiksha'. They deserved only this with the prudence Yudhisthra had. It is, Krishana mentioned, because of Yudhisthra only that they joined Kaurvas in gambling leading to their exile for thirteen years and now again he was repeating the same foolishness after winning the rajya killing crores of people and now when only one remained, he was prepared to hand over the rajya to him for nothing. Even if Bhima fought with Duryodhana, he was not sure that he would win then how Yudhisthra had offered Duryodhana to fight with anyone of the Pandavas and in case of defeat, shall return the rajya to him. Bhima then assured his victory over Duryodhana. It was then decided that Bhima shall fight with Duryodhana.

At that time, Balrama also reached there from pilgrimage and having known of the fight between Bhima and Duryodhana, he decided to stay back to see the fighting as Duryodhana was his disciple in 'gada-yudha'. Balrama then explained about his pilgrimage and importance of each of the tirathas in detail. Balrama further added that he had heard from Narada about the defeat of Kaurvas and Duryodhana's fighting with Bhima. So he came to see this fighting. Balrama told that he had heard from rishis that anyone, who died in Kurukshetra, got swarga. Therefore, all, who gave up their lives in the Mahabharata war, shall go to swarga. Then Duryodhana and Bhima appeared in the battle field with their kawach on to fight with gadas. They both challenged each other. There were bad omens for Duryodhana. We have seen that whenever some great man was to die in the battle, there were bad omens for him. So how correct omens in those days were can be imagined. Even today, people start new works seeing good omens and bad omens do take place when some bad things are to happen—one may now believe it or not. At first they both got engaged in rebuking each other (Tongue war). Then Bhima attacked on Duryodhana and Duryodhana faced him. Both were expert in 'gada yudha'. Both had injured each other but had still been fighting, courageously. At one stage Bhima was unconscious. Pandavas then became very upset. After some time, Bhima attacked with gada on Duryodhana on his ribs. Duryodhana sat on ground. But shortly afterwards he got up and got enraged on Bhima and attacked on Bhima. Bhima too again attacked on Duryodhana, who fell on earth but again attacked on Bhima. While the fighting was going on, Arjuna asked Krishana as to who of the two was more brave. Krishana told that they both had coaching from the same teacher but Bhima was more brave and Duryodhana had put better effort. Krishana warned Pandavas that Yudhisthra's commitment of handing over rajya to Duryodhana, if he could defeat any of the Pandavas, could put them into difficulty and all efforts so far made would become futile. Yudhisthra had made this fight another gamble. Bhima then threw the gada on Duryodhana and broke his thighs as a result of which Duryodhana fell on earth and was defeated. Gods, who had come to witness the fighting, went to their respective lokas. Pandavas said that Dharitrashtra's sons had called Pandavas as impotents and now having killed them all, they had shown their worth. Having seen that Duryodhana had been killed by hitting on thighs, which was not allowed according to the laws of 'gada yudha', Balrama became furious. Then he said that Duryodhana did not have an equivalent in 'gada yudha' and Bhima had hit him wrongly. Balrama ran towards Bhima with his plough in his hand. Krishana, however, checked him and pacified him telling him that one's elevation was of six kinds—

1. Elevation of self.
2. Elevation of a friend.
3. Elevation of friend's friend.

4. Loss of enemy.
5. Loss of enemy's friend.
6. Loss of enemy's friend's friend.

If the condition of anyone or any of his friend is contrary to what is stated above, then one should feel humiliated in his heart and try to redress the same at the earliest. Pandavas' were their relations and friends. The enemies had done many wrongs to them. In the universe, it is kshatriyas' Dharma to fulfil their promise. Bhima had in the sabha, when Pandavas had been defeated in gambling by cheating them, undertook that he shall break Duryodhana's thighs in the war. Maitreya too had passed a curse on Duryodhana that Bhima shall break his thighs. Bhima is, therefore, not to be blamed and it should not enrage him, Krishana told Balrama. Balrama told Krishana that pious persons follow the Dharma but their efforts are mitigated by greed and ambitions. Therefore, the person, who kept a balance in following Dharma, satisfying greed and desires, is really a happy man. Bhima had harmed the Dharma and the justification put forth by Krishana was his creation only. Krishana told that he might take it that Kalyug had started and then consider the undertaking of Bhima. Today Bhima had been able to fulfil his undertaking. Krishana further told that it was Duryodhana who advised Karna to kill Abhimanyu from the back, when he was without chariot, without a dhanush but still engaged in his protection. Duryodhana had been a sinner right from his birth. Bhima had promised to break Duryodhana's thighs thirteen years back and Duryodhana should have remembered it. He wanted to kill Bhima by jumping on him and it was in that position that Bhima had to throw his gada hitting his thighs. Bhima could not, therefore, be blamed.

This indicated the extent of detailed laws of war available in those days and those laws were complied with. Their breach had to be justified, if it took place, either when similar breach had been caused by the other party or due to some other reason. Yudhisthra said that with the help of Krishana and the last effort of Bhima, Duryodhana had already died when he, out of greed, started depending on sinners and keeping the well-wishers away from him. He did not part with their share of rajya to Pandavas even after continued persuation by Bhishma, Darona, Vidur, Dharitrashtra and Gandhari, leading to this war and then inspite of detailed laws of war having been laid down at the beginning of the war to be followed by the two parties, Duryodhana started breach of the same in killing Abhimanyu. Krishana further told that Duryodhana adopted a wrong path that is why all his brothers, relations and helping rajas had been killed. He—

1. had his consultants like Shakuni, Karna etc., who had a biased mind against Pandavas.
2. served poison to Bhima and subsequently threw him amidst snakes.
3. desired to kill Pandavas in Lakshagriha.
4. cheated Pandavas in gambling.
5. sent Pandavas in exile for thirteen years.
6. attacked on Pandavas while in exile. Although he himself had been captivated by Gandharvas. Arjuna got them released at that time from Gandharvas. Further Jayadratha desired to kidnap Daropadi, while in forests.
7. attacked on Raja Virata but Arjuna let them go inspite of having defeated them.
8. had taken the assistance of asuras in the war. After Duryodhana had been killed, Pandavas had the overall control on Kaurvas' base camp. They, therefore, went there along with Daristdumana, Satyaki, Shikhandi, Yuyutsa, Daropadi's sons etc.

Krishana then asked Arjuna to take out his Gandeeva Dhanush and all astras from the chariot and he himself too should get down from it. Then Krishana too got down and left the reins of the horses. Then the godly vanar went away from the flag of the chariot and the chariot got burnt. All the Pandavas were surprised to see it and Arjuna fell in the feet of Krishana. Krishana told that the chariot had already been burnt by various astras but it continued in its form because of him only. Yudhisthra expressed his obligation for Krishana and said that it was because of him only that they had been able to have victory. Krishana advised that for the night they should stay out of the camp. All Pandavas, Krishana and Satyaki went out from the camp. Yudhisthra then requested Krishana to go to Hastinapur to pacify the aggrieved Gandhari as he only could do that job. Vyasa Muni too shall be there. Krishana, therefore, went to Hastinapur. Pandavas again requested Krishana to pacify Gandhari as all his sons had been killed and Yudhisthra feared facing her after having been responsible for the death of Gandhari's sons lest she should pass on some curse on Pandavas.

On entering Hastinapur, message was sent to Dharitrashtra by

Krishana about his arrival. This is necessary as per normal protocol, when one raja enters the rajya of another raja and wants to meet him. Even now where a plane of any head of state passes through another country's space, a message of respect is conveyed to that country. Krishana entered Dharitrashtra's mahal as a humble person (without any assumption of victory etc.). Vyasa Muni was already there. He touched their feet and paid respects to Gandhari. Krishana then started weeping taking Dharitrashtra's hand in his hand. This is necessary when one goes to condole. After weeping for sometime, they washed their faces and had achman (taking water for self purification). Krishana then told Dharitrashtra that all that had happened was destined to be like that. He stated that Pandavas had passed thirteen years in exile tolerating great inconvenience, but they were not given their part of kingdom as promised before they proceeded for forests. They had even come down from their demand of their part of rajya to only five villages but even that was not accepted. Then war was the only solution. It is because of that default that crores of persons had been killed. Even Darona, Bhishma, Vidur etc. had requested Duryodhana for a peaceful settlement but he did not buzz. Now the rajya and the dynasty shall be retained by Pandavas only and they would be able to get all that is expected from the Pandavas only. Krishana told that Yudhisthra was his great admirer as he himself knew it and he had been under great grief on all the killings in Mahabharata. Krishana also requested Gandhari to understand the situation in which war had to take place and she had herself told Duryodhana that, "victory is where Dharma is". Gandhari told that so far she was in great rage against Pandavas but after listening to him, she had got pacified. She said the raja was old and blind. So Krishana only was the one, on whom he could depend. Gandhari then started weeping. After sometime, Krishana took leave from Dharitrashtra and Vyasa Muni and requested them not to worry any more. He also said that Aswatthama had got a bad idea of killing Pandavas during night.

10
Sauptik Parva

On the other side, Kripacharya and others went to Duryodhana and sat on earth before him. They felt sorry for what had happened viz. that a chakravarty raja was lying on earth unattended, counting his last days. It is all as destined for each one. Duryodhana agreed that it is the principle of nature that everyone has to die one day. He was fortunate to have died in the battle-field, while fighting and should not be worried at all. Aswatthama told that Pandavas had killed his father in a cruel way but he was more worried now to see Duryodhana dying. Aswatthama undertook to kill all Pandavas and Panchalis. On this, Duryodhana took water and coronated Aswatthama as his Senapati. In Hindus there is a system for doing every job. Now as proper arrangements for coronating Aswatthama as Senapati could not be made, Duryodhana took water (as water is considered to be most sacred of all things) and with this applying 'tilak', he coronated Aswatthama as the Senapati of his army. This job could he done by a raja only and Duryodhana being still alive, could do it, after taking approval of Kripacharya. Aswatthama then left that place. Aswatthama, Kripacharya and Kritvarma went to a hiding in forests lest Pandavas could find them. Dharitrashtra had been crying in agony. How he, who ruled the entire universe, could now live at the mercy of Yudhisthra. In the forest, Kripacharya and Kritvarma slept but Aswatthama, being in rage, could not sleep. He had been thinking that Pandavas were rather brave and he could not defeat them in the battle and at the same time he had undertook before Duryodhana that he shall kill all Pandavas and Panchalis. So if he fought with Pandavas, he shall be killed. He should, therefore, kill them cheatingly when they would he sleeping during night after having been relieved of the war tension on their victory. Although such an action was against the laws of war, yet Aswatthama could find out some provision in war ethics saying that enemy could be attacked, when their army is tired ; is scattered ; taking meals; going somewhere; or entering some special place; sleeping in night; the Senapati having died; commanders having divided and who are in confusion.

परिश्रान्ते विदीर्णे वा भुजाने चापि शत्रुभिः,
परस्थाने वा प्रवेशे वा प्रहर्तव्यं रिपोर्बलम्। (1/53)

and निद्रार्तमर्ध रात्रे च तथा नष्टप्रणायकम्,
भिन्नयोधं बलं यच्च द्विधा युक्तं च यद्भवेत्। (1/54)

Thinking this, Aswatthama decided to kill the Pandavas along with Panchalis, while sleeping during the night. He then awakened Kripacharya and Kritvarma. Hearing Aswatthama's plan, they felt ashamed of taking such an action and could not give any reply. Kripacharya then told him that all persons were bound by fate and action and nothing else and any action is complete with both of these and not with either of these and out of these, too, fate is more powerful.

न हि दैवेन सिध्यन्ति कार्याण्येकेन सत्तम,
न चापि कर्मणैकेन द्वाभ्यां सिद्धस्तु योगतः। (2/3)

He further told that Duryodhana was greedy and without any farsightedness. He neither accepted anyone's suggestion nor pondered much on any problem. He ignored his well-wishers and consulted wicked persons and developed enmity with Pandavas inspite of everyone having checked him from resorting to such enmity. They have got such bad ideas because they followed him. This shows how a bad company changes one's mind. Hearing what Kripacharya stated, Aswatthama became upset and said that everyone thought that he was the most intelligent and acted according to his way of thinking.

पुरुषे पुरुषे बुद्धिर्या या भवति शोभना,
तुष्यन्ति च पृथक सर्वे प्रज्ञा ते स्वया स्वया। (3/3)

The thinking, however, at times changes according to changed times. Therefore, environments change the thinking accordingly. Now even being expert in bow-operation, if he does not take revenge of his father's killing, then he shall not be able to face the brave persons. Therefore, he shall kill all Panchalis in their camp itself and then kill Pandavas too while asleep. Kripacharya advised him to take rest during the night and next day they shall accompany him to battle-field and kill all people.

Aswatthama told him that a person, who is worried, or enraged, or thinking about many jobs to be done or involved in some fulfilment cannot sleep and he was involved in all these. So he could not sleep. He, therefore, shall kill all enemies, while they were asleep and then only shall heave a sigh of relief and sleep. Whereas Aswatthama justified his thinking of killing the enemies, when asleep by quoting shlokas from shastras, Kripacharya too quoted the provision in Dharma that Dharma does not provide for killing the persons, who are asleep; who have kept aside the armaments; who have left the chariot and horses; who have taken refuge; who have untied their hairs and whose means of transport have been destroyed. Therefore, killing of Panchalis, when they would be asleep, would be strictly against all canons of Dharma.

Aswatthama told that whatever Kripacharya had said was alright but Pandavas themselves had caused breach of canons of Dharma in having killed his father when he had put down his arms. Similarly, Bhishma had been killed when he had put down his arms. Duryodhana too had been killed against the laws of war in the presence of all of them. Therefore, all were adharmik and sinners. Then Aswatthama started on his chariot but telling him that they were with him in all sorrows and pleasures, Kripacharya and Kritvarma too followed him. They reached the camp, where Pandavas and Panchalis had been sleeping. They stood outside the gate of the camp, where they saw a strong and ferocious person standing to safeguard the camp. Aswatthama fired godly astras on him but these did not have any effect on him. Aswatthama tried many weapons but all were ineffective. When all his armaments were finished, he saw towards sky and saw many Vaishnavas there and Aswatthama resorted to praising of Shiva. Shiva then provided him with a sword. Aswatthama then entered the camp from a backdoor and reached Daristdumana's bed room, where he was sleeping. He made him awake by a kick. Daristdumana recognised Aswatthama and before he could get up, Aswatthama caught hold of his hairs and threw him on the earth and started crushing him. Daristdumana, however, asked him to kill him so that he could attain salvation. Aswatthama then killed him crushing. The queens of Daristdumana started crying along with his army. The army surrounded him but Aswatthama killed them all by Shiva's sword. Yudhamanyu tried to face him but he too was killed. Aswatthama attacked on other kshatriyas sleeping there and killed them all. Then the sons of Daropadi came there and attacked on Aswatthama. Shikhandi too joined them. Aswatthama killed all Daroapdi's sons and Prativindhya, Sutsoma, Shatanika, Shrutkarma, Shrutkirti, Shikhandi, Virata's army, Drupada's sons and grand sons and others, who woke up and came to fight with Aswatthama and rest fled from the camp. The three then came, where Duryodhana had been killed. They saw Duryodhana still alive but restless. They started crying for him after seeing his condition. Then Aswatthama told Duryodhana to listen to him if he could and told that only seven persons (Five Pandavas, Krishana and Satyaki) were alive on Pandavas' side and three (Aswatthama, Kritvarma and Kripacharya) were alive on Kaurvas' side and rest all on Pandavas' side had been killed. Hearing all this, Duryodhana came to his senses and told them that what they all could not do, they three had done and having satisfied with this killing, left the universe. Dharitrashtra was already shocked on hearing the news of the death of Duryodhana.

Next morning, Daristdumana's sarthi narrated what had happened during the night to Yudhisthra. Hearing the death of Daropadi's sons and others, Yudhisthra fell on earth and became unconscious. He then started crying that he had lost the battle after having won it. He said sometimes meaningful things become meaningless and vice versa. So their victory had been converted into defeat.

Yudhisthra was upset, Daropadi had been crying on her sons' death. They demanded death of Aswatthama. Bhima left to kill him. Daropadi undertook to die if Aswatthama was not killed. She resorted to hunger strike. Yudhisthra then told her that her sons had died fighting as is the Dharma of kshatriyas and now in case Aswatthama was killed in forests, then how shall she be made to believe it. Then Daropadi told that there is a 'Mani' in Aswatthama's forehead since his birth. If that 'mani' is brought and put in her hand by Yudhisthra then only she shall live. Daropadi put her condition before Bhima too. Bhima left finding the signs of the chariot of Aswatthama. Krishana told Yudhisthra that Bhima should not have gone alone to kill Aswatthama. Then Krishana, Arjuna and Yudhisthra followed him. Bhima could find Aswatthama at the bank of Ganga and he challenged him. Aswatthama threw Brahmsatra on him. To undo the effect of Brahmastra, Arjuna also threw another Brahmastra. The entire mankind started suffering because of the effect of the two Brahmastras. To undo the effect of the two Brahmastras. Narada and Vyasa munis appeared there and thrashed them for having used the Brahmastras, which could destroy the entire universe. These Brahmastras must be some very powerful bombs like Hydrogen bombs of present day. Then Arjuna withdrew his Brahmastra, which had already made Aswatthama's Brahmastra ineffective. Vyasa muni then asked Aswatthama to hand over his 'mani' to Yudhisthra after which Pandavas shall allow him to live.

Aswatthama gave that 'mani' to Pandavas. Simultaneously, Aswatthama fired another godly astra to destroy the foetus in Uttara's (Abhimanyu's queen) womb. Krishana told Aswatthama that Uttara had been blessed by a brahmin that when Kaurvas shall have finished in a war, then she shall give birth to a child, who shall be named Parikshit. Aswatthama told Krishana that the foetus could not be saved even by him. Krishana told that the astra shall be effective and Uttara shall give birth to a still born child but then he shall attain a long life. This is how in our ancient times bombs were made and to make the same ineffective another method was available like the bombs and anti-bomb appliances of the present day. Krishana then passed a curse on Aswatthama that for three thousand years, he shall be left alone in the forests. Aswatthama left for forests and Pandavas handed over the 'mani' to Daropadi and consoled her.

Yudhisthra asked the reason for the death of all his sons and army-men. Krishana told that Aswatthama had worshipped Shiva, the God of God Vishnu and Shiva only had given this power (sword) to Aswatthama and with that power only Aswatthama had killed all persons.

Dharitrashtra had been crying on the death of his sons. Then Sanjaya told him not to worry as there was none to console him at that juncture.He advised him to perform last rites of his elders and sons. Dharitrashtra accepted that it was the result of his not having agreed to the peace proposals put forth by Muni Narada and Krishana. Vidur too consoled Dharitrashtra as this had to be the result of the war, which had to take place because he did not agree to the peace talks. He should now take it easy as it was the desired end of kshatiryas to die in battle-field while fighting and now arrange for the last rites of the dead ones. Vyasa Muni too came and consoled Dharitrashtra telling him that it was all destined to take place like that. Dharitrashtra said that it was a curse to have born as a human being and then greater curse to get married and have children as all sorrows are the outcome of a married life and children.

Pandavas came and met Dharitrashtra along with Krishana, Yuyutsa and Satyaki. All pandavas paid respects to Dharitrashtra calling their names. Dharitrashtra embraced Yudhisthra. Dharitrashtra was very much in rage for Bhima. Krishana could sense it. So he kept Bhima aside and instead placed his iron statue before Dharitrashtra. Taking the statue as Bhima, Dharitrashtra crushed that statue and having been injured by the statue, he also fell. Sanjaya picked him up and told him that he should not have done so. Then Dharitrashtra realising his mistake of having killed Bhima, started crying for Bhima. Then Krishana told that Bhima was still alive and what had been broken was the statue only. Krishana told him that he should not have been so much upset because of Bhima having killed his sons as Druyodhana was not to survive even if Bhima had not killed him. Krishana told Dharitrastra that all that killing had taken place because of him only as he could not reach a peaceful settlement with Pandavas ignoring his sons. In fact he himself was biased against Pandavas.

Then after taking permission from Dharitrashtra, Pandavas with Krishana went to meet Gandhari. When she came to know that Yudhisthra wanted to meet her after killing all his enemies, she planned to pass a curse on him. Vyasa Muni had known this fact. So he came from Ganga straight to Gandhari. Because of special power imbibed in him, he could know the inner feelings of any person. It is nothing but the extreme of psychology, through which we can read the mind of the people to some extent even now. He told Gandhari that she should have patience. He reminded her that during the last eighteen days, Duryodhana used to come to her everyday and asked for her blessings to be victorious in war and everyday she used to say "victory is where Dharma is". Therefore, she should check her rage. Gandhari said that she was not biased against Pandavas nor does she want them to be destroyed but the shock of her sons' death had upset her. Like Kunti, she had an ardent duty to bring up Pandavas. In fact all this killing was the result of the conspiracy of Duryodhana, Dushashana, Karna and Shakuni. Pandavas, therefore, could not be blamed for it. But the behaviour of Bhima in 'gada yudha' with Duryodhana, whom he had hit on the thigh, could not be approved. Hearing this from Gandhari, Bhima told her whether, bad or good, he had taken this action in his defence. He, therefore, should be excused as any action in self defence is excusable even today in the jurisprudence. Duryodhana had also behaved with Pandavas against the Dharma in trying to kill them in Lakshagriha; cheating them in gambling; insulting Daropadi in sabha; then in exile for thirteen years; trying to kill them while in forests and finally in killing Abhimanyu when he was without chariot, without arms standing on earth, by six Kaurva chiefs. Therefore, whatever he had done was not bad in ethics. Gandhari accepted whatever Bhima had told. Duryodhana had done all bad deeds but now he too had done a thing not permitted by laws of war. He too is, therefore, a guilty person. Regarding drinking Dushashana's blood, Bhima told that brother's blood is like one's own blood and if one could not take his blood so cannot take brother's blood too and the blood he had taken remained upto his throat only and did not go down to his abdomen. He had to do it to fulfil his undertaking when he was very much in rage at the time of insult of Daropadi. Bhima further said that she did not check her sons when they had been acting in an ill-way toward them and now finding fault with Pandavas was not desirable. Gandhari then said that he had killed all her sons. He should have spared at least one son, who was not guilty. Then Yudhisthra came and told her that he only was responsible for all the killings. She should, therefore, pass curse on him only, as he did not now want wealth or rajya. Yudhisthra wanted to fell on Gandhari's feet. Then from behind the bandage on her eyes, she saw Yudhisthra's nails of the feet. These became black. It shows that for one's actions, one should not just feel sorry but should at first project the reason behind such actions to satisfy the aggrieved party and then only feel sorry for the part remaining un-explained. Further, since it is difficult for a person to accept punishment for his actions as he thought it a proper action, someone else could own responsibility for the same. In that case the extent of rage in the mind of the aggrieved person gets reduced. So here, on Yudhisthra having owned responsibility for all the killings, Pandavas were let off by Gandhari except that Yudhisthra's feet's nails became black. Then Kunti and Daropadi too came there and wept after paying respects to Gandhari as she was older to Kunti and like mother to Daropadi. Kunti consoled her, who had lost her one hundred sons.

Vyasa took Gandhari and Dharitrashtra to the battle field in Kurukshetra, where all killings took place and through a special power, made them see the killings there. Her daughters-in-law were also there crying on the death of their respective husbands. Gandhari then told Krishana that having seen so many people killed, she had a feeling that all five ingredients viz. earth, water, air, agni and space, which go in the making of a human being, have vanished from the universe. No body could think that Bhishma, Darona, Karna, Jayadratha, Abhimanyu etc. shall be killed in the battle. Seeing her daughters-in-law crying, she cursed herself to be most unfortunate. Then seeing Duryodhana dead, she became unconscious and fell on earth. She stated she was more worried to see her daughters-in-law and grand daughters-in-law weeping there. Bhima's taking blood of Dushashana was an inexcusable action. Gandhari had been crying after seeing the dead bodies of each of her sons and Darona, Karna and others. She told Krishana that her sons had died when he had been unsuccessful in his attempt for a peaceful settlement and returned to Uplava. At that time itself, Bhishma and Vidur had told her not to have any affection with her sons (as they shall all die now). She blamed Krishana how he had just brushed aside the fact that Kaurvas and Pandavas had died fighting in the battle-field, when he had capability of making both parties agree to some settlement and he could have avoided all this killing and destruction. He, therefore, intentionally permitted this to take place and should, therefore, face the consequences of this wrong action on his part.

She passed on a curse on Krishna that within 36 years (two years for each day of Mahabharata, which continued for 18 days), all his family members, and ministers shall die fighting within themselves. He shall wander in the forests and shall be killed unceremoniously. His daughters-in-law shall also weep on the dead bodies of his sons. Krishana smilingly accepted the curse for the destruction, which had already started and it was all planned by him only as none else could kill the Yadavas. Pandavas were aggrieved hearing that all yadavas shall die fighting within themselves. Krishana then asked Gandhari to have patience as she herself was in a way responsible for all that had taken place. She had encouraged Duryodhana for all his evil actions. Duryodhana was biased and jealous of Pandavas. He was over greedy and had all the vices. Now she wanted to brief for him and put the blame for his misdeeds on others. This was not correct. Then even otherwise one should not worry for the dead, wasted out commodity and passed time. Further, kshatriyas produced children to die while fighting. She, therefore, should console herself as her sons had died while fighting. Gandhari then kept quiet.

Dharitrashtra asked Yudhisthra to tell him the number of persons killed in the war. Yudhisthra told that in the war total number of the dead was one Arab, sixty-six crore and twenty thousand (1,66,00,20,000). In addition twenty four thousand, one hundred and sixty five sainiks were missing. Then Dharitrashtra asked the condition of the killed persons after their death. Yudhisthra told that those, who had given up their lives delightedly shall go to Indra Loka; those, who lost lives unintended, shall go to Gandharva Loka; those, who begged for their lives but still killed, shall go to Guhyak Loka; those, who were rendered without any arms and still faced the enemy and have been killed by them, shall go to Brahmloka and those who had been killed due to any reasons, within the four-walls of the battlefield, shall have rebirth in Kurukshetra. On Dharitrashtra asking how he had known all this. Yudhisthra told that during his stay in forests, he had met Lomash Rishi, who had imbibed in him this power. Then on Dharitrashtra's request, Yudhisthra ordered for the final rites of all the dead. Then suitable pyres were made out and all Kaurvas. Pandavas, Rajas had been put to funeral with all protocolic requirements. The dead bodies of all others were put together and were burnt after pouring ghee, sandal, flowers etc.

The above narration shows that in those days there was advancement in technology in India which could maintain the accountal of all those present in the battle-field; those, who died and those who were missing. Also there was some science to know the category, each dead got in the 'parloka' and those who got rebirth, also confirming the theory of transmigration of soul.

When the last rites of the dead had been completed, including the performance of 'Jalanjali', Kunti came running and told pandavas that Karna too was their eldest brother as he had born from her, when she was virgin and so could not disclose this fact so far, and should be offered final rites as such. This surprised and put to grief all Pandavas. They blamed Kunti for all killings as if she had told this fact earlier, Mahabharata would not have taken place as in that case, Karna would have been on their-side and then Duryodhana would not have dared fighting with pandavas. Yudhisthra then performed Karna's last rites himself.

11
Shanti Parva

When the war was at the head, Karna had given the word for fighting on behalf of Duryodhana against the Pandavas. In this way, Yudhisthra stated that Kunti was responsible for the war as if she had disclosed this fact earlier, then Karna would have been on Pandavas' side and with Karna and Arjuna being togehter, no power in the world could have faced them and Kauravas would not have dared to impose the war on them. In fact Yudhisthra stated that he was already suspicious about Karna's genesis as his both feet were like those of Kunti and he had all through been pondering on this secret and finding Karna brave enough, Duryodhana had always been jealous of Pandavas and so after finding Karna equally brave and humiliated by Pandavas, Duryodhana immediately got him on his side and elevated him as the Raja of Angadesha.

Having seen Arjuna more expert in the art of dhanush operation, Karna went to Darona and requested him to teach the use of Brahmastra, but Daron did not want anyone to be equal to Arjuna, his pet disciple in dhanush operation. He, therefore, declined to accede to Karna's request, saying that this could be known by a brahmin or a Kshatriya and none else. Karna had then gone to Parshurama and told him that he was a brahmin and requested for telling him the use of Brahmastra. Parshurama coached him. But during that period once Karna killed a cow taking it as a ferocious animal and accepted his mistake before the brahmin, who was the owner of the cow. Brahmin, however, passed a curse on him that during his battle with a raja, whom he wanted to defeat, the wheel of his chariot shall get sunk in the earth and his enemy shall at that time kill him. Further, once, when the Guru Parshurama was sleeping with his head in Karna's lap, one scorpio had bitten Karna, resulting in lot of bleeding. When Parshurama got up and saw so much bleeding, he could know that a brahmin, as Karna had told him to be, could not tolerate so much pain and he must be a kshatriya. He asked him the correct position and on Karna having told that he was a Soot's son, Parshurama passed on a curse on him in view of his having told a lie that he shall be able to remember the case of Brahmastra so far as he does not fight with his equal in the battle and till he fell prey to death. At such a situation, he shall not remember the way of using the Brahmastra. Narada then narrated the bravery of Karna, who had defeated all rajas and arranged the yagya by Duryodhana, short of Aswamedha yagya, and defeated Kalingraj, kidnapped his daughter and married her with Duryodhana. Karna had thus become very popular in the universe. Having seen him invincible, Indra, who was fond of Arjuna, being his father, begged of the kawach and kundal of Karna as so far as Karna was wearing them, no one could kill him. In exchange, Indra had given him a shakti, which would certainly kill one person on when it was fired. Karna had kept that shakti to be used on Arjuna, but then Ghatotkachha had created so much tyranny in Kaurvas that Karna had to fire that Shakti to get rid of Ghatotkachha by Krishana's manipulation and in such a situation only Karna could be killed by Arjuna.

Kunti had gone to Karna before the start of the war to request him to join Pandavas, who were his brothers but Karna could not agree to such a request as it would have caused breach of trust for Duryodhana at that juncture but he had assured Kunti that he shall not kill any other Pandava except Arjuna and so she shall have five sons always— her four sons and either Arjuna or Karna. This secret was disclosed by Kunti when Pandavas had gone for the final rites of all their relations that Karna was their brother and so they should perform his final rites too. At that time, Yudhisthra felt very depressed and passed on a curse on all women that they shall not be able to keep anything secret upto themselves. It is, therefore, seen that—

1. One does get upset when faced with a situation in which one gets a benefit after a lot of sacrifice as Yudhisthra got kingdom after the killing of crores of persons, including all Pandavas' sons and Kaurvas.
2. at that time one needs someone to console him. Here this job was done by all rishis, Krishana and other Pandavas.
3. Although, to be fair, the guru should welcome imparting education to all his disciples, Darona refused to coach Karna the usage of Brahmastra as he was neither a brahmin nor a kshatriya. Such an action was unbecoming of a guru.

4. It was unprotocolic on the part of Karna to have gone to Parshurama to have coaching from him telling him that he was a brahmin. Telling such a lie to a person of Parshurama's dignity, had got him the curse.

5. In Mahabharata, the person, who was to be held responsible for the war, goes on shifting.

   (a) Duryodhana was responsible as he did not part with Pandavas' share of kingdom on their return from the forests.

   (b) Dharitrastra was responsible as he did not over-rule his son Duryodhana and passed on the kingdom to Pandavas as he too was having a weakness for his sons.

   (c) Karna was responsible as, if after he had known that he was the eldest brother amongst of Pandavas had joined Pandavas, Duryodhana would not have dared to start the battle.

   (d) Kunti was responsible as, if she had told Karna at an earlier stage that he was her son, then he would not have to face humiliation at several places of not being a kshatriya, and would have been with Pandavas and Kauravas would not have gone in for war.

   (e) Yudhisthra was responsible as, if he had not agreed to start gambling with Kaurvas, the Pandavas would have continued with their rajya and would not have gone to forests and consequent declining by Duryodhana to part with rajya to them.

6. It was bad for Kunti to have given birth to Sun's son Karna, when she was still not married and then to save herself from the charge of breach of virginity, she kept this fact a secret throughout, causing a lot of killing.

So, Yudhisthra was still worried about so many killings. He could not reconcile to a situation where Dharitrashtra had always been biased against them even when the Pandavas had always respected him. All present there consoled Yudhisthra to now reconcile to accepting to govern.

Arjuna told that it was kshatriya's Dharma to attain the kingdom after defeating the enemies. Since they had been victorious in the battle, the kingdom was their earned one and had now to be governed. Non-governing of the attained kingdom is a sin and breach of trust with the praja. Non-acceptance of the governance, and resorting to live by begging is only for the persons, who had no other means of their livelihod; who is utter poor; who does not have a name in the universe; who is without a family or yet who is not brave enough to have other's kingdom or wealth etc. These were not applicable in the case of Yudhisthra, who should resort to governance. Further, it is the kingdom or the wealth, which makes friends, brings relatives closer, and which gives a good name to a person in the universe, and with wealth one could have all attainments. But Yudhisthra continued to harp on adopting vanprastha or sanyasa.

Bhima then told that for kshatriyas, there was Rajdharma to be complied with and one could resort to vanprastha or sanyas at the appropriate age only. At that juncture, after having caused killing of crores of people, it would be breach of trust reposed by people to govern them. So far as the killings were concerned, they had to take place in any battle, where a kshatriya had to fight to regain his due. Here, the fighting had to be resorted to as Kaurvas did not part with the share of Pandavas in the kingdom as had been undertaken by them at the time of Pandavas' exile for thirteen years. The best thing in Yudhisthra's interest now was to resort to governance.

Nakula told that for them the time now was to lead the life as a 'grihastha' and for a kshatriya, governance had to be resorted to in leading the grihastha' life as grihastha ashrama was the best of all ashramas in Hindu philosophy as in this ashrama, one could resort to enjoy the satisfaction of all senses and still attain salvation by doing good to the mankind and by complying with the tenets of the Rajdharma.

Sehdeva advised that vanprastha had to be resorted to after breaking off from all universal ties and not by giving up the wealth alone. If, therefore, one could remain aloof from affection and other indulgences, one could as well attain salvation by remaining in the universe and doing Rajdharma.

Daropadi also advised to resort to governing by a brave hand (Rajdanda). At the beginning of the battle, it was considered that all the persons on enemy's side, including elephants and horses shall be killed and then they shall govern the entire world. Now what was the cause for giving up the rajya, obtained after so much killing and sacrifice. Such a thinking now was cowardish only. Living on alms and universal friendship is for brahmins to adopt and not for kshatriyas, she said. Yudhisthra should, therefore, be ready to rule as advised by all other Pandavas too.

Arjuna then said that it is the might of the king that rules; it secures all wealth; controls the criminals; saves the praja from being exploited by one-another; and saves the country from enemies. The raja punishes various persons by his might—brahmins by humiliating them; kshatriyas for being paid sufficient to keep body and soul togehter only; vaishas by imposing pecuniary fines on them but shudras cannot he punished. They can only be put to service. Bhima reminded Yudhisthra of the sufferings, they had undergone in living in forests for thirteen years including working as servants of Raja Virat for one year and the humiliation suffered on that account by Daropadi, Yudhisthra and others.

Yudhisthra said that one should not remember the past sufferings, time and again, as this refreshes the sufferings without remedying the same. Yudhisthra told Bhima that he had within self, the greed, non-contentment, bravery, pride, etc. Therefore, he was after the kingdom and its governance but he was of the view that the emperor, although the owner of entire universe, has only to feed one abdomen and nothing else. Why, then, should one have so much greed for things, which shall ultimately be left for others, particularly when all human beings are considered as part of the almighty God only. They have arisen because of him and shall ultimately get absorbed in him. But then Arjuna said that many people get their hairs cut and wear sadhuish dress to take alms but they still continue involved in worldly requirements. There is no use of adopting such a life. It is, therefore, better to live in the universe as a 'grihastha' and comply with the tenets of one's Dharma, which is governance for the kshatriyas. Even Raja Janaka, who was considered to be well aware of all fundamentals of abdication, had not been able to absolve himself from worldly attachments. There was, therefore, no use leaving the universe without absolving oneself from its attachments. To this, Yudhisthra replied that he very well knew the philosophy of 'Dos and Donots' and when he speaks of adopting vanprastha, he means complete renunciation from the world. Therefore, one should engage oneself on everyone's well-being and absolve from worldly ambitions, leaving the traditional way of living together with desire for wealth and live happily. A true man on attaining the highest position by his tapsya; attains that truth through his knowledge and leaving aside the selfishness, enjoys a very pleasant life. Arjuna, however, told that they had born in kshatriyas and God had bestowed particular duties on the people of different varnas. So a kshatriya, according to that rule, has only to govern and kshatriyas not discharging that ordained duty are sinners of the breach of canons of Dharma. Muni Vyasa also agreed to what Arjuna had said that is to continue in 'grihastha ashrama' and discharging the duties of 'Rajdharma' as a kshatriya. Vyasa further told that 'grihastha' is one 'ashrama', which is very tough to live as per Dharma and one, who is sensually weak, cannot live as 'grihastha'. It was, therefore, for him to chose and live as 'grihastha' only. Vyasa also told him the ingredients of Rajdharma, which are performing yagyas; attacking on enemies; never be satisfied with wealth; always be ready to punish the criminals; always be proud of governing skill; protecting the subjects in all respects; attaining knowledge of all vedas; tap; good moral living; more and more collection of wealth and spending. Profit or loss, and death and life have to be accepted from time to time and one should not feel happy or sorry for either of the two.

पर्यायतः सर्वमवाप्नुवन्ति,
तस्माद् धीरोनैव हृष्येन्न शोचत्।। (25/31)

Yudhisthra still continued condemning wealth and rajya. He said wealth imbibes greed, theft, affection, enmity, rage, rebirths, separation from close relations, discontentment, etc. Therefore, it is better, one is absolved from these as early as possible. Yudhisthra was even prepared to give up his life if he was not able to come over the worldly involvements, rather than getting more and more involved in these. He was sorry that for the sake of attaining the kingdom, he had to tell a lie saying Aswatthama was dead knowing fully well that, who had died was only an elephant and what he meant was Darona's son. This led to his guru believing him and giving up arms and ultimately his death. This, he had said when his guru thought that he was only truth-speaking and would never tell a lie. He had, therefore, made up his mind to give up his life and all others were free to do whatever they wanted to do. Vyasa muni, however, futhere discouraged him from taking the step of giving up his life as although one feels pleasure in lying idle but its end is harmful and one feels annoyed in doing job as any job requires labour but its result is good. So, to die, may appear to be easy now but its result will not be good and pleasures, wealth, praise, kingdom etc. are attained by active persons and not by lazy ones. So far as the result after death is concerned, one cannot see swarga or narka (heaven or hell) while alive. These can be assumed to be existing as per shastras. Therefore, one has to act as per shastras, which teach of action as per one's Dharma.

Krishana had been listening to the dialogue between Yudhisthra and other persons so far but it is Krishana, who inspired Arjuna to fight in the battle field and now was his turn to inspire Yudhisthra to stand up and accept kingship. Krishana told that he should not worry now as by worrying one becomes weak and those, who had died, could not become alive. Fighting was the Dharma of the kshatriyas. He should, therefore, take these deaths as normal phenomena of Rajdharma and should not worry about the deaths caused in the battle otherwise no kshatriya shall be able to fight with his enemy and protect the subjects from foreign invasion, which was his duty. Krishana narrated the incident of deaths in various battles that had taken place from time to time and how those rajas, who fought those battles, had attained salvation by their actions as rajas. Rama was one of them, who treated his subjects as his sons. During Rama's reign:-

1. No one became widow or orphan in young age.
2. Rains took place on time leading to rich crops and harvests.
3. There were no famines.
4. No one died of drowning in water; none was burnt and none was suffering from chronic diseases.
5. People lived from hundred to thousand years, and all got their wishes fulfilled.
6. What to speak of males, even females had no quarrels.
7. Entire praja lived in peace and comfort.
8. All people led a contented, fearless, pious, and independent life. Here independent life has been indicated which means that there was no unnecessary pressure on public from the raja.
9. Even the trees developed fully and cows gave sufficient milk. This indicates that there was proper protection of trees and the cows were adequately fed.
10. After living in forests for fourteen years and subsequently attaining rajya, Shri Rama performed many Aswamedha yagyas, which not only established his suzerainty over his vassal states but also got a lot of wealth as presents and led to his salvation ultimately.

So Yudhisthra should also now accept emperorship and hold Aswamedha yagyas to attain salvation rather than going to forests in vanprastha or giving up his life in despair, which was an action for the cowards to adopt. Further, since even Rama had to ultimately give up his life, so should he live as emperor and let death come at its time. Krishana also gave instances of other great rajas, who had to face many difficulties but still they ruled and ultimately got salvation too. That, therefore, is the surest way of attaining salvation for kshatriyas to adopt 'grihastha' and ruling as per 'Rajdharma'. The word 'kshatriya' had come from the word 'kshat' i.e. protection from sufferings and the word 'raja' came into being from the word 'rajan' that is providing all pleasures to people. This took place during the regime of Raja Prithu, who ruled to the satisfaction of his subjects and then attained salvation. Therefore, Yudhisthra should also now rule as per Dharma and attain salvation rather than flying away from the ordained duty.

Then Vyasa further told that bringing up and protection of his subjects was the Dharma of a raja. Further, he told that so far as the killings were involved, there could be four reasons—

1. All deaths took place because of the inspiration for those killing imbibed in the rajas by God.
2. The people were responsible for all those killings.
3. These were because of the ego of the people so killed.
4. It was all destined to take place like that only.

If as per no (1) God is considered responsible for all killings, then God should be considered responsible for all good or bad actions and God only should face the consequences. That way, Yudhisthra should not owe responsibility to himself for all killings.

If he considered that all the killings were by human beings only then he should take it that he had killed only the ill-doers and they have got the result of their doings only as per their fate.

If it is considered that the deaths took place because of the ego of certain persons, then this fact was already known before the start of the war as Duryodhana, by his ego, did not part with the share of Pandavas in the kingdom. He, therefore, got the result of his ego and others died because they assisted Duryodhana in the fulfilment of his bad ego.

If it is accepted that it was all in fate, then he should not worry as he was only a means and all deaths took place because it was destined like that only and all those who died had died because of their bad designs and it was the ordained duty of the raja to punish the bad designers. He should not, therefore, worry for having punished the criminals as per tenets of 'Rajdharma'. Vyasa Muni also narrated that such killings in battles are not restricted to this universe alone. These are stated to have taken place between gods, between gods and asuras and between gods and the rajas of this universe and in all these battles, killings did take place and still Indra rules as raja and asuras too ruled when they became victorious. Further, monitoring of death is the job of the 'Kala' (काल) and he completed this job through various rajas. Such deaths had to take place whether there was Yudhisthra or no Yudhisthra. He should not, therefore, owe any responsibility to himself for all those deaths. Also during the entire battle, Pandavas had been fighting for their rightful share in the kingdom and those, who fought against them, did not recognise that share. They have, therefore, been killed for favouring an adharmik cause. Yudhisthra should not, therefore, worry for such killings nor is this a cause for any repentance. Even Manu had indicated in Samriti devising the four varnas for mankind that the kshatriyas' job was to fight, either for protection of the kingdom from outside aggressions or for expansion of the kingdom and in either case, killings shall take place but these killings are as per Dharma of the kshatriyas.

Yudhisthra asked Vyasa Muni to narrate to him the concept of Dharma, particularly 'Rajdharma', after having heard all the above persons and having made up his mind now to resort to governance but he was still confused thinking that the concepts of Dharma and Rajdharma were contrary to each other. Vyasa, however, advised him to go to Bhishma if he desired to know all about Dharma as he had the treasure of these concepts having life-long experience. Yudhisthra, however, considered himself guilty of having got all his relations killed, some even against the rules of war, including Bhishma, Darona and Duryodhana. He, therefore, had no courage to approach Bhishma now. Krishana, however, advised him not to go on repeating about the killings, again and again, as sufficient discussion on the subject had already taken place. He should, therefore, now act as per Vyasa's advice. Yudhisthra then got up in the interest of all and went to the capital with Dharitrashtra in front. Dharitrashtra had to be kept in front and followed by others as so far Dharitrastra was the raja till Yudhisthra took over from him although in fact after the war was over, Pandavas had gained the kingdom. While entering the capital, Yudhisthra, as per religious protocol, worshipped all gods, paid alms to brahmins and others and then boarded the chariot. Again, as per protocol, Bhima controlled the chariot, Arjuna held the umbrella, Nakula and Sehdeva held chanwars and thus all the five brothers boarded on one chariot. Yuyutsa followed Yudhisthra, Satyaki, Krishana and Vyasa too followed them. Dharitrastra was in forefront. Then there were elephants, horses, troops on foot, soots, and others. The capital had been adequately decorated and all citizens welcomed the Pandavas. There were flowers, perfumes etc. all through. Ten lakh people were standing on road sides to welcome them. After all the subjects had already tasted the peaceful living in Yudhisthra's rajya before he was exiled to forests. Ladies were on the top of their houses as per social protocol.

After entering the mahal. the first job was to pay respects to family gods and so he worshipped them. With the guru and Raja Dharitrashtra, he worshipped the brahmins and paid alms. They blessed him in turn. Amongst the brahmins, there was one rakshas Chanwar, dressed as a brahmin. He rebuked Yudhisthra. He cursed Yudhisthra for having killed all his brothers, relations and many rajas to attain the kingdom. The other brahmins disowned him and put him out from amongst them. All were quiet on this development. The brahmins then themselves killed him. Then Yudhisthra had been coronated. For coronation too, proper protocol is laid down—

1. Yudhisthra sat on the golden Sinhasana facing east.
2. Satyaki and Krishana sat on their seats facing Yudhisthra.
3. Bhima, Arjuna, Nakula, Sehdeva and Kunti sat on their seats around Yudhisthra.
4. Then ministers, and Senapati came to pay respects to Yudhisthra along with the Purohit.
5. All material required for coronation had been brought.
6. At first Krishana was worshipped and he applied 'tilak' to Yudhisthra. Then Dharitrashtra and others applied the 'tilak'.
7. Bands were on. Yudhisthra accepted all blessings. All brahmins were worshipped and alms given and brahmins in turn offered their blessings. Yudhisthra then ordered that everyone, who had faith in him, should respect Dharitrashtra and he himself shall also be in his service and treat him as the owner of the entire kingdom. Yudhisthra then dispersed all to go to their respective houses.
8. Bhima was coronated as the Yuvaraja.
9. Vidur was appointed as special adviser.

10. Sanjaya was appointed to check up all that had been done, all that was yet to be done and to monitor the receipts and expenditure of the kingdom.
11. Nakula was made incharge of army establishment.
12. Arjuna was made incharge of suppressing all enemies.
13. Purohit Dhaumaya was put on ecclesiastical duty.
14. Sehdeva was asked to remain with the raja as his escort.
15. Further duties were assigned to all as deemed fit by the raja.

Here, it has been established that the assignments were allotted by the raja himself keeping each person's worth in view. Then was the turn of final rites of all, who had been killed, i.e., the 'Shradha', (श्राद्ध) ceremony. He himself along with Daropadi performed 'Shradha' of Darona, Karna, Daristdumana, Abhimanyu, Ghatotkachha, Virata and other close relations, Drupad, Daropadi's sons etc. and all other rajas, who were killed leaving none in the family to perform their Shradha. Yudhisthra then praised Krishana and attributed the entire victory to him as he was all in all in the war. Yudhisthra also allotted the residences to all, Pandavas and others with the approval of Dharitrashtra and asked them to have rest now since they had great sufferance, injuries etc. in the war and shall meet them again the next day. Duryodhana's mahal was allotted to Bhima, Dushashana's to Arjuna, Durmukhan's to Nakula, Durmukha's to Sehdeva, Yuyutsa, Vidur, Sanjaya, Sudharma and Dhauma continued to live in their respective abodes already with them.

Then again alms were given to brahmins and others and then Yudhisthra went to Krishana and praised him as the God incarnate. Krishana praised Bhishma and asked Yudhisthra to go to him as he was now counting his days, to pay him respects, remove any misunderstanding in his mind and ask for his blessings and advice to govern and live in the universe. Yudhisthra then agreed to go to Bhishma with Krishana in the forefront as he was not able to face Bhishma. Bhishma had the boon that he would die when he wished. So he was waiting for the sun to come in certain direction. Sun had now come in that direction and Bhishma had got absorbed in God almighty, when Krishaṇa and Pandavas reached there. Already Narada, Atre, Vashistha, Shandilya, Brihaspati, Shukracharya, Gautama etc. rishis and gods were there around Bhishma. He was praying to Krishana, as incarnate of God. Then Krishana, Pandavas, Kripacharya etc. reached Kurukshetra, where dead bodies (parts of the bodies of human beings, elephants, horses etc.) were still scattered in the field. Bhishma was already lost in thinking about Krishana at the period of terminal before death. Seeing Krishana before him, he paid respects and praised him. Krishana too blessed him with the knowledge of all the three lokas and came back to Pandavas.

Kurukshetra was famous as Parshurama had performed last rites of his ancestors with the blood of kshatriyas he had killed and now crores of people had been killed in the battle at the same place. Parshurama had killed the kshatriyas and he had born as incarnate of God, particularly for killing all kshatriyas, as the kshatriyas, in those days had departed from their Dharma and had indulged in luxuries and all sorts of sensual satisfactions after extracting money from the public. Immediate inspiration was the enmity with raja Sahastrabahu. Parshurama killed Sahastrabahu and his sons and subsequently killed all kshatriyas twenty one times. The kshatriyas available at that time had born subsequently only.

Krishana and Yudhisthra came to the place, where Bhishma was lying. Yudhisthra and others got down from their chariots and appeared before the munis sitting there. They respected the munis and then bowed before Bhishma. On Krishana enquiring if Bhishma was feeling pain in his body, Bhishma replied that he knew it was all as per destiny. Krishana then told that all Pandavas were sorry for all the killings and requested him to tell them the Dharma of all varnas and the way for salvation through yoga and Sankhya philosophy as he only could redress all doubts in this regard. Although Pandavas, particularly Yudhisthra, were well-versed with all Dharmas, what had been asked and replied to here is for the benefit of the people at large. Similarly, Bhagwat has been narrated as dialogue between Parikshit and Shukdeva for the benefit of all people and Ramcharitmanas is the dialogue between Shiva and Parvati. Shiva had even told Parvati that although she knew all that had been asked for but it was for the benefit of all people. Then Bhishma and Krishana praised each other and Krishana requested Bhishma again to tell Yudhisthra about Dharma redressing his doubts. Bhishma not being at ease, showed his inability but then Krishana granted him the power to speak and to come next day. They went and slept. Krishana used to get up when the night was left for about three hours that is at about 4 A.M. and finished his daily chorus. Then Pandavas and Krishana came, where Bhishma was lying. Yudhisthra ordered all others to go from there as he wanted to talk to Bhishma on secret matters. Krishana told Bhishma about who were left alive after the battle viz. Pandavas, Krishana and Dharitrashtra. They all expressed their sorrows before Bhishma. Pandavas did not dare ask anything from Bhishma. Then Yudhisthra told that except Krishana, none else could dare talk to Bhishma. The Pandavas had fear for not following the laws of war in the battle and Bhishma had known it all. Krishana at first enquired about Bhishma's well-being. Bhishma told that with Krishana's grace, he was alright. Krishana told that he knew all about Dharma and could satisfy Yudhisthra but he wanted it to be narrated by Bhishma only and, therefore, he had passed on his power to him for narration to Yudhisthra. May be because Krishana had already consoled Yudhisthra but had no effect and now hearing it from Bhishma, Yudhisthra might feel satisfied. So it was arranged to be narrated by Bhishma. There is a principle in ethics that one, who is trusted and considered capable of having knowledge of certain matter, should only tackle the same. In Manas too Rama himself had told about his bhakti etc. and other matters of philosophy were narrated either by him or by big rishis etc. Krishana assured Bhishma that whatever he would say in reply to Yudhisthra's questions shall be recognised as correct in the universe. Bhishma then asked Yudhisthra about his question but he was still not daring to ask. Krishana told that in view of the killings and the modus operandi adopted in the battle, Yudhisthra feared any curse being passed on him and so he was not coming close to him. It is a religious principle that a sinner cannot go closer to rishis and God lest he should be reprimanded or cursed. Bhishma then assured that Yudhisthra had done his job in the battle as is required of the kshatriyas, so he should not feel guilty of the killings in the war.

Yudhisthra told that he had heard the Rajdharma to be the best but he considered this as a burden. He, therefore, requested Bhishma to tell him about Rajdharma. Bhishma asked him to listen to the Rajdharma or about anything else he desired to ask him. The duties of the raja are —

1. He is to keep his subjects happy as his foremost duty and for this purpose he should worship gods and respect brahmins.
2. He should always be toiling hard, as a raja without hardwork cannot solely depend on fate.
3. Although hard work and fate, both are considered essential for accomplishment but he considred hard work as more important of the two.
4. He should continue to make efforts for taking a job in hand, complete it and not giving it up half way.

5. The raja should be truthful so as to win the confidence of his people.
6. The raja should be benevolent but tough towards criminals.
7. He should not develop quarrel with brahmins as brahmins shall destroy the kingdom.
8. But if a well educated brahmin too takes up arms then the raja should fight with him religiously and arrest him and warn him to behave and if even then he does not improve, then he should be exiled rather than killed.
9. The raja should be kind to the people of all varnas and keep them happy.
10. The raja should not only be kind, the people should have fear from him too, as the mean persons insult the very kind raja if they have no fear.
11. The raja should give up all addictions like gambling, sleeping during the day, jealously, rivalry, drinking, womanising, hunting etc.
12. The raja should give up all sensuous involvements. except as necessary for a 'grihasta'.
13. The raja should be courageous in inflicting punishment on criminals.
14. The raja should not involve himself much in amusements with servants as then they start insulting the master; do not discharge their duties well; ask for undue favours; curse the raja for minor things; may forge raja's authority; talk ill of the raja; may not at times obey the raja; may disclose secrets and weakneses of the raja to others; start wearing raja's clothes etc.
15. The raja should always be industrious and should not sit idle.
16. The raja should be able to decide when to fight and when to have friendly alliance.
17. There are eight important organs of a raja—raja, ministers, friends, treasury, country, fort and army. The raja should kill anyone, who acts against the interest of the rajya.
18. A guru, if he is proud of his position and acts in a way unbecoming of his position, he should be punished.

19. The raja should not unnecessarily extract money from anyone and arrange to give, whatever due to others in time, as any payment made after it became due, reduces confidence of public in the raja.

20. The raja has not only to protect the people of all varnas but see that they comply with the tenets of their respective Dharmas.

21. The raja should not have blind confidence in any one even if one is quite trust-worthy.

22. The raja should himself analyse and take decision in cases of alliance, battle, position of enemy. In case of battle, if the enemy is stronger, then an alliance should he resorted to; if weaker, then he should be attacked. If enemy is stronger and he attacks, then the raja should take action for his protection. If the invader is of equal strength then the raja should adopt double standards, apparent and otherwise. In case of stronger enemy, the raja should take help of other rajas and then face the enemy.

23. The raja should not extract money from gentlemen and should extract from criminals as punishment.

24. The raja should give alms to deserving people from time to time.

25. Those people, who are of confidence, should be adequately awarded so that they could not be purchased by others.

26. The raja should behave with such people from outside and inwardly alike.

27. The raja, who doubts on everyone's integrity and extracts money from all, is killed by his own men.

28. The raja, who earns favour of his people is helped by them in case of external aggression etc.

29. The raja should ensure protection of life and peoperty of all people.

30. The raja should impart justice in case of all disputes without any favour to anyone.

31. There should be proper arrangement for education, hospitals, fearless travelling, fruit gardens, good roads, water arrangements etc.

32. Then the foremost job is to appoint spies in the country—in

markets, meeting places, on high ways, in palace, in residences of all ministers and bureaucrats and in other countries.

33. The raja should not ignore his enemy even if he is quite unimportant.

34. The raja should keep secrecy in dealings with enemies, organisation of army, things not to be known by public, appointment and posting of spies, plans for invasions, attacks etc.

35. For the sake of protecting the life of his people, the raja should not care even if he is to give up his life.

36. The raja should take care for the salvation of his people too, as a matter of morality and not as Rajdharma. Rama had advised his people the way to attain salvation but had left to the people to abide by his advice or not in that regard.

37. The raja has also to act as per sam, dam, dand and bhed (साम, दाम, दण्ड, भेद) principles in all matters. He should take care that his ministers etc. are not attracted by other rajas on their side.

38. The raja has to see that his treasury is full. If there is no money, then he should raise by extra cess or by getting from other rajas after attacking and defeating them. He should also draw proper agreements with his vassal states for regular payment of contributions.

39. There are four occasions of attacking other rajas—(1) Dharma Vijay, to extend one's Dharma to other areas. Generally it is used to be by pursuation and not by force. (2) Economic Vijay, to raise money for the rajya (3) Asra Vijay, to annihilate the sinners/ rakshasas and (4) Trivarga Vijay for extending the kingdom.

40. The rajas have to have sufficient stocks of food-grains and other essential commodities in the fort as well as in towns. He should also secretly have stores of poisonous commodities and raptiles etc. to harm the enemy in case of attack.

41. His commanders should be well-versed with formation of army (व्यूह रचना) and breaking the same.

42. He should be well-versed with laws of war etc. and should be quick in taking decision when a breach of the same is called for

in case of self defence.

43. His forts should be well-protected by trenches, poisonous gases, electric current passed in walls, brave troops to protect the same.

44. The raja should arrange proper procedure to be followed in courts and the persons managing the same so that justice is granted to all culprits and petitioners.

45. There should be well laid down codes of procedure to be followed in courts and punishment to be awarded for all kinds of crimes.

46. Adequate number of hospitals with competent doctors be provided to take care of the health of public.

Yudhisthra then asked about the Dharma of all the varnas, and the ashramas to be followed by the people of all Dharmas and the common Dharmas to be followed by the people of all varnas. Varnas and ashramas are the fundamentals of Hindu Dharma and it is for the raja to ensure that these are followed by all people. If it is ensured, then there shall be all peace and pleasure in the kingdom. Bhishma replied that the canons of ethics applicable to people of all Dharmas are no rage, truth speaking, proper distribution of wealth, be contented, be prepared to pardon, leading a pious life, no jealousy, leading a simple life and helping the infirms, reading vedas and shastras (Here the study of vedas and shastras has been indicated for the people of all varnas). It was only subsequently devised that shudras and ladies were not entitle to the same. This had also been dismantled by Tulsidasa in Ramcharitmanas, where he authorised all to resort to Bhakti and study of shastras. The brahmins were, however, required to be thorough in knowledge of vedas and shastras as they had to teach the same to others. The brahmins should also take alms but not ask for the same. Similarly, the kshatriyas should give alms but should not beg. He should perform yagyas but should not perform the same for others. He should read but should not teach; should care for all people; should impose punishment on criminals and face external aggression. The vaish is to give alms; study shastras and vedas; perform yagyas and earn money in lawful way, grazing and rearing of animals; trade; industry; bearing up of brahmins, kshatriyas and shudras by milk and other essential commodities; payment of 1/6th of the products to government exchequer. The shudras have to serve the people of all the other three varnas and the people of all the three varnas should contribute to shudras' livelihood. Shudras should not have wealth of their own and it is always under their masters' ownership. Shudras could read shastras and perform yagyas. Varna was opted by each person as the word (वर्ण) denotes and one could change from one varna to another. Brahmcharya, Grihastha, Vanprastha and Sanyas are the four ashramas provided for in Manu Samriti. The jobs required to be done in all the ashramas by the people of all varnas have also been indicated in that Samriti. In brarmcharya ashrama, the persons of all varnas used to go to gurukula leaving their homes; live on bhiksha; obey the guru; lead a simple and pious life and study all shastras. After basic education, one had to opt for the further studies of the vocation he was to adopt viz. a brahmin had to study further; a kshatriya had to learn fighting, governance etc.; the vaish was trained in trade, industry, animal rearing etc. One, who did not fit in any of the above, adopted shudra's varna. Since, the varna was as per one's option, as per capability, he did not have any grudge against the people of other varnas. After brahmcharya ashrama, and completion of studies, one enters grihastha; gets married, earns livelihood for the family, production and rearing up of children ; leads a contented life ; have control over his senses and desires ; should not have jealousy against others and lead a pious, truthful and simple life. After grihastha, when the son has got a grand-son, one should proceed to vanparastha. This was necessary so that the charge of kingdom, industry, trade, etc. is passed on to the sons, when they come of age. This served two purposes— one to now try to attain salvation and another to peacefully abdicate from worldly involvements lest the sons throw them out like Aurangzeb had put his father Shahjahan in captivity to gain throne and Shahjahan had to pass his remaining life in an awful condition. After vanprastha, there is sanyas, when one should have full control on senses; should not have any worldly ambitions and coach Dharma to others. Sanyas in fact is extended vanprastha itself.

Kshatriya Dharma has been indicated as best of all Dharmas as in this varna one is responsible for protection of all; put all in their respective Dharmas; care for the well-being of all and ultimately caring for the salvation of all his subjects. He is respected by all his subjects. The kshatriyas, who are after wealth and do not care to spend it on public and lead a luxurious life themselves are stated to be bad and should be removed. That is why Parshurama had to come as incarnate to kill all kshatriyas, who had involved themselves in luxuries; extraction of money from their subjects etc. Therefore, if the raja discharges his duties well and ensures others to comply with the tenets of their respective Dharmas, the raja earns the result of the actions of the people of all other varnas.

There are three ingredients of a rajya— the raja, its people and the kingdom. In case there is no raja, the people would fight with each other and there will be all chaos. The people should elect their raja,— either on the basis of who succeeded if he was capable, or another capable person not in the line of successors and in case of failure of these both sources then from other country but the raja adopted from other country, should give independent life to his new subjects and should not keep them as the slaves. In case of foreign aggression, entire public should come forward to help the raja. We lost in Rajput period as people thought that fighting with the enemy was the job of the raja with his army only and other people kept aloof. In this way fifty percent women 25% children and old persons and 3/4 of the balance 25% remained aloof from the aggression. So only about 6% people faced the enemy resulting in the defeat and establishment of foreign rule in India. Our shastras provide for all people to face the foreign aggressor. Similarly, in case of financial help to the raja too, all people are to rise to the occasion although there is provision for such people being compensated subsequently when the raja becomes financially stable.

Raja was respected by all. In case of curse passed by rishi's son on Raja Parikshit that he shall be bitten by a snake after seven days, the muni rebuked his son that giving punishment was the job of the raja and not of public, particularly brahmins and if the raja himself was culprit then God or the public shall punish him such as Rama had to have separation from Sita on public allegation for having kept Sita with him even after she had stayed in Lanka for a long period. Therefore, whereas the raja had to care for his people, the people too loved the raja and the raja as per his Dharma, already explained, cared for the proper protection and brought up of the people.

For proper protection of people from external aggression and internal criminals, the raja should—

1. At first have control on himself and then make efforts to win the enemies.

2. Keep army in forts, on borders of the kingdom, and in towns and villages. In all parks, forests, in the mahal and around the mahal.

3. Get the antecedents verified of all in Government job as troops or on civil duties.

4. Put spies all around, who should have direct access to the raja. The spies could be from trades, infirm, women and people of

all vocations so that they are not doubted by others while doing spying duty.

5. Enter into peaceful settlement if the enemy is stronger after consulting his senapati and ministers.

6. Appoint the ministers out of capable brahmins, kshatriyas and vaishas.

7. Not allow his weaknesses to be known by his enemy and should find out enemy's weaknesses.

8. Keep a check on the production from mines, salt, earning from boats, in markets etc and ensure rajbhag from these productions.

9. Take refuge in the fort when attacked by enemy if he is not able to face him.

10. Keep his reserved forces in secret places like forests etc.

11. Keep a watch on production in farms and their evaluation and contribution to government exchequer.

12. Install proper topkhana etc. on all gates of the forts and the towns and the raja should himself monitor the same.

13. See that there is no fire during the day and all cooking should be during the night only.

14. Send, beggars, vehicle drivers, cunnels, bunaties and dramatists out of the towns and villages during the war as they could be spying for the enemy.

15. Provide proper cantonments, residential accommodation, storage of foodgrains, kawach and armaments, water wells, pliable roads for army and keep them secret.

16. Particularly take care of self, friends, ministers, country, town and villages.

Bhishma told that the raja should know all laws of war and their application as per Dharma. In Satya yug, it was all Dharma; in Treta it was seventy five percent Dharma; in Duapar fifty percent Dharma and in Kalyug there shall only be twenty five percent Dharma. So in wars too all decisions should be taken accordingly but during peace he should act as per Dharma only. For the well-being of the praja, the raja —

1. Should act as per Dharma.

2. Should be God-fearing.
3. Should collect wealth without undue extraction.
4. Should have pleasures within limits.
5. Should be sweet in talking but should not be humble.
6. Should be brave.
7. Should give alms but not to non-deservings.
8. Should be courageous but not crude.
9. Should not ally with bad characters.
10. Should not fight with his brothers.
11. Should have spies of integrity.
12. Should get his job done without harming anyone.
13. Should not antrust secret jobs to others.
14. Should not praise himself.
15. Should not snatch money from gentlemen.
16. Should not take refuge under mean persons.
17. Should not punish the criminals without proper investigation.
18. Should not divulge the secret of governance.
19. Should not distribute wealth amongst misers.
20. Should not trust the people of non-integrity.
21. Should protect his wife without bias.
22. Should be pious and not hate anyone.
23. Should not be a womaniser.
24. Should take tasty and simple food.
25. Should not be rude and be respectful to respectable persons.
26. Should serve the Guru ingenuously.
27. Should worship gods without any vanity.
28. Should collect wealth in an honourable way.
29. Should be affectionate to all without any ego.
30. Should be well-versed with his job but should act as time warranted.

31. Should not console or give undertaking simply to get rid of the people.
32. Should be kind to everyone without any consideration.
33. Should not harm anyone without knowing the facts.
34. Should not feel sorry for killing the enemies.
35. Should not enrage on anyone suddenly.
36. Should be benevolent but not to criminals.
37. Should stand up when brahmins come, pay respected and thereafter serve them.
38. Should egage a capable Purohit and take his advice on all important matters. The Purohit too in turn should keep the raja apprised of all important happenings in the kingdom, in mahal and in other countries of interest of Raja. Since brahmin and kshatriya have both born out of Brahma, they should make joint efforts in bringing peace and Dharma in the kingdom.

Bhishma told that except for brahmins, the raja had the lien on the wealth of all other people. The raja, therefore, can ask for the wealth from anyone in case of need and compensate him later on. This has been made a part of the Dharma so that anyone may not have any objection in parting with his wealth for the cause of the kingdom. The best governed kingdom is one in which people of all varanas act as per their respective Dharmas. The raja is, as per shastras, held responsible for no rains, famines, early death, chronic diseases, death of son before father, death of husband in young age rendering the wife as widow without any means of livelihood, protection of life and property of people from external aggressions and internal criminals.

As already indicated, the institution of varnas was generally to be followed but a person of one varna could change over to another, depending on his capability as Muni Vishvamitra had become brahmrishi from kshatriya. Similarly, if a brahmin is not able to make his both ends meet, he can opt to become kshatriya and if even as kshatriya, he is not able to earn livelihood, then he can opt for vocation of vaish varna but the brahmin as vaish should not trade in meat, drugs, intoxicants, salt, alcohol, cow, other animals, horses etc. Exchange of commodities is allowed as per Dharma but if such exchange is by force then it is not Dharma. For alms-giving, tapsya etc., one should not have jealousy against others. For annihilating crime, people of all varnas are allowed to take up arms against the criminals. Brahmin too is not considered adharmik if he takes up arms for the protection of the people of other varnas. Similarly, for self-defence taking up arms is not adharmik or a crime. Anyone, who protects others is to be honoured even if he is a shudra.

On Yudhisthra asking that one requires help of others even for the petty jobs then how the raja alone arranges entire governance, Bhishma told that the raja is helped in the governance by his friends, brothers and sons, ministers and other advisors. But sometimes friends become foes and vice versa. Therefore, the raja should keep an eye on all his foes and friends through his spies and should not have blind reliance on anyone. He should be always alert in respect of a nominated yuvaraja or the person, not so nominated, but aspiring to take over the kingdom on raja's death because for the sake of attaining throne, such persons can harm the raja in one way or the other. The raja should entrust a job to one person and to two or more as there is always difference of opinion in more than one person. Similarly, only deserving persons should be made ministers. They shold be from high family, contented, brave, gentlemen and be able to differentiate between 'dos' and 'donots'. The raja should have fear from his familymen like one have fear of death. As a raja cannot tolerate the uprising of a neighbouring raja so a familyman does not tolerate the rising of another familyman. The raja should, therefore, keep them always in good humour but put his spies to keep a watch on them. There have been instances where a raja could save the kingdom from his relations only on account of receipt of timely information from his spies. Ala-ud-din is one such instance, where his uncle wanted to usurp the throne but the spy apprised Ala-ud-din in time and then the uncle was killed. Krishna also told that there are various kinds of close relations, who are not well-wishers, second, who are well-wishers, but are not well-educated and then there are people, who are well- wishers and well-educated but do not have any control on themselves. Secret matters should not be discussed or divulged to them. Sometimes the raja gets confused whom to help and whom not to help as the mother of two gambler sons wishes victory for one but does not wish the defeat of the other. In such a case, one side has to be adopted. The raja should also encourage the ministers, who are responsible for extra revenue to the exchequer and keep a watch on the ministers, who mis-appropriate the exchequer money. In such a case, the persons, who apprise raja of the mis-appropriator should be provided with adequate protection as such persons have risk of their life from such mis-appropriators. If an employee commits some mistake because of carelessness, he may be excused once and a watch kept on his future behaviour. Further, all in the darbar had to be under protocol in entering the darbar, sitting in the darbar, talking in the darbar, walking in the darbar and leaving the darbar. It shows the extent of protocolic requirements then laid down for each and every occasion and each and every persons.

> दर्व्याहृताच्छंकमानो दुष्कृताद् दुराधिष्ठितात्,
> दुरासिताद् दुर्व्रजितादिगितादंग चेष्टतात्। (82/30)

When a group of persons is involved in a particular misdeed against the rajya, the raja should hold discreet enquiry and if the misdeed is established then action should be taken against them one by one as one time action against all may give a chance to all to unite and harm the raja.

On Yudhisthra asking about the requirements of a ministers, Bhishma advised that they should have control over senses, truth speaker, pious, simple, conteneted and well-versed in expressing themselves. They should be out of brahmins, brave persons, contented, courageous and be with the raja in case of difficulty. They should be with good family background, able to express themselves fearlessly and devoted to the cause of the rajya and should not be miser, crude, shameless, and corrupt. The raja should give up a group of persons if one is able to serve the purpose meaning thereby that the minimum possible number of persons should be put on Government jobs. The ministers should be able to keep secrecy in all consultations by the raja. The raja should also have secret consultations with his ministers, when none else is there so that responsibility could be fixed up in case of any leakage of secrecy. This shows the philosophy of accountability and responsibility in Government jobs in those days.

Yudhisthra further asked the requisites of a town, where raja should live. Bhishma advised that the town should be with—

1. A fort.
2. Sufficient foodgrains godowns.
3. Sufficient space to store arms and armaments.
4. A strong wall all around it.
5. A trench full of water all around it.
6. Sufficient place to put elephants, horses and chariots.
7. Sufficient place for intelligent persons and artists to live in.
8. Adequate water arrangements.

9. Persons well-versed in religions and other matters.
10. Brave persons, who could be recruited in army.
11. Proper laid down roads, streets, squares, bazaars,.
12. Good courts and judges.
13. Peaceful environ.
14. Free from violence or riots.
15. Proper arrangement for lighting.
16. Proper music system on play.
17. Sufficient number of traders, industrialists, brahmins, shudras and other utility personnel.
18. Sufficient number of temples.
19. Sufficient space for constructing houses for ministers and other officers.
20. A cantonment.
21. Proper place for raja to reside with his family men.
22. Doctors, vaids, chemists etc.

The raja should himself meet the spies, have secret consultations himself, decide the quantum of punishment to criminals, control the exchequer, make important appointments of ministers, high officers and senapati and commanders of the army. The kingdom should be distributed in villages, blocks of ten villages, twenty villages, one hundred villages, on thousand villages and appoint their mukhias accordingly. The mukhia should handle the criminals at the village level itself and decide the quantum of punishment, send the report to the mukhia of ten villages of important happenings. Similarly, the mukhia of ten villages should report matters to mukhia of twenty villages and so on and last but not the least, all reports of important matters should reach the raja. Similarly, the accountal of production and revenues of the rajya should be kept at all levels. The mukhia should be adequately paid. Nagar Prabandhaks should be appointed to take care of peace and prosperity of the town. Spies should be fixed in all villages and towns so that the mukhias do not indulge in bad practices or harass the people. They should see that traders do not charge high rates for commodities and do not underweigh or under measure them. The raja should also take care not to extract more money from the people as may be difficult to bear. In case of any emergency or foreign aggression etc., the entire population should be moved to rise to the occassion through the multi-tier management system indicated above.

For raising revenues for the exchequer, the raja should see that the exchequer is sufficiently full but should not harass people to extract money as in that case they will either leave the rajya or rise against the raja. The extraction should, therefore, be within tolerable limits.

1. He should raise money from all alike and not in a discriminatory way.
2. The raja should raise revenues from agricultural products, which is the main source of income, on a fixed proportion basis (one-sixth of the produce) and should reduce it in case there is no rain and consequently no production or less production.
3. The raja should not allow drinking centres, prostitution and their brokers as they harm the nation.
4. Except for emergent times, the raja should not raise extra money from the people.
5. The raja should not be extravagant in spending on personal account. The raja in fact can spend on his personal account out of the wealth collected as presents or war damages and not out of the rajbhag from the products. It is said that once when Yudhisthra wanted to hold Aswamedha yagya, but he did not have sufficient fund for this purpose, he then had to meet such expenses out of the gold ornaments/utensils thrown by people of other raja after yagya. Aurangzeb used to do some job to raise money with his hand in a symbolic way.
6. The money raised from pubic should be prudently spent on army or other public welfare jobs.
7. Raising money from mines, forests, lakes, boating, trade cess industrial production cess etc. The raja has the authority over all mines, forests etc and any income from these sources is that of the raja only. He should, therefore, keep a watch that these resources are not misappropriated by public.

In case a raja desires to annex territory of another raja, he should—

1. Put in the mind of the people of the territory to be annexed as if he was their raja and shall protect their life and property. They should either start paying him or fight with his people. In this way if those people accept his suzerainty, well and good,

otherwise he should fight and subdue them.

2. Should suppress all in case of any opposition.

3. Not fight with a raja without kawach. One raja should rather ask anohter raja to attack on him and he shall attack too.

4. If he comes in kawach then he should wear kawach too. If another raja comes with army then he too should have army with him.

5. If the other raja adopts some deceitful methods in fighting, then he too should adopt such methods.

6. If the other raja fights as per laws of war then he should also follow the same.

7. A troop on horse should fight with another on horse; a commander in chariot should fight with the other man in chariot and so on.

8. If the enemy is in trouble then he should not be attacked.

9. Also one should not attack on a defeated enemy.

10. Poisonous arms should not be used.

11. If one person wants to kill another person in battle then he should not have rage against him but fight on equal footing.

12. One should not attack on a weak issueless preson.

13. In case of breakage of Dhanush, breakage of chariot, death of sarthi, or the enemy is arrested, then he should be sent home.

14. An enemy without wounds should not be spared.

15. A raja should not adopt deceitful way if the other is fighting according to Dharma.

16. A raja should not attack when kawach of the other is torn out or when one surrenders his arms.

17. A raja should fight with another raja only.

18. A raja should check up the way of fighting, types of armaments of the enemy.

This shows that we had detailed laws of war at that time. These laws permit the battle with deceitful method if the other party adopts such method that is how when the rakshasas had been fighting with 'maya' the gods too had to adopt such methods to do away with the 'maya'.

Prithviraj excused Mohammed Ghori several times when he was defeated as this was the rule of battle but since Muslims had not been following the rules of law, Ghori and his armymen should have been killed as was done by Ghori subsequently when he was victorious. If prithviraj had killed Ghori and his men, it would have created fear in Muslims and they would not have dared establish their rule in India.

As already indicated, the concept of election of the raja is not alien to India. According to vedas and samrities, the raja and the members of his council are to be elected ones but threre are some short-comings in this sytesm. Bhishma told that greed and rage are the two reasons for creating enmity amongst the families, ganas, and rajas.

In a republican state, even the sons and brothers are punished if they indulge in immoral actions. The people are provided with high education and are owned when they have finished their education. The people of republic are always prepared to work for the state as spies, ambassadors for secret consultation, framing of constitution for the republic, and collection of wealth for republics. Such republics, therefore, always progress. These people are intelligent, brave, courageous, and hardworking and devoted workers, always caring for the uplift of the republics. They are all rich, knowing the usage of armaments and help the people in trouble. Therefore, the raja should honour all principal authorities in the republic as they have to bear the burden of governance. All the people of the republics are not supposed to be knowing the secrets of Government. Therefore, only principal authorities are entrusted with secret jobs or consultation on secret matters. The people of the republics should work combinedly for the welfare of the state otherwise they shall get divided leading to chaos and anarchy.

Any uprising or riot or persons responsible for creating division should be immediately suppressed. If the elders in a family do not suppress the quarrels in the family, then that family shall get destroyed. All should work for the republics without any fear or favour as these destroy the republics. All may be treated equal in a caste or family but all cannot be equal in intelligence, bravery, hardwork. The enemies always try to create division amongst the people of the republics by paying money etc. It is, therefore, ardent duty of the people of a republic to remain united.

There is a detailed narration of the duties of the parents and their children as per social protocol. It provides for the children to be obedient to parents and the guru. The children should carry out the jobs entrusted by parents or guru without giving a second thought to their orders. Such children need not follow any other Dharma as parents and guru make the children perfect in all respects, fit for complying with the Dharma of their respective varnas. Out of the parents and guru too, the guru is considered superior as the parents only give birth to the body but the knowlege imparted by the guru makes the children rise in this universe and attain ultimate salvation as the habit of serving parents and guru continues as service to almighty, helping in attaining salvation.

Yudhishthra asked about truth and non-truth and how one should comply with the requirements of truth. Bhishma told that there is nothing above truth and no Dharma is without truth but there are situations where telling lie in fact works as truth, such as saving anyone from trouble or where truth puts someone in trouble. On such occassions, one should not resort to truth but tell a lie. Therefore, a man acts as per tenets of Dharma if he acts after adjudging the result of truth or lie. Dharma is 'Dharma' because it upkeeps all. It saves from downfall and protects life. Dharma also protects and brings up the people. Further—

1. Dharma teaches non-violence.
2. It teaches non-raging, truth, tapasya, alms-giving, control over senses, not seeing ills in others, not talking ill of others, not being jealous of others. According to Brahma, these are the ingredients of Dharma and one, who complies with these, attains salvation.
3. One should not tell about the wealth of a rich man if someone wants to have this information with a view to steal the same. One should not talk in such a situation but if the robbers force for divulging it, then one should tell a lie and it is treated as Dharma.
4. If taking oath can save one from the clutches of a criminal, then such oath taking is Dharma.
5. If a money-lender presents some one as witness regarding the amount owed by the other person and if witness does not support his true claim, then the witness is a liar.
6. But one can tell a lie in case someone's life is at stake, at the time of marriage, to save others' wealth or for protecting Dharma.

7. One should not, however, tell a lie in case of establishing the crime of a criminal even if it leads to punishment of death to the criminal.

8. If a person has become asura, leaving Dharma, and wants to lead his life cheating others, such a person, must be punished even if such punishment is death. In such cases one should not tell a lie.

9. One should not tell a lie to save the wealth earned by corrupt practices.

10. It is not a sin to get a sinner killed by telling the truth regarding the sins caused by him.

Yudhisthra then asked about the qualifications of the secretary, senapati, and other Government servants. Bhishma told that raja should check the truthfulness, piety, simplicity, temperament, knowledge of shastras, morality, family background, control over senses, strength, taking pity, image, and capacity to pardon, of his servants before appointment and post them on jobs according to their capability and afford them full protection. The raja should not fix up any minister without proper verification of antecedents as the raja cannot be happy after having appointed a mean person as his minister. Raja should, therefore, appoint ministers, who are from high family, adequately educated, intelligent, well-versed with art and science, having full knowledge of shastras, tolerant, citizen of the same country (It is pertinent to note that the considedration of citizenship for appointment as minister or high officials in Government service is not a recent concept. It was much in prevalence even as per our shastras in ancient times), grateful, having control on his senses, devoted, well- wishers of the master and his friends, contented, non-greedy, non-lethargic, keeping spies in the country, expert in visualising the situation for alliance or battle, well-versed with Rajdharma, finances, popular in towns and villages, expert in army formation (व्यूह रचना), construction of trenches and tunnels, expert in inspiring courage in army, reader of what is in others' heart, specialist in finding proper time for attacking the enemy, knowing the ways of elephants, horses, without pride, pious, dear to all, charming and attractive, having leader like personality, non-rude, humble, sweet tempered, sweet in talking, brave and able to take decision as warranted by situation. The kingdom of raja with ministers as per above requirements expands day in and day out. The raja should also meet the above requirements in addition to his Rajdharma as already indicated. A man of a mean family, if gets high post, he becomes arrogant. The raja should assign job to his employees according to their capability to get best results of their performance. The raja should make continuous efforts to protect the exchequer in full liquidity, godowns should be full of food-grains, the arsenal should be full with latest armaments and the army should be well-versed in their usage. The most important job of the raja is protection of life and property. He should be benevolent, diplomat, manipulator, true, Dharmik, knowing weakness of the enemy, able to create division in enemy's kingdom, knowing proper usage of sam, dam, dand and bhed (साम, दाम, दण्ड, भेद) policies, invading enemy's kingdom at proper time, well-versed with war strategy, efficient in governance with the help of his ministers, proper treatment and providing encouragement to his officials and be alert always in respect of enemies and other happenings in the kingdom, awarding punishment to criminals, maintenance of army in good spirit always, thinking of the well-being of his subjects in this universe and after death, protector of all Dharmas and making adequate arrangements for education and health etc.

Yudhisthra asked the way out for a raja, who has many enemies; his friends leave him and the army and treasury is also wasted out; helped by a good for nothing ministers and who finds no way of survival. Bhishma told that the topic of Dharma is very sensitive. One can know it by pondering over shastras after listening to the same. A raja gets destroyed if he extracts money from the public even when the public is in trouble. One becomes wise on going through shastras. If the treasury of a raja is lost, his strength is lost. In such a situation, the raja should collect money from the public (particularly from resourceful persons) and return the same when position is comfortable. This amounts to public borrowing of the present day, which is adopted by all countries. After collection of money, he should act as per Dharma. As it is only in difficulty that a man should find out any way out even if he has to be little adharmik. This is only for the kshatriyas, who are in trouble and expect getting money from the public otherwise it amounts to begging and begging or adopting the vocation of vaisha or shudra is not ordinarily permitted for an kshatriya as after the kshatriya becomes well off subsequently then these vaishas are converted into friends and sometimes a friend becomes enemy. Therefore, the position of a friend or enemy gets on changing from time to time based on change in circumstances. The raja should accordingly take a decision to have confidence or otherwise, according the situation. One should have friendly alliance to the extent possible even with the enemies but should not still have blind confidence in anyone. Such a prudent decision can only save the person in trouble otherwise he shall be completely ruined. There is a saying that intelligent enemy is better than a non-intelligent friend. Therefore, intelligent enemy, if made on his side, shall be very helpful whereas a non-intelligent friend can hit him down any time.

"श्रेष्ठोहि पण्डितः शत्रुर्न च मित्रमपण्डितः" (138/46)

In fact none is friend or foe, it is the self interest which makes a man friend or foe and the interest goes on changing from time to time. After the job is over then one does not recognise the other. Therefore, the job should be left incomplete in such situations so that there is always hope of the work being done.

न कश्चित् कस्याचिन्मित्रं न कश्चित् कस्याचिद् रिपुः,
अर्थतस्तु बिद्धयुन्ते मित्राणि रिपवस्तथा ।

(138/110)

Therefore, one should enter into friendly alliance because some sanctity is always attached to written agreements. Even then it should be kept in mind that a person of wavering mind cannot be a regular friend or a foe as his affinity shall continue changing depending on the interest involved at a particular juncture. Even the real brothers or husband and wife love each other because of self interest. One should not, therefore, take any relation as selfless and money is the base of all affinities. Friendship should, therefore, be with well-to-do persons only without wavering mind. There can also be a situation in which a raja might have friendly alliance with an enemy and fight with a friend because some misunderstandings go on multiplying and it would be difficult at a later stage to sort them out. Also, one should always try to ward off any fear in time and should not be left to be sorted out later on as later on it may result in one having to enter into fighting as in such a case the person from whom one may have fear might think that he could be easily subdued if put to fighting.

So far as the dealings with enemies are considered, one should try to keep them in good humour but continue to prepare oneself to face them, if such an occasion arises and should never have confidence in him. Even those, who are trust-worthy, should be seen with suspicion everytime without exposing oneself. There can be enmity between rajas and other persons on five accounts—

1. For women.

2. For house and other properties.
3. For harsh speaking.
4. Due to dynastical malice.
5. Because of some untoward incidence, which took place in the past.

In the above situations, the person or raja should not have confidence as such in a person as he shall always have ill-feeling against another person/raja. Such a feeling cannot be subdued by harshness, softness, discussion or on the basis of provision in shastras. It ends only after one of the two parties is eliminated. One should, therefore, be always careful from enemy's side. Bhishma also advised that—

1. If a person has got both his legs injured then the injuries shall further develop if he walks even though carefully.
2. One should eat only as can be assimilated, so friendship should be to the extent of under-standing.
3. Destiny and hardwork are interdependent on each other. The liberal persons always act as per Dharma and impotents depend on destiny.
4. One should keep oneself busy. One, who leaves doing any job and lead a lethargic life, kills himself.
5. One should act by dint if his intelligence, knowledge, strength, power and courage.
6. Even a small amount in the hands of an intelligent persons, gets on increasing day-by-day and heaps of wealth in foolish hands become zero.
7. One should leave a mischievous wife, bad sons, polluted relations, and ill govered country.
8. False friendship cannot become perpetual.
9. If the praja remains depressed, then raja cannot prosper too.
10. The raja should always he ready to punish the culprits. This keeps the praja disciplined.
11. Intelligent raja should uproot the enemy at the earliest occasion.
12. The enemy should not be trusted even after entering into alliance with him.
13. An intelligent raja should completely surrender before a powerful enemy but take revenge, when he is weak that is he

should act as per environ.

14. One should not have good relations with ungrateful persons.
15. Warding off the action in good time and hoping to have good time in future, does not make a person happy.
16. The raja should punish even the Guru if he acts against the tenets of Dharma.
17. One should not keep balance of borrowed money, ailment, fire and enmity as the same can erupt further any time.
18. The work in hand should not be left unfinished and should not take up in hand a work, which it is not possible to complete. In other word one should not try to cross a river, which it is not possible to cross.

Dharma and conduct are the products of brain and are deciphered by brain only. An intelligent raja, wishing to conquer other areas, works as per Dharma but the same action or Dharma becomes Dharma at one time and adharma at another. One should, therefore, properly understand this dualism. An intelligent person should at first start his plans secretly and subsequently only disclose the same otherwise it may be taken in other sense. Further, some people are learned and some only pose as being learned. The raja should, therefore, take into confidence the actually learned persons only.

Also the immature people cannot properly analyse the Dharma and adharma. Therefore, only matured persons should be kept for consultation on Dharmik problems. The Dharma cannot be visualised only by speach or by brain but it is decided on the basis of combination of the provision in shastras and its proper analysis. It can, therefore, be safely conculded that the result of the analysis of provision in shastras by brain is to be taken as correct thing to be adopted. Such an analysis has already been carried out by our rishis and brahmins. Therefore, advise of the brahmins and rishis should be taken as the best guide.

Yudhisthra further asked about the genesis of sin and how a person gets inclined to commit a sin. Bhishma told that 'greed' is solely responsible for all sins being committed.

1. All sins, adharma, and troubles in man's life as also in the rajya arise out of greed only.
2. Out of greed only one gets enraged.
3. Out of greed one is down with all kinds of passions.

4. Out of greed one becomes proud, arrogant and rude.
5. Greed puts a man as a slave of other persons.
6. Discontentment, shamelessness, destruction of property, decay of Dharma, worries, and disrepute are caused because of greed only.
7. Thefts, rapes, ill-talks, habit of ill speaking about others, rise of passions and ambition, violent thinking, violence, over talkativeness, jealousy, all kinds of sins, interest in bad jobs and involvement in undesirable actions are all caused because of greed.
8. A person cannot get rid of bad actions in childhood, youth and even in old age because of the basic element of greed in him. A greedy person can never feel contented. He is never satisfied with whatever amount of gains he had attained.
9. A person, who had controlled his sensual feelings, should overpower affection and greed otherwise all other bad elements shall get imbibed in him.
10. Even if a man has studied all vedas, he does not get rid of worldly troubles because of greed.
11. One forgets the morality and starts abusing or cheating others.
12. In a way a greedy person can be called a non-disciplined one.
13. Those who are same in happiness and sorrow and are always truth-speaking persons. ready to take up good jobs, who only give and do not take, are kind to others, are Dharma protectors, do not threaten others, always follow the correct path, are always above the instinct of greed and are worth being followed.

On Yudhisthra asking about negligence, Bhishma explained that—

1. The person, who commits sins out of negligence and does not even understand the disadvantage caused to him because of negligence, is not liked in the universe.
2. He suffer and faces many troubles because of negligence.
3. He goes to hell.
4. Jealousy, happiness, sorrow, affection, passions, rage, lethargy, wishes, enmity and sinful conduct, all arise out of negligence.
5. In a way negligence and greed can be taken as same thing as negligence arises out of greed and till one is relieved of greed,

one's negligence gets on escalating and because of greed and ignorance one can never attain salvation and have rebirths from one specie to another.

6. One reaches death earlier because of negligence.

7. Contrary to negligence, different kinds of Dharmas have been narrated because of knowledge.

8. Further, control over senses is in the root of Dharma. Every person or raja, who has control over sensual feelings, would be able to have control over greed and negligence too. Such a person is successful in this universe and ultimately attains salvation as control over senses leads to truthfulness, non-violence, simplicity, piety, ragelessness, sweet in treatment, no rudeness, no jealousy, since all these things arise for the fulfilment of sensual feelings. Such a person is appreciated by everyone in whatever varna or ashrama he might be. Such a person need not even go to forests for vanprastha or sanyas and can lead his life as a 'grihastha' too.

9. Tapasya is another means of attaining salvation. The creation of universe by Brahma is by tapasya. Anything can be attained by tapasya. Tapasya does not necessarily means going to forests and sit in samadhi. In fact complying with the requirements of the respective varnasharama Dharma by a person is tapasya. Non violence, truthfulness, control over senses, to be contented and remaining same in happiness and sorrows is tapasya only.

10. Truthfulness too is part of the tapasya as indicated above. Truthfulness includes true to his Dharma, true to profession, true in the behaviour with not only human beings but also other beings, true to raja and brahmins, and excusing others on their faults. For a raja, protection of life and property of his people from external aggression and internal criminals, is his Dharma and in complying with the requirements of this Dharma, he may have to kill the enemy and his men in war and punish criminal too but these actions are true projections of the discharge of his duties by the raja.

11. In this context, the control over all faults is an important part of Dharma too. These faults are rage, passion, affection, jealousy, acting against the provisions in vedas and shastras, desire to kill others (violence), pride, greed, arrogance, miserliness, finding faults in others. A person or a raja has to have control over

these normal faults in human beings. These faults lead to all adharmik actions by a person and, therefore, have to be controlled fully.

There is then the narration of various kinds of sins and their repentance. In our shastras, various kinds of crimes have been indicated as sins (irreligious actions). Some of the crimes are taken care of by the raja and the criminals are punished but there are some crimes pertaining to morality or where the crimes are not detected by the raja's persons. In such cases, the people can release themselves from the results of such crimes by atonement/repentance. The way of repentance on each kind of crime has been indicated like if a brahmin prepares for a yagya and the yagya material is stolen. they should be paid by raja to enable the brahmin to complete the yagya. Similarly, a hungry brahmin who has not taken meals for 6 months can steal foodgrains / money from other persons sufficient for that day's meals and the raja should not punish him for such thefts rather arrange for his livelihood in future. The brahmin can cross the troubled period by mantras and havan, kshatriya by his strength and vaish and shudra by money. Any yagya etc. should be followed by proper dakshina. A lie spoken in humour, before wife, at the time of marriage, for the well-beings of the guru and for saving one's life is not considered unethical. No repentance is called for drinking, killing a brahmin and relation with guru's wife but only death releases the person from such a sin. Killing an infant in pregnancy is washed off if one is killed in battle. Killing a pregnant lady involve in the sin of killing two brahmins and accordingly repentance should be undertaken. One should feel sorry if small insects are killed unknowingly. A lady sleeping with other persons, should be got bitten to death by ferocious dogs.

Yudhisthra, after going to his home during the night asked Vidur and his brothers as to which is best, second best and third best out of Dharma, Artha and Kama (धर्म, अर्थ, काम) and how to have control on these. Vidur replied that tapasya, sacrifice, faith, yagya, to excuse, to have pity, truth and control over passions are the roots of Dharma. The possession of these is the way to salvation and earning praise in this universe. In fact Dharma has been adopted by rishis for attainment of ultimate aim. In Duapur, Dharma possessed the top position; Artha, the second position and Kama, the last. Arjuna told that Artha was the best as even Dharma could be attained if Artha is there and passions could be satisfied by Artha alone. Dharma and Kama are, therefore, attained if Artha is there. So Artha is at the top, Dharma at number two and Kama at number three. Nakula and Sehdeva too agreed that Artha was at the top position as it is most difficult to have Artha and Dharma and Kama could be attained if Artha is there. Therefore, the man should earn Artha in a Dharmik way and spend on attaining the satisfaction of Kama. Bhima told that a man without Kama (desires) can neither put himself in attaining Dharma nor in attaining Artha. Even rishis resorted to tapasya keeping some desires in view. Kama has a variety of purposes and Kama (desire) is necessary to attain something before the same is actually attained. As butter is the essence of milk and curd, so Kama is the essence of Dharma and Artha. Therefore, satisfaction of Kama is the attainment of Dharma and Artha too. Bhima further told that according to him one should try to attain all the three (Dharma, Artha and Kama) simultaneously. Therefore, a person trying to acquire all the three is best; who tries to acquire two is of middle class and who tries to have one only is of lowest class. Yudhisthra then told that although they all were well-versed with the tenets of shastras and could reach a solution after proper analysis and they knew logic too, he had heard them all and according to him a man not involved in any virtue or vice or earning wealth or Dharma or non-indulging in Kama, is above all faults and he attains salvation. According to Brahma too, a person involved in worldly passions, can never attain salvation. A man above these passions can only have 'mukti'. Therefore, a man desirous of attaining salvation, should not do any good or bad to anyone. God has entrusted everyone with his job called his Dharma. All the brothers were happy to listen to Yudhisthra.

Bhishma then told next day about the persons with whom a person or a raja could have friendly relations and with whom he should not have such relations. One should not have friendship with persons, who are greedy, rude, adharmik, cheat, mean, cunning, sinner, suspicious toward others, lethargy, crooked, dilatory, a condemned, one leaving at the time of trouble, condemnor of vedas, non-alert, always wanting to snatch other's wealth, shame-less, enraged, jealous, drunkard, ungrateful, violent, who cannot have control on sensual feelings, and ill-speaker of friends etc. One should have friendship with persons from high family, talking sense, well-versed with art and science, knowing vedas and shastras, non-greedy, grateful, man of moral character and principles, having good friends, non-tiring, having control over senses, industrious, without any addiction, popular in public etc. Further, those, who act as per Dharma can be made friends. Ungrateful are the worst of all as they can ever kill the friends and his relations.

Yudhisthra asked Bhishma to now tell about the people in various ashramas. Bhishma told that vedas provide for the way to attain salvation, while in any of the four ashramas. There are many ways to be Dharmik and there is no action without a reaction. This theory is there in our vedas and shastras.

सर्वत्र विहितोधर्मः स्वर्ग्यः सत्फलं तपः,
बहुद्वास्य धर्मस्य नेहास्ति विफला क्रिया। (174/2)

A man, who, has attained finality in Dharma following certain methods, should continue to work on those methods only and by following those methods, he gets renunciation from the universe. Since this universe is full of faults, one should try to attain salvation following the path of Dharma. Yudhisthra further asked how a man should console himself in case of loss of wealth or death of wife, son or father. Bhishma told that in such a situation, one should take it that the universe is full of sorrows and with a view to eliminate sorrows, one should devise means of controlling one's senses so that there is no pain of the sorrows.

नष्टे धने व दारेवा पुत्रे पितरि वा मृते,
अहो दुःखमिति ध्यायंशोकस्यापचितिं चरेत्। (174/7)

In an incidence, the son of Raja Sainjit had died and he was upset because of that death. Then a brahmin told him why he was so upset like a foolishman, as a day shall come when others shall be sorry for his death. He told that everyone has to go from where he has come. The raja asked about what could make him not to worry in even such cases: The raja told that even though knowing that happiness and sorrow come and go, one becomes very happy on some gain and very lost in case of any sorrowness. The brahmin told that people of all shades have been facing sorrows in this universe. He was alone. There was none, whom he could claim as his own and none else could claim him as his own. There was none affectionate to him or vice versa. Even this body was not his own and all other commodities were as much his own as the same belonged to others. Therefore, he was not worried about the existence or otherwise of those commodities. In this universe, people meet and set apart. Similarly son, wife, other brothers etc. meet, they become affectionate but one should not very much involve in them as the separation from them one day was definite. His son had come from a particular situation and had gone to another specific situation. Neither of the raja and the son knew each other. Then why should there be any shock for the loss of that son. In the universe, non-fulfilment of the ambitions is painful and the elimination of that pain is the happiness. This cycle of happiness and sorrow continues.

This body is the basis of all sorrows and joys. The persons have to face joys or sorrows as a consequence of his actions by his body. The man is surrounded by various relations and separation from any of those relations causes pain to him. Man commits so many wrongs for the sake of wife and sons but he alone has to suffer for all those wrongs after death and none else shares the same. Everyone feels pain on separation from relations but he should take it that sorrows and joys, life and death are all governed by destiny. The only persons happy in this universe are either those, who are foolish or those, who are beyond the reach of thinking. The foolish cannot make out good or bad result of his doings, so he ramains happy and he who has attained 'gyan' and do not have jealousies is also happy as he does not differentiate between happiness and sorrow. A person in between the two becomes happy on good news and is upset on hearing bad news. There are thousands of situations causing sorrow or happiness but intelligent persons are not affected by the same as they are same in all situations— good or bad. Therefore, as and when, one gets rid of the ambitions to that extent he is relieved of the pains and as he involves himself in worldly attainments, he has to suffer for the same although he may not feel so when he indulges in the same. The joys in this universe are not even 1/16th of the joys attained after salvation.

One should, therefore, not caring for the joys of this universe, retire from the same and try to attain salvation at all costs as the joys of this universe are for a small period of life only whereas the joys of the salvation are perpetual. When one does not have any fear from anyone nor anyone is afraid of him and he neither has ambition for anything nor has disliking for the same, then one attains salvation. Therefore, those, who get rid of worldly involvements, really get happiness. The instance of Pingla prostitute is quoted in this connection. Pingla had wanted in vain for his customer, who did not come. Then she thought of God, who is always there and got absorbed in him getting rid of all sorrows of the universe and got eternal joy. The raja was further told that one is upset on non-fulfilment of the hope and if there is no hope then there is no pain too. The raja then felt satisfied, got rid of the pain and started living happily.

Bhishma further told that anyone, who sacrifices everything and does not keep anything to himself, he is happy as possession of things causes unhappiness. Therefore, a person, who does not possess anything, who is pious and has attained vairagya is happy and none else can be happy in this universe. Non-possession is better than having the rajya of the entire universe. But if a person is not in possession of anything and has ambition to have everything in the universe, cannot remain happy as he shall always be making efforts to have worldly possessions. Similarly, a rich man is either greedy or remains enraged leading to a situation in which he can never remain happy. He quarrels with everyone; he has fear from everyone lest his wealth is stolen by them; he remains upset to have more and more and since there is no end to such collections, he remains always worried. Therefore, one cannot have pleasure without sacrifice. In fact the very ambition of having wealth causes sorrows for a person although he feels satisfied in having more and more wealth aparently but then the wealth creates fear in his mind lest someone might steal it or if it is stolen then he cannot console himself of that loss and so dies an untimely death in pain only. He does not attain peace even after death. Therefore, if a person wants pleasure, then he shall have to give up accumulation of wealth. Even a person, who, out of frustration for not having been able to accumulate wealth, gets detached from such ambition of collecting wealth, gets pleasure in life and after death he would die in peace. On the contrary, if anyone gets everything, he desired and then gives up the same, he is more happy than a person, who is not able to get anything and then gets detached. Bhishma told that joys and sorrows; loss and gain; favourable and unfavourable situations and life and death are all as per destiny. Therefore, rather than worrying for the same, one should have belief in destiny and be happy. In Hindu religion as also in other religions too one gets rid of sorrows on account of loss, death etc. when it is attributed to destiny. Same thing has been written in Ramcharitmanas too.

"हानि लाभ जीवन मरण जसु अपजसु विधि हाथ।"

Yudhisthra further asked out of brothers, fate, wealth and intelligence, on whom should a person depend upon. Bhishma told that the greatest refuge for a person is that of intelligence as intelligence gets a person everything and leads to the well-being of a person. Bali got everything by his intelligence after everything had been taken away by Baman God. Similarly, Prahlad, Neemuch etc. became prosperous because of intelligence. By intelligence one can earn wealth, by intelligence one can control the senses and by intelligence one can attain vairagya and ultimately salvation.

Now let us see how the mankind came into being. Brahma was produced by God to create the universe. He first created brahmins, Marich, Prajapatis etc. Then he created truth, Dharma, tap, vedas, conduct and purification system. Then he produced gods, asuras, gandharvas, snakes, yaksha, rakshasas and spirits and then the human beings. Then the human beings started fighting within themselves. They, therefore, had to be put in an organised way. Manu distributed the mankind into four varnas—brahmin, kshatriya, vaish and shudra. In satya yuga, there were only brahmins. When brahmins started involving in worldly indulgences, then kshatriyas came into being to regulate them. Subsequently as some of the brahmins started cattle grazing, trade etc., vaish were created and those, who could not adjust in any of the above three, became shudras. But since all had their origin in brahmins, they were never denied the right of yagyas, bhakti and reading religious books. Subsequently, respective jobs were assigned to the people of all the varnas, so that there was no overlapping in the discharge of their duties and it was identified as the varnadharma. Everyone, working according to varnadharma, was entitled to attain salvation provided he acted as per dictates of ashramas too. Brahmins were to study vedas and shastras, perform yagyas, accept alms, coaching the varnadharma to the people of other three varnas. They were to be truth-loving, non-jealous toward others, non-rude and with all moral ethics. Those, who were to become kshatriyas had to be brave, interested in fighting, giving alms to brahmins and protection of life and property of the people from external aggression and internal criminals. Those, who, after completion of vedas' studies etc., showed interest in trade, cattle grazing, agriculture, storage of foodgrains etc. became vaishas. The people of all the three varnas had to be pious, clean and truthful. Those, who could not put themselves in above three vocations and were neither clean nor pious, became shudras. If a shudra had attained brahmin-like qualities, then he was no more a shudra but became brahmin. Similarly, people of other varnas could also shift to other varnas after acquiring qualities laid down for those varnas. In this way, although everyone had to proceed as per dharma of his varna, he could change over to other varnas as per his capability. Further, since each person opted the varna of his choice according to his capability, he did not have grudge against the people of other varnas. It was only later that one was recognised by birth and not by the capability as also one could not change the varna subsequently along with the fact that varnas gave place to many castes in each varna, that water-tight compartmentisation started and people of one varna started having grudge against the people of other varnas and strict division, not only on the basis of varna, but on the basis of caste prevailed. In that case, people did not know the varnadharma and in many cases the cast-ridden society did not even know the varnas they belonged to what to speak of non-compliance of varna-dharma and everyone started doing whatever suited him, primarily within the persons of the first three varnas. People of shudra varna, were completely out-cast. Therefore, in course of time, they started having grudge against the people of other varnas and started revolting against the duties and treatmet meted out to them by the persons of other varnas. Since division in varnas was the basic ingredient of the Hindu society, having all its laid down qualities and option to shift from one varna to another after attaining the qualities of the changed varna, the non-observance of the varnadharma led to the anarchy and chaos in society and ultimately in the country. It is basically the non-observance of varna-dharma that India had been subdued by the Muslim conquerors leading to the establishment of Muslim rule for over 600 years.

Let us now consider the other basic ingredient of Hindu society namely the ashramas. Narrating what a person should do from birth to death with a view to prosper in this loka and attain salvation after death, Manu had divided the span of life into four ashramas--Brahmacharya, Grihastha, Vanprastha and Sanyas--of 25 years each, taking the average life of a man as 100 years. A person, acting according to varna-ashrama Dharma, was definitely to lead a peaceful and comfortable life in this universe and ultimately attaining salvation. In brahmcharya asharma, one had to lead a simple, pious life, reading vedas and other shastras, imbibing vedic sanskaras, control over sensual feelings, worshipping God, obeying the guru, living in gurukula away from house and the persons of all varnas living together without any distinction or bias against one another, living on bhiksha (begging) collected and received from the guru after entire collection was entrusted to him. In this way, patience, sacrifice, equality amongst all, obedience, submission, non-arrogance etc, were imbibed in the students. This worked in them till the end of their lives. Therefore, the concept of equality is nothing new to India. It was ever existing in the country.

Grihastha is the second ashrama. After the students have completed their education in brahmcharya ashrama, they enter 'grihastha' ashrama. In this ashrama, one attains satisfaction of Dharma, Artha and Kama. The 'grihastha', therefore, with a view to attaining these three, collects wealth, gets married, produces and brings up children. In fact it is only in this ashrama that one puts himself to the dictates of his varna and is called the root of all ashramas. One has to do yagyas, entertain the guests, give alms to brahmins and to other deserving persons and lead a contented life.

After 'grihastha', one enters into vanprastha. He hands over the household to his son/sons, who by now have become capable of handling the same. In case of a raja, the children come of age and start thinking of becoming raja. It is, therefore, better if rajya is handed over to the capable son otherwise he would throw away the raja (father) and capture the throne, which shall be bad for the father as Aurengzeb had succeeded Shahjahan, putting Shahjahan in house-arrest. Therefore, to avoid such a situation, in Hindu Dharma, the provision of vanprastha has been made. Like the raja, the vaish should also entrust trade etc. to the sons and adopt vanprastha. In vanprastha, one gets completely detached from worldly involvements, live on whatever is available in the forests and devote the entire time to the cause of God. He visits various tirathas, meets rishis, munis, attends satsang and lives as a man, who has renunciated everything—wealth, son, wife, house and other belongings—and live with control on all senses. Wife can accompany in vanprastha, if she does not want to stay with the sons and desires to lead an ascetic life with the husband.

In sanyas, which is fourth and last ashrama, one can either enter after vanprastha or direct from brahmcharya ashrama. Since in vanprastha, the persons would have already got used to the living in forest detached from all worldly involvements and having control over all senses, it would be easier to follow the requirements of sanyas ashrama. Besides what a vanprasthi is required to do, a sanyasi has to visit the towns and villages too frequently but does not stay there permanently rather he cannot stay for more than five nights at one place, and coach Dharma to the people of that place. He lives on bhiksha and accepts bhiksha to the extent of his that day's requirement only. Again in sanyas ashrama, one devotes to the cause of almighty God and attains salvation after death. This is how in Hindu Dharma, care has been taken not only to make the person prosperous in this universe but also attain salvation after death.

Bhishma further narrated the persons, who are of good morality and who are immorals. The persons of good morality are those who—

1. Do not ease or urinate on road, in streets, amidst cows, and in foodgrains.
2. Take bath after easing etc. in the morning and complete worshipping the God.

3. Do not sleep after sun-rise and resort to worshipping in the morning and evening.
4. Take meals after washing feet, hands and mouth, facing east, keeping quiet during eating and take whatever is available without condemning the same. Then again wash hands after finishing meals. Should not sleep with wet feet in the night.
5. Entertain the guests and see that the food served to guests and family-men is the same. The food should be taken in the morning and evening only and not in between. Serve food to brahmins and take remaining only.
6. Perform yagyas and havans. Do not go to woman other than their wives.
7. Do not take non-vegetation meals.
8. Entertain the guru, when he comes.
9. Do not see toward rising sun, a naked woman, other than his wife and have marital relations with the wife only at appropriate period. It shows our knowledge of gynaecology in ancient period.
10. Visit the Tirathas and worship God and ask for the well-being of acquaintances, whenever they meet.
11. Use right hand in all Dharma-related jobs like yagya, giving alms etc.
12. Do not urinate facing the sun. Do not see excreta. Do not sleep with wife on one bed and do not take meals with her in one plate.
13. Do not interfere in others' personal matters, way of worshipping God and way of living.
14. Live as per his varnashrama Dharma.

Yudhisthra wanted to know about soul (Atma) and Parmatma. In this connection, Manu had told Brihaspati that there are two bodies in the person—one this gross body with hands, legs etc. and another subtle body within the bulky body called the soul (atma). As, while in dream, the gross body is asleep, and the subtle body keeps wandering, after leaving this gross body on death, the subtle body gets into another gross body. A person, by dint of his ambitions, goes on living in this universe and so goes on committing sins. The sins come to an end after the ambitions are over and one gets absorbed in Him. The gross body goes on involving itself in worldly indulgences, treating this as happiness although ultimately it results in sorrow. If, however, the subtle body (Atma) in gross body leaves all ambitions of fulfilment of sensual feelings and gets absorbed in God, then there is salvation and the atma then does not get into another specie. Absorption in God is important as by saying a good bye to fulfilment of sensual feelings, one does not attain detachment from the worldly involvements. This is attained only on absorption in the almighty. God is above all sensual feelings of smelling, touching, seeing, hearing etc. and only the pious soul reaches him and gets a feeling of closeness to him. Question then arises as to how one could reach that almighty. It was told that in case of a trouble, whose remedy is not available, one should have thinking about the panacea for all troubles as by thinking about the trouble again and again, it continues getting generated and then starts affecting the health of both gross and subtle bodies. The youth, beauty, life, wealth, non-ailment and meeting the beloveds are mortal and one should try to get rid of these attachments as such attachment only leads to sorrows. The trouble, which is faced by all, should not be a cause of worry for a single man but still try to get rid of the same. In the life, sorrows are more than the joys and a person involved in fulfilment of worldly ambitions is in continuous trouble. A man, who does not care for sorrows and joys, gets absorbed in God and then there are no sorrows for him. For reaching the God, the brain has to get rid of thinking about worldly involvements and enter the heart. In that situation, he falls into samadhi and then reaches God. Like the five senses are away from the subtle body, God is away from nature and the subtle body after crossing natural instincts only reaches God. One becomes happy following the tenets of Dharma and falls in infamy in getting involved in worldly indulgences.

Therefore, one should leave the indulgences and the moment the minute body is away from these indulgences, he finds Brahma everywhere and then attains salvation getting rid of rebirths' cycle otherwise it goes on changing from one specie to another. When one reaches Brahma, one can only feel the closeness but cannot explain or narrate the same. Therefore, by knowledge, one trains brain, by brain one reaches heart and by heart one realises the existence of almighty and then by further advancement, he attains his closeness. God is everywhere, every time and soul (subtle body) is also ever existing. It is, therefore, only the question of the meeting of the two and this is possible where soul is free from all sensual and worldly involvements.

Bhishma then narrated the Paramyoga, the basis of attaining salvation. Once one pupil asked his guru to advise him where he had come from in this universe, from where others have come and also to tell the supreme truth (परम तत्व). The guru told that it was the spiritual truth and essence of all shastras. Truth, knowledge, yagya, patience, control over senses, simplicity and supreme truth are all parts of Krishana only. He is also known as Brahma, Mahadeva and Vishnu too. Same Brahma had come as incarnate in Krishana. The guru considered the pupil eligible to listen to it. The guru did not narrate everything to everyone. He first considered whether the questioner was eligible for it or not and finding him eligible only, he taught what was asked for. On the outset Krishana is the Brahma. He has created the entire universe. He, at the beginning of the universe, created vedas, shastras and Dharmas, which lapsed at the end of each yuga and were then recreated by rishis by dint of their tapasya.

The rishis, gods, asuras had known the almighty. As one lamp lightens many others without any effect on it, so the nature produced many things and still continues unaffected. Out of the nature, the supreme truth is also born. This gives birth to pride. Pride produces space and space produces air; air produces fire and fire produces water. They all combinedly produced the beings and other commodities of the universe. Then there are five gyan senses, five action senses, five sensual feelings and one mind—sixteen in all. They get destroyed in course of time. Ears, skin, tongue, eyes and nose are gyan senses; hands, legs, anus, sex and speech are five action senses. Sound, touch, taste, beauty, and smell are five sensual feelings and these are common in all beings. Then there is mind. Mind is in existence everywhere. These sixteen elements worship the almighty through soul, which is not visible and can be seen only by yoga. So by the sixteen senses, we recognise and see the soul and by soul, the Parmatma and having seen Parmatama, the human being gets absorbed in him and attains salvation. But the sixteen senses run towards the involvements of universe and thus go away from the soul. When, therefore, soul is recognised by these sixteen senses, the soul proceeds toward's the almighty. In other words, when the sixteen senses leave the universal involvements and come closer to soul, the soul gets closer to Parmatama. The pious persons always adopt this method of reaching Parmatma via soul, when soul is above the three ingredients—happiness, rage and sorrows or satoguna, rajoguna and tamoguna respectively. This body comprises of five ingredients, earth, air, water, fire and space and satva, rajo and tamo gunas are imbibed in these five ingredients and go on increasing and decreasing as per one's actions. One should keep continuous efforts to leave tamo and rajo gunas, although this body gets attracted by these gunas more, and reach satoguna only to attain salvation. Happiness, happy alliance, loss of suspicions, courage and rememberance are all satogunas. Passions, rage, pride, greed, affection, fear, tiredness, sorrows, and unhappiness, are rajo and tamo gunas. A person gets effected by rajoguna and indulges in adharmik actions getting involved in worldly passions and attachments. Under influence of tamoguna, he becomes greedy and enraged and acts accordingly getting always lost. A person with satoguna, always yearns for satvik actions and becomes quite pious and bright with knowledge and faith.

Bhishma then told that human being is best of all the beings and brahmins are best in human beings. Brahmins are well aware of the supreme truth and atma-Parmatama relation. The following of the Dharma to supreme truth leads a person to absorption in almighty. Speech, body, piousness, to excuse, truth, courage and remembrance are the ingredients of Dharma, which alone enable one to reach Brahma. Dharma differs from varna to varna and ashrama to ashrama. Brahmcharya ashrama is toughest of all. A Brahmchari has to keep aloof of rajoguna and tamoguna, should not take and listen about women, should not see a naked woman as that leads to rajoguna arising in him. If passions arouse in a brahmchari, he should reduce intake of food for nine days. If the passions still do not subdue then he should take bath in a river and if there is nightfall, then he should take bath in a river. There is a vein passing through the heart, through which passes the semen of the man taken out from the entire body in case the passion arouses. If a brahmchari, sees a woman, comes in her contact or gets aroused after thinking of a woman, his semens come out either by over-eating or when passions arous in thinking of the women during sleep or when one is awake. One should, therefore, keep his mind in control by acting without any consideration. In this way he is able to reduce rajo and tamo gunas and acts as per his wishes. If a man is able to preserve semen in youth, he would be well off in old age and a well matured person is able to strengthen his will power as time passes and this power does not get reduced ever. Such a person, with strong will power, is able to kill all his faults and is able to control all his sensual feelings and ultimately gets absorbed in almighty God. Therefore, one should act as per command of mature mind, body and brain to reach the almighty.

To save oneself from nightfall, the brahmchari should give up sleeping as during sleep, one gives chance for rajo and tamo gunas increasing and satoguna being subdued. When one keeps awake, one is able to control his sensual feelings and preserve semen, which helps in creation of satoguna and will-power.

A man, who does not know about God, visible things, nature and man, he cannot get absorbed in almighty God. These can be known through Dharma or control over sensual feelings and detachment from universal involvements. A well-matured person should at first understand nature and the man and then the supreme truth. Once he has known the supreme truth, the closeness to almighty God is not far off. The nature and the man are the creations of this universe, which can be realised from normal activities in this universe and indulgence in the three gunas—sato, rajo and tamo. As already indicated, the reduction of rajo and tamo, in the creation of man and nature leads to recognition of God by dint of having satoguna only. The Brahmchari is also supposed to exercise tapasya by heart and body. Brahmcharya and non-violence are bodily tapsyas and control of speech is heart's tapasya. The knowledge attained by these tapsyas is only responsible for killing tamo and rajo gunas and increase of satoguna. Those, who, subsequently, take refuge under God, reach the goal of salvation and do not have to again come in the universe on rebirth. By semens only self-consciousness can be attained. Since self-consciousness is part of the body then it should remain in body after death too but it does not happen so. Self-consciousness goes out of body after death. Therefore, self-conscious soul is different from the body. As even non-believers too cure themselves by remembering gods through mantras etc. and if according to them soul is also considered to have vanished with death, then their deeds too shall have no effect after death and then there shall be nothing like sufferance or enjoyment as per deeds and the person shall born on rebirth with a clean slate without having to do with the deeds before death in previous life. But since this is not so and one gets the specie on rebirth according to one's deeds in previous life, this confirms existence of self-conscious soul distinct from body, and soul does not vanish with the death nor does it take any shape. It only enters in another specie without changing itself. Those, who take body as soul too, they only suffer in life and can never get peace in their lifetime as they shall always be after happiness through sensual or bodily feelings, which are only farce.

Therefore, those persons, who are desirous of attaining salvation, they should give up self, affection, involvement in worldly passions and over-ambitiousness as without sacrificing these, they cannot reach the desired goal. In shastras, the sacrifice of wealth is stated to be by yagyas and actions, sacrifice of passions by vrats and bodily pleasures by tapasya and sacrifice of everything (self, affection, involvement and passion) by yoga. This is the climax of sacrifice. Having established that body and soul are separate entities, body may be categorised as kshetra and the self-conscious soul as the kshatraja. The kshetraja exists in body but is not effected by the actions of the body or kshetra. It only carries the deeds from kshetra (body) only after death.

To clear the entire narration, it is said that this matter had been discussed by a brahmin with Raja Janaka, when Raj Janaka had stated that he had absolved himself from worldly attachments. The brahmin put Mithila Nagari to fire. Raja Janaka was not upset at all and told others that he had a vast treasure of self-consciousness and the burning of Mithila Nagari had no effect on him. The brahmin also heard Janaka saying so and understood his inner feelings. He again made the Nagari as before as the brahmin was God himself, who had come to test the consciousness of Janaka. Brahmin then disclosed his identity and blessed Janaka that his brain be always indulged in self-consciousness and he would remain renunciated from worldly passions and attain supreme truth. God then went away. This is the God and Jeeva relation, where God goes on testing the Jeeva of his convictions and having crossed the test , the Jeeva is duly blessed. The writer has here indicated that one can live in 'grihastha' and still renunciate worldly involvements and attachments. Yudhisthra desired to know a person, who, while living in 'grihastha', with his wife, could control his senses and cross worldly indulgences remaining aloof and with courage as such a person was difficult to be found. Bhishma pointed out that Brahmrishi Deval was one such person. He was well-versed with vedas and shastras and was active, dharmik and worshipper of gods and brahmins. He had one daughter Suvarchala, who was full of all qualities, neither very short nor very tall or thin. She came of marriageable age. The father thought of marrying her with a learned brahmin, who should be tapasvi and unmarried. The daughter, however, said that her husband should be blind and at the same time should have eyes. Father was surprised how a person could be blind and at the same time having eyes. The girl, however, said that she had said so duly thinking over the matter and wanted such a husband only. She asked father to call eligible brahmins and she shall select one. The rishi asked his pupils to call all eligible bachelors. The pupils gave publicity to the proposal. Many brahmin boys came there. The daughter told the gathering that a blind with eyes could only be her husband. The brahmins condemned her as 'mad' and went away. Then one Swetketu rishi came there after listening to the entire incident. Deval entertained him and asked his daughter to accept him as her husband as he was quite learned and well-versed with vedas and shastras. The daughter saw him duly raged but Swetketu told her that he fulfilled her requirments as he was a blind man but being without any doubts he had got eyes too. The eyes are those, which see the Parmatama through the inner senses and knowledge and having those eyes, he is a man with eyes too. He had been doing all jobs in the world but being self-conscious he did not indulge in the same and had a contented life depending upon what is there in fate. He was also able to make up the livelihood for both. Suvarchala then accepted him as her husband but actual marriage as per shastras, she said, shall be held by his father, for which he shall ask her hand from her father. Here the matters of protocol involved are that the husband should be to the requirements of the bride; he should be able to feed her and the bride should only accept him in principle but, the marriage was to be held as per shastras' provision with the consent of the father, for which the groom to be had to ask for the bride's hand. The rishi then worshipped the groom Swetketu and married her daughter with him in the presence of other munis with promises taking water in hand. Therefore, the marriage was held as per shastras and shastras provided for marriage to be witnessed by other persons. All promises as per shastras had to be either before fire or water. Rama had undertaken friendship with Sugreeva before fire and with Vibheesan taking water in hand. At present too marriages are complete after Saptpadi around fire. Swetketu asked his wife to live as a wife as provided in shastras. She should act as desired by him and then he shall do whatever she asked for. He also asked her to forget the egos that so and so work was hers, and so and so not her's. So she should have pride and affection and he too agreed to live in the same fashion. They produced several children, worshipped the gods and lived without any dispute. Once Suvarchala asked her husband, who he was.Then the husband told that she already knew that he was a brahmin then what else did she want to know. The wife replied that she wanted to know it from his heart but husband said that heart did not speak and it neither had any name or gotra. this is relevant to the body only. The brahmin further told that for attaining salvation, one have to realise self first and then he goes to God's loka. Such a person is yogi and his bhakta. Therefore, one in 'grihastha' had to live in the universe according to the dictates of the society. He too had been living like that only. Man boasts of 'me' and 'mine' but it is only out of confusion. As the earth and space seem to be different but are in existence because of one another, so man and Brahma, though appear differently, are one and the same. Like soul, Brahma cannot be seen or felt or touched but can be known only by self consciousness. Having heard the institution of self-consciousness and its relation with Brahma, Suvarchala felt satisfied. They lived in peace doing all worldly jobs and entrusted all jobs to almighty God and after living for long, attained salvation. In this way, the 'grihastha' can lead their life in the universe living as husband and wife and still attain salvation. Main thing is the control over senses and mind otherwise one cannot have self realisation without which it is not possible to have closeness to God and so no salvation too. Control over senses and mind leads to there being no miserliness, no rage, contentment, not thinking about others' faults, simplicity, having mercy on all beings, truth-speaking, non-jealous and no worry for the sorrows . Such a person has no enmity with anyone. He remains alike when praised or when condemned, with moral conduct, happy and courageous. Such a man gets fame in the universe and then attains salvation.

Bhishma further told that a person has three debts on his head—one toward parents, second toward rishis or guru and the third towards God. After birth, the debt toward parents starts and on living in gurukula to have education, the debt towards guru is caused and then by living in the universe, favours are asked from God. So that is the debt towards God. Now after one produces children, he is absolved from the debt towards parents. Study of vedas and shastras and then coaching others obsolves him of the debt towards rishis and gurus and performance of yagyas, absolves him from the debt towards God. Therefore, one should complete the 'grihastha' ashram and having absolved oneself of the three debts, enter the next ashramas i.e. the vanprastha or sanyas.

Shukdeva asked his father Vyasa as to how a learned person knowing the contents of vedas and holding yagyas could know Brahma, who could neither be imagined nor presumed to be existing or whom even vedas do not prescribe with any definite shape etc. Further, he asked by which out of sankhya,yoga, tap, brahmcharya and full sacrifice, or intelligence, one can realise the Supreme truth. Vyasa replied that one cannot have self-realisation wihtout full sacrifice, education, tap and cantrol over senses. All ingredients in making a being are the first creation of God. It is at first made with earth; perspiration and liquids are formed in the body by water; eyes are given by fire and life is given by air and nose, ears etc.; holes are because of space. These parts have their respective senses and are called five gyan senses. Their functions are five other senses and over and above these ten senses is mind that governs all these senses.

The mind takes the senses towards indulgence in worldly passions but the soul rules over the mind if that is under control. Then one gets absolved from the effect of senses too and remains under control. The soul is in other words the part of Parmatama too and when the senses are under control then there is the combination of soul and Parmatama otherwise the soul does not reach Parmatama. Then there is the 'Kal' too, which is always after taking the soul out of the body, whenever it finds appropriate time but having absorbed in Parmatama, the function of the soul cannot be questioned by 'Kal' too as Parmatama is the 'Kal' of 'Kal'. Such a union of Atma and Parmatama is by 'yoga'. Then the yoga is the union of all senses, mind and brain with the soul. For this, the senses have to be kept under control leading to the control of mind and brain too. For this purpose, the mind has to be brought round and entrusted to soul. This can be done by control over senses first and then by practice it can be done. Once it is done, then one can have the feeling of closeness with Brahma. A yogi, who practises the control of senses, brain and mind by Atma, could reach the stage of Samadhi, when he forgets everything of the universe and gets absorbed in Brahma within a period of six month. By practice again the duration of the Samadhi could he extended by-and-by. This would he possible in forests, caves, temples or even in a quiet corner of the house.

Then Shukdeva asked the position of human being while he is active in doing his jobs and while he leaves doing his jobs. In other word these are 'Karma' and 'Gyan'. Further, by doing 'Karma' with consideration in mind, one gets involved in worldly indulgenses and by 'gyan' one gets absolved of the same. Even some people consider that by control on senses, they have attained 'gyan' even when mind and brain have not been under control. Such a situation is that of semi-gyan and in such a situation, whereas one enjoys the life, one cannot attain salvation. So it is complete 'gyan', i.e., control over senses, mind and brain through soul only, which can take the person to absorption in Brahma, giving him the attainment of salvation. Vyasaji further told that human body, senses and mind etc. are vanishable and these exist with the existence of soul of 'kshetraj' only. These do not know about soul being immortal but the soul knows them. So the first thing is that senses and the passions over-power the same. Thus mind is powerful and controls passions and mind is controlled by brain and brain is controlled by soul. Nature controls the soul and nature is controlled by Parmatama. Therefore, there is a hierarchy of all these— one being stronger than the other or the controller of others in hierarchy of senses , passions, mind, brain, soul, nature and then

Parmatama. One has to have control over senses, passions, mind and brain to realise the Atma and then Atma has to reach Parmatama through the channel of nature. Absorption of Atma in Parmatama through the nature is the yoga. For doing any action 'Karma', there are three channels. At first the person makes up a mind for doing certain job,then brain analyses and confirms its doing or dropping; then the soul considers its good and bad points and then only gives clearance for doing it. So like the present day hierarchy in administration, there is hierarchy in one's body too. After the clearance by soul, the orders for execution of the job again pass in reverse direction through the entire hierarchy as in the ascending order. Then there is the combination of clearance of good or bad deeds by the soul. The clearance of bad deeds leads to destruction or more and more indulgence in worldly attains or tomoguna, clearance of some and with-holding of others bring one to rajoguna and clearance of only good deeds and withholding of bad deeds leads to satoguna or closeness to the almighty and ultimately salvation. Having achieved satoguna, one does not indulge in passions of the universe even in the company of wife, sons etc. as Janaka had been living in 'grihastha' without any indulgence in worldly involvements. Deeds undertaken without any consideration wash off the earlier deeds executed with consideration. Therefore, there is a provision of vanprastha and sanyas, when one embraces God by full control on senses, passions, mind, brain leading to the union of soul and Parmatama, which, though can be undertaken during 'grihastha' but it is very difficult to attain such a control while in 'grihastha', where he had been enjoying all these fulfilments all through, eversince he entered 'grihastha' ashrama after brahmcharya.

Now we come to passions (काम), rage (क्रोध) and pride (अभिमान) on which rests the entire human being with the mind. One, who is able to control these elements, would cross the pains of old age and death but one, who, with a view to have pleasure, indulges in these elements, goes on getting more and more involved after which there is no retrace or coming back except with the help of strict observance of yoga tap controlling all senses, mind, brain etc. As already indicated, the body comprises of earth, water, air, fire and space. The jobs of earth are providing a base, reproduction, smell, further extension, establishment. The jobs of water are to provide coolness, liquidity, taste, rotting, greasing, tongue, freezing etc. The jobs of fire are to provide heat, burning, cooking, lighting, sorrow, to alight, to sharpen, to rise above etc. The jobs of air are to talk, to walk, strength to listen, extraction of wastes and urine from the body and to work. The jobs of the space are noise, absorption, having holes, to take refuge of a non-being, non-rotting, seeing, hearing, etc. The jobs of mind are courage, analyse, cleverness, to remember, to assume,to excuse, to determine good or bad points, The jobs of the brain are to destroy good or bad instincts, to think, to console, to remedy, to doubt and to decide.

Yudhisthra then asked what is death, how does it take place, who dies, why death takes place. Bhishma told that when brahma created universe, many beings were born so much so that even Brahma did not like so many beings to exist. There was no space left where there was no being. Then all started getting choked. Then Brahma thought of reducing the beings. After thinking over the problem for a long time, he produced fire and started burning the universe with that fire. Then God Shiva came to Brahma. Brahma told him to ask for any boon. Shiva told him that he had himself created this universe and now he was destroying it. He should not, therefore, burn them. Brahma told that he was not in rage nor he desired to destroy the universe. What he wanted was to reduce the burden on earth by killing some, as earth has been after him for reduction of burden on her. Shiva asked him to be cool as this fire shall destroy everything on the earth which may neither be the intention of earth nor of Brahma and think of some other alternative to reduce the burden of earth. Shiva then asked Brahma to recreate the burnt beings etc. Brahma then recreated them and in this way the system of birth, death of each being was fixed and accordingly birth and death started taking place at the fixed time as rostered by Brahma at the time of birth of each being.

Yudhisthra wanted to know what Dharma is, whether it is the deeds to attain pleasure in this universe, or it is the deeds to enjoy after death or it is the deeds executed to enjoy in this universe as also after death. Bhishma told that compliance of tenets of Dharma give pleasure in this universe as also after death. The sinners, however, do not observe the tenets of Dharma. Therefore, they have agony in this universe as well as after death although initially such people may have some pleasure. The sinners do not follow Dharma even when they are in trouble and the compliers of the tenets of Dharma do not plead for causing sins even while in trouble. Further, one should not usurp the wealth of others. Some people usurp others' money by dint of their strength but when they become weak, they take refuge under Dharma only. Therefore, since one is neither always strong nor weak and as such one should not be rude or crude in one's mentality. One, who does not commit any fault, is not afraid of anyone. A person with good moral character does not have anyone's fear and remains happy always. Alms-giving is also a Dharma although some people call it the Dharma by the poors to extract money from the rich but the same rich people too consider alms taking or giving as a Dharma. Therefore, one is neither rich nor poor always. The situation goes on changing. One should not behave with others in a way that one does not want to be meted out to him. When the money with one is more than one's requirement, one should lend to others. For this purpose, God has provided for lending the money on interest.

अतिरिक्तैः संविभजेद् भोगैरन्यानकिंचनान्,
एतस्मात् कारणाद् धात्रा कुसीदं सम्प्रवर्तितम्। (259/23)

Further, the man should stick to the way of living as adopted by gods or to depend on Dharma for the sake of earning more money. Whatever is gained from others on good behaviour is Dharma itself and a bad behaviour earns adharma. This, therefore, is the difference between Dharma and adharma. But Yudhisthra did not agree to the definition of Dharma indicated by Bhishma. He, on the contrary, stated that Dharma creates the beings, Dharma brings them up and causes their uplift but Dharma cannot be judged from the provision in vedas only. For a man in trouble, Dharma is different from that for a man in good position. This fact cannot be known from vedas. As the water in a small pond is finished after a few cows have taken it and that of canal finishes after it is used for irrigating agricultural farms, so is the position of vedic Dharma, which shall vanish with the advent of kalyug, because in kalyug some people shall act as per Dharma to meet the selfish ends; some in others' interest and still some act on Dharma due to some other reason. Therefore, Dharma in kalyug is different from Dharma in other yugas, like Darona fought in departure from his varnadharma and Viswamitra being a kshatriya became brahmrishi. One may prosper by following one tenet of Dharma while the other may suffer because of the same. So Dharma changes with time, and from person to person. Dharma can be applied in kalyug by—

(1) Working for the well-being of others and be friendly to all.

(2) Not cheating the people.

(3) Neither opposing others nor begging from anyone. Nor have ill-will against others.

(4) Being strict in one's dealings and not interfering in others' jobs.

(5) Having same treatment with all and not biased in favour or against others.

(6) Not seeing towards bad things; not listening to bad thing and

not being attracted towards passions.

(7) Not having any fear from others nor trying to be of any fear to others.

(8) Following the way followed by matured persons, who have sons and grandsons and conduct themselves according to the provision of shastras.

(9) Following the Dharma of non-violence and neither killing beings nor selling them.

(10) Doing one's job and leaving the result to God.

(11) Not resorting to be rude or crude towards fellow beings.

(12) Doing all jobs looking into Dharmik or adharmik aspect imbibed in the same.

(13) Not becoming greedy as greed leads to individual in all sorts of bad deeds to earn more and more money.

(14) Performing yagyas as per shastras without any consideration as yagyas with consideration become adharmik.

(15) Following the policy of ahinsa but the raja should not resort to ahinsa in case of battle with the enemies where a lot of killings are a must or in punishing the criminals otherwise the criminals shall live in the kingdom causing nuisance to others.

Now we come to attaining closeness to Brahma by usage of available resources in all ashramas. This is—

1. By following the way presented in vedas.
2. By sacrificing the available resources leaving greed and using resources for giving alms and indulging in deeds of well-being of others and spending without any consideration.
3. By acting as per Dharma applicable to each ashrama in which the human being is placed at a particular time in equal behaviour with all, being content, pious, simple, unassuming, and God fearing.
4. By following the way of truth.
5. By worshipping God without keeping any consideration in mind.
6. By resorting to vedas and shastras as following Dharma may not be a clean path to be followed.
7. By following Dharma prescribed in shastras applicable to each ashrama.

8. By properly analysing good or bad actions and resorting to only good jobs.
9. By being contented and prepared to sacrificing everything.
10. By being kind to all beings, excusing others, being simple in living, and controlling the sensual feelings.
11. By giving up all fulfilment of passions in the universe as could come up on possessing more money like drinking, womanising, being cruel to others, gambling etc.

Yudhisthra then asked replies to four questions—

(1) How does one become sinner?
(2) How does one follow Dharma?
(3) What forces one to adopt vairagya?
(4) How does one attain salvation?

Bhishma told Yudhisthra that although he had the knowledge of all Dharmas yet he was asking these questions for the general benefit of the public at large and to raise his image in public. He told that (1) The human being first wishes to enjoy hearing, touching, seeing, tasting and smelling good things. Then he develops special taste for one of these and develops liking for the same and tries to achieve the same and starts enjoying other feelings and develops taste for some and hatred for others. Then one falls into greed and then in affection for the same. Then his brain goes away from Dharma and showingly only shows his love for Dharma, earns wealth by cheating others and puts his entire brain to achieve more and more wealth inspite of being checked by guru, relations etc. and goes on working for the same and even projects some provision in shastras to confirm his conviction. But the people know of his faults and the sinners like him follow him. Such people can have pleasure in this universe and not after death. Such people become sinners. (2) So far as Dharmatama people are concerned, they get the share of Dharma as and when they work for the well-being of others and thus attain salvation. A person, who is able to analyse good and bad things, starts following good persons only by satsang etc. Then his brain gets absorbed in good things only and puts himself in Dharma and earns friendship of such persons only and then attains salvation after enjoying life in the universe in all respects. (3) Such persons do not become very happy even after having attained Dharma, and proceeds toward vairagya distracting himself from sensual feelings. (4) Then they take the universe as mortal and try to achieve pleasure after death. This is how they start preparing themselves for attaining salvation. They leave sensual feelings and all works leading to commitment of sins and proceed as per tenets of Dharma leading to attainment of salvation. It, therefore, shows that either one can proceed to own pleasures in this universe by submitting oneself to all kinds of sensual enjoyments falling in greed etc. or care for the life after death and adopt a life of Dharma leaving all sensual enjoyments and thus attain salvation.

One, who proceeds to attain salvation have to leave rage, greed and resort to sacrifice, courage and truthfulness. Then one enters the field of yoga, then samadhi and ultimately absorption in the almighty, and does not then have to revisit the universe in any specie otherwise one shall have to change from one specie to another and then still another and so on till ultimately he adopts the way of Dharma and attains salvation. Thus being neither belongs to anyone nor anyone belongs to him. It is only after the being adopts one body, he starts loving that body and falls into the trap of pleasures and sorrows relating to the feelings by that body on the basis of sensual attractions and thinks in terms of immortality of that body and its enviorns forgetting that the life was to end and was not for ever. When at some stage he realises the mortality of life, he runs to take refuge under some immortal support that is Dharma to make him reach the almighty God.

Yudhisthra then asked a personal question that the Pandavas were very rude and crude. They had killed their brothers, relatives and gurus for the sake of attaining kingdom. The greed, therefore, made them do all these undesirable actions. Raja Janaka, who had said that he was passing a very nice life as he did not have anything of his own nor did he have affection for anything and that even if entire Mithila was burnt, he did not lose anything. Such a situation is achieved when one has reached above the stage of any greed and in such a situation since he does not own anything, he does not have to worry for its loss too. Also when one sacrifices everything, he does not develop any greed and thus gets all pleasures in life.

Death is a must for everyone, whether he is follower of Dharma or otherwise. The only difference between the two is that a person not following Dharma reborns after death in another specie and thus continues in that cycle, changing one specie after another whereas the person following salvation and when he is thus successful in his efforts, he is absolved from the cycle of rebirth. The universe is nothing but a 'mayachakra' instituted by God and one revolves in this 'mayachakra' by continuous indulgence in worldly involvements, born again and again and one who gets absolved from these indulgences, gets closer and closer to almighty and ultimately absorbing in Him.

There is protocol followed by gods too in their day-to-day dealings. It is said that once Prajapati Daksha held a yagya in Himalayas. All Prajapatis, Gandharvas, apsarss, Prithvi, all gods, rakshasas, nagas, Aditya, Vasu, Narada, rishis etc. as were invited, had reached in the yagya. Dadhichi saw that all gods, rishi etc. were there but shiva was not there. He told that no yagya is Dharmik without Shiva having been worshipped. Then in meditation he saw Shiva, Parvati, Narada etc. and he felt satisfied. He was definite that all gods had joined in not inviting Shiva. Dadhichi left the yagyashala and said that one is sinner if one worships the unworshipables and does not worship the worshipable. He said God Shiva is the creator of entire universe and protector of them all and, therefore, they shall all see Shiva present in the yagya. Daksha said that he knew many Rudras around here and does not know any Mahesh besides these Rudras. Dadhichi told that he did not recognise anyone other than Shiva as Rudra and since it is true, the yagya shall get destroyed. Daksha, however, said that Vishnu is the only God above all others and he, therefore, shall worship God Vishnu only in the yagya. Parvati, was worried how she could manage Shiva getting his share in the yagya. Shiva, however, told her that since the yagya without Shiva had annoyed her, he shall produce a person, who shall destroy the yagya. He accordingly produced that person and asked him to destroy the yagya. He destroyed the yagya in no time. That person was subsequently known as Virbhadra. All gods present in the yagya became upset. There was all chaos everywhere. Then Daksha, Brahma and other gods asked him who he was. He indicated that he had been directed by Shiva to destroy the yagya and the lady accompanying him was Bhadrakali sent by Parvati to assist him. He advised them all to take refuge under Shiva. They then praised Shiva. Shiva appeared. He was worshipped and then he restored the yagya. This episode indicates that:—

(1) Even gods have to undertake performing yagyas to please the other gods.

(2) There is a system of sending invitation cards as are sent to relations and friends in marriages etc. social functions or political functions like republic day parade etc.

(3) Those, who are not on good terms, are not invited in the yagya, functions etc.

(4) That uninvited god/persons left out of enmity get enraged and take revenge. Here Shiva not having been invited by Daksha, got enraged and destroyed the yagya. Therefore, it is better to go taking all along with oneself.

(5) Rather than continuing enmity, one should submit or have alliance if the god/person so annoyed is more powerful. It is definite that such annoyance shall get mitigated in course of time and in this way the purpose shall be served, and then the ultimate result is always to the benefit of all.

On Yudhisthra asking obout spiritualism, Bhishma told that earth, air, space, water and fire go into the making or unmaking of a person. The person lives and acts in this universe because of these five elements. After death all these elements get mixed up in the universe in their respective elements, and rejoin again on rebirth. So there is some other element to join them and break them. That is soul (Jeevatma), which functions in combination of other senses created by five elements indicated above. So the body of the five elements and senses is the living person with soul. Soul never dies with the death of the human being and joins another specie of the same five elements and senses. The body and soul are creation of the overall Lord Parmatama. So the soul is part of that Parmatama and the relation between soul and Parmatama is the spiritualism. How the soul gets absorbed in Parmatama has already been discussed in detail. So it is spiritualism which enables atma to get absorbed in Parmatama and thus attain salvation.

Yudhisthra further asked that all human beings in the universe go on having fear of sorrows, pains and death. Bhishma was, therefore, requested to tell some way of becoming free from such a fear. Bhishma told that similar question was raised by Narada to Samaga rishi, when the latter advised that he did not have any fear because—

1. He knows the past, present and future of all elements. Since it is same for all, he is not afraid of any situation—sorrow, pains or death.
2. Like other living beings, serious natured, unhonoured and progressive persons, he too was living. So there is no difference in him and others.
3. Those with thousand of rupees live, those with hundred also live and those who do not have a single rupee also live and he too lived with them all.

4. All happiness and sorrows taking place as per dictates of Dharma or fate, one should not worry in case of sorrow and feel very happy in case of happiness.
5. He had, therefore, left worrying for the sorrows and had rather tried to keep his senses under the control.
6. Having pride, greed, getting enraged etc. are, therefore, of no use as all have to live in the universe in their respective species and environ and since all sorrows are followed by joys and all joys are followed by sorrows, he did not feel overjoyed in the event of happiness thinking that sorrows are not far away. Therefore, he remains same in all sorrows and joys.
7. Since wife, sons, relations etc. cannot help one get rid of pains, one has to face, there is no use of keeping any attachment with them and try to get away from those pains by less and less involvement in the universe as involvement causes sorrows and pains.
8. The dear things give happiness, happiness in turn raise pride and pride in turn leads to Narka. It is, therefore, better one leaves all these three—happiness, pride and way to 'narka'.
9. Once one leaves wealth and ambitions, one gets rid of greed and affection and after that one is free to move in the universe without any worry.
10. Like a man, having taken Amrit, does not have fear of death, he too did not have any fear of death, adharma, greed and other fears.
11. He has come to this conclusion after prolonged tapsya. Therefore any environ of sorrows does not worry him.

This is how one can get rid of all fears and sorrows and pains as concluded by our rishis etc. So getting absolved of the sensual feelings is the root cause of getting rid of all sorrows and pains in this universe. A man involved in worldly pleasures, although gets momentary pleasures, is not aware that because of those pleasures, he was getting closer to the perpetual sorrows and riddance from those sorrows is the salvation, which can be attained by vairagya, which in turn is possible only after detaching oneself from wealth, wife, son, home, sensual pleasures etc. As every action has a reaction, so every deed gives good or bad results. The results have to be faced even if one at first having done all bad deeds subsequently resorts to good deeds. In that case the account of good and bad deeds has to be settled respectively for each of the two.

Bhishma also told that the wealth gained by brahmin out of alms; by kshatriya out of conquests; by vaish earned out of agriculture, trade, and by shudras by serving the people of other three varnas, is a matter of appreciation by all in the universe and its investment in jobs relevant to Dharma gives the best results. If a brahmin is not able to earn livelihood out of his profession, then he can resort to the vocation of kshatriya or even of vaish but not of shudra. Similarly, a kshatriya can take up vaish's vocation and a vaish can work as shudra. Subsequently they can come to their original varnas' job, when position eases. Similarly, a shudra can resort to agriculture, cattle grazing, trade or industry for earning his livelihood. But whatever vocation is adopted, one should follow the Dharma of that varna and should be recognised as such in the society. That is why at the time of Sita Swayamber, arrangement for seating of the public was made according to their then existing position and not as per varnas.

"उत्तम मध्यम नीच लघु, निज निज थल अनुहारि"।

This shows the strictness in following the Dharma of one's varna and at the same time flexibility in changing from one varna to another and recognition in the society accordingly. One should not, however, do the work of another varna while remaining in one varna such as Darona, while remaining as a brahmin resorted to kshatriya's job in taking arms against the Pandavas. This was wrong as per ethics of varnashrama Dharma.

Similarly, in the case of ashrama, after brahmcharya, one enters 'grihastha' and falls in the rut of earning livelihood, producing children, running the household in whatever varna one is placed. After 'grihastha' one should resort to vanprastha and sanyas as without these one is not able to attain salvation. In this way one has to lead a tough life as brahmchari and then a leisurely life as 'grihastha' and again tougher life as vanprasthi and sanyasi. This shows that in Hindu Dharma, right from the beginning, one is told about non-attachment with worldly involvement and one should be able to renounce the same anytime without any grudge. In 'grihastha', one is trapped by greed, pride, affection of children and under these cloaks one starts earning money by wrong actions etc. to fulfil the requirements of family but at the same time keeps in mind that he should not very much indulge in these as after sometime he had to resort to vanprastha leaving all that had been collected in 'grihastha'. In other words the advent of vanprastha and sanyas checks one from much indulgence in worldly involvements as he is aware that he is to leave them all here. In vanprastha, everyone has a right to perform tapsya irrespective of the varna he belonged to. In other words there is no sanctity of varna and all are equal in brahmcharya and again in vanprastha and sanyas. So one does not feel much difference between the people of various varnas as this difference was temporary limited to about 25 years of 'grihastha' only and then all are equal and continue to be so upto death. That is why when a rishi had put a shudra pupil on his asan and Balrama had killed him, when he saw the shudra on rishi's asan, Balrama was considered to have earned the sin of a brahm-hatya (killing of a brahmin) and Balrama had to repent for it. Therefore, per force, a person, irrespective of the varna, he belongs to, does not involve in worldly indulgence during 'grihastha' ashrama since he had again to leave them on vanprastha/sanyas and does not fall in much affection of family created by him, which too is for a short time and had to be left in course of time.

Everyone has a right of tapsya as tapsya leads one to swarga and all are equal on way to swarga and one rises above the concept of varna, ashrama, caste etc. in vanprastha or sanyas, in performing tapsya or yagyas in changing from one varna to another on attaining the qualities of the other varna. It is, therefore, in the end, the deeds—good or bad—which count and not the varna or ashrama or even caste. Even a raja. who has not walked on earth and had been in all leisures and pleasures, has to leave all those leisures and pleasures and live in forests like all others, eating as available in forests and sleeping on earth etc. The raja, therefore, does not completely give up laborious or strenuous life even when he rules so that it does not become very difficult for him when he resorts to vanprastha. Our Dharma (even in 'grihastha') also teaches to have full control on senses and keep oneself detached from worldly attractions during 'grihastha' ashrama.

Yoga shastra: Yudhisthra asked to be told about the difference in sankhya and yoga shastras. Bhishma told that persons well-versed in sankhya praise sankhya and those well-versed in 'yoga' praise yoga system. The yoga people say that no one can attain salvation without accepting the existence of Ishwar. Therefore, Ishwar only grants salvation. Sankhya people on the other hand say that after knowing all existing situations, one who absolves himself from passions, attains salvation after death.

This is clear to all and attainment of salvation in any other way is not possible. Therefore, they call sankhya way as the way to attain salvation. Persons of each of the two ways to attain salvation project their respective arguments and counter-arguments. The yoga people accept only visible proof and sankhya followers accept what is provided in shastras. Apparently both ways appear logical. Both ways have been recognised leading to salvation. Purity, piety, tap, being kind to others etc. principles have been recognised by both. The yogis attain salvation by absolving themselves from affection, attachment, love, passions and rage, by yoga. In this way the yogis absolve themselves from all worldly attachments and attain salvation. In fact the strength of yoga kills all passions in the human being but one, who is weak in yoga, continues involved in the worldly passions unless he becomes a strong yogi. A yogi who, by thinking of God, gets absorbed in God, attains salvation. The constant thinking lead one to absorption in God in samadhi and leave this body. This is the best way of attaining closeness to the almighty. In samadhi a yogi joins his soul with Parmatama by establishing the same in navel, throat, forehead, heart, chest, front portion of the body, eyes, ears and nose. He finishes all his bad and good deeds and attains salvation through yoga. To attain yoga, one has to take simple vegetarian food, get rid of all passions, rage, heat, fear, sorrow, affection, discontentment, high ambitions, sleep, lethargy and resorts to reading and thinking of God and realising the self through his brain. It is a tough way of attaining salvation but if one once reaches the stage of yoga, it is not difficult for him to get absorbed in God.

Sankhya way has been described by rishis like Kapila. There does not appear to be any lacuna in this way of attaining salvation.

According to sankhya, there are five bad elements in a human being. These are passions, rage, fear, sleepiness, and breathing faults. One should kill rage by excusing, passions by sacrifice, sleepiness by adopting satoguna, fear by sacrifice of ignorance and breathing fault by eating less. The sankhya people absolve themselves from worldly involvements and tamo and rajo gunas by resorting to acting as per sato guna and thus get salvation. The senses in the body feel various passions and their satisfaction. These only help in self- realisation as with the help of these five only, the soul gives up the outwardly passions after feeling the same. God is in Jeevatma with all gunas—tamo, rajo and sato—all elements like brain, mind, space, air, fire, water and earth and with all other things. Mind, senses, and good and bad deeds of the human beings follow the Jeevatma. But when Jeevatma crosses the effect of these senses and nature, it gets absorbed in God and attains salvation. All brahmins, gods and others desirous of having peace, praise Parmatama only. The yogi and sankhya people, all praise the same Parmatama. Only difference is that yogi praise him as a body corporate whereas the sankhya people assume him as almighty without any form etc. and in whom Jeevatma gets absorbed after self realisation. The yogis attain salvation by getting absorbed in Ishwar whereas in sankhya the atma, which is a part of Parmatama, meets and enters Parmatama.

The main power of yogis is to remember God through meditation. Now this meditation is of two kinds—one by concentration of mind and another by Pranayam. Further, Pranayam is of two kinds—Saguna and Nirguna. Where the mind remembers Saguna God, then it is Saguna pranayam and where it thinks of Nirguna God, then it is nirguna pranayam. The person should sit in pranayam after taking bath etc. and removing the mind from other worldly involvements thinking of the almighty God through self realisation. Such people get closeness to the almighty after continuous yoga. The yogi should restrain himself from all kinds of indulgences, should eat less and should have control over senses. He should bring round his mind and concentrate in soul. At that time since he has already cut off from all sensual feelings, he reaches the almighty having no connection with the mortal body. Such meditation is possible only by courageous, intelligent people having faith in vedas and shastras and on constant meditation through pranayam, they reach the almighty God. As against yoga, sankhya needs more concentration and thinking. Sankhya people tell of sixteen elements called vikaras (विकार). There are sixteen senses, eyes, ears, nose, tongue, skin, voice, touching, beauty, taste, smell, to speak, hands, legs, genital organ, and anus and one mind. Then there are eight natures comprising of five ingredients used in the formation of the human being which are earth, air, water, fire, space, and brain, ego and soul. So these are twenty-four elements. All these elements are controlled by soul. Which is 25th element since soul is part of Parmatama, Parmatama too is treated as 25th element. Thinking of Parmatama and absorption of soul in Parmatama leads to salvation. This is what people call as sankhya.

Yudhisthra asked to be told as to how the human being leaves the mortal body (स्थूल शरीर)—and how the subtle body (आत्मा) leaves the mortal body and how one attains salvation without leaving 'grihastha' ashrama. Bhishma told the dialogue of Janaka and Sulabha in this context. In old days janaka was the raja of Mithila puri. He was treated as sanyasi even while living as a 'grihastha' in his kingdom. Also there was one sanyasin Sulabha. She heard about Janaka knowing well of attainment of salvation. She went to him fully dressed up as a beautiful girl. Janaka welcomed her in the Darbar and asked about her introduction but she only told her mission and evaded telling her introduction. Her mission was to enquire about salvation. At first to know whether Raja Janaka was well-versed with it or not, she entered the brain of Janaka. Protocol requires that before putting a question to anyone, one has to enquire whether that person was capable of giving answer otherwise one was likely to be misled. So she entered in Janaka's brain. On the other hand, Janaka had been insisting on her for telling her whereabouts as protocol requires one to know the bonafides of a person before interacting with him/her as also to know the extent of her knowledge in the field she had been questioning. She then disclosed her indentity. Janaka told her that—

1. He does not involve in worldly indulgences.
2. Everyone was equal for him—one who harms as also one who gives some happiness.
3. He is happy even in trouble.
4. The ways to salvation are spiritual knowledge, spiritual sanyas and spiritual way of conduct. Some people say that knowledge is means of attaining salvation while others say action is the means of attaining salvation. The yogis have, however, told that with restraints from indulgence in worldly passions, one can attain salvation even while in 'grihastha' ashrama and with malice thinking even a sanyasi cannot attain salvation.
5. One acts on the way he is aware of to attain an object.
6. One, who leaves 'grihastha' ashrama finding it faulty and goes to other ashramas, is not completely relieved of the fault he saw in 'grihastha'.
7. One cannot attain salvation simply by putting on sadhu's dress, getting shaved like sadhus and taking a kamandle. One has to get rid of worldly passions and sorrows and happiness. One cannot attain salvation either in poverty or in excesses. It is the knowledge (ज्ञान) which bestows salvation on a person.

(8) He was not involved in worldly indulgences inspite of his engagements in Dharma, wealth and passion (धर्म, अर्थ, काम) of rajya.

He then said that beauty, youth and innocence were obstacles in becoming yogi but she still with these weaknesses was a yogi, was surprising. If a person even after becoming yogi believes in the above worldly attractions, then his/her having become a yogi, is of no avail—

1. If she had done it to hide herself, even then it was not desirable.

2. Further, her sitting in charming way amidst the sabha was not becoming of a sanyasi.

3. The rajas boast of their leisures and pleasures; the brahmins boast of their knowledge of vedas and the women boast of their beauty, youth and fortune. She should have, therefore, thought of these things before coming in that sabha and should have at first told the purpose of her visit and her capability in that direction.

Sulabha replied that by seeing a person only one should not conclude the purpose of his/her visit and should not presuppose the advent passion on seeing a beautiful lady. But one should act in any direction only after knowing him/her fully. She said she was above passions, rage, greed, shamelessness, and would not, therefore, talk on these actions. Since raja had asked her whereabouts, she would tell that she was above all worldly involvements. She knew yoga and sankhya and was well-versed with all ways leading to salvation but she had come to him to know more about these as their knowledge is never complete. She had, however found that he was not worthy of yoga and still he was proud of being above life. A person, on way of salvation, should treat all things as places of indulgence and then analyse one's position. That way he was not a complete vairagyi as—

1. For entire earth, there is one raja but he lives only in one country, within country too he lives in one town, within town too he lives in one palace, within palace too he lives in one room and in one room too he has to use only one bed and out of that one bed too, his wife has a right to half of it. So the raja actually is owner of half bed only.

2. In his leisures, pleasures, needs and other jobs too he is not independent as others have to provide the same to him. He is, therefore, involved in all these.

3. Even in deciding alliance of battle, the raja is not independent, he has to depend on the advise of his ministers, commanders etc.

4. The raja may be considered to be independent in passing any orders for the kingdom but there too he can be checked by his ministers etc. and he may be forced to take back his orders or amend the same. There is, therefore, no independence there too.

5. In taking bath, in taking meals, taking even water, in sleeping etc., he takes assistance of others. Therefore, he is not independent.

6. The beggars etc. ask for alms from the raja but the raja has to consider the position of his exchequer before giving alms to them even though the beggar may be a genuine person to be given alms.

7. The raja has always fear in his mind from enemies, other rajas, his praja, his officers and ministers lest anyone should revolt against him. He even fears his sons and wife lest they should revolt or disclose some secrets, known to them, to others.

8. Everyone is a raja in his house and is a family head. They punish some and are kind to others. Therefore, they are all like rajas.

9. Everyone has to face ailments, troubles. Wealth, wife, sons and servants are available with others too like the raja. Then how is the raja different from others, she asked.

10. Raja considers his rajya, treasury, town, army, ministers as his own, but it is only an assumption. No body can say them as his, as anytime, an enemy may conquer and they all shall then belong to him.

11. If there is no praja, then there is no rajya too. When there shall be no rajya, no Rajdharma and if no Rajdharma then how can he attain salvation.

12. There are thousands of situations in which a raja is pained. She told that she was not sure of his own body then how could she think about the mental situation of other persons. How then did the raja say that she had entered the sabha in a wrong guise. It is on the contrary, the raja himself, who was wrong in assessing her.

13. It is, therefore, essential for any man or raja to at first judge what to do and what not to do; what to say and what not to say before acting on it. The raja had already fallen from 'grihastha' Dharma if he considered that he had been a sinner in having seen or touched a woman and cannot now attain salvation too. He was, therefore, neither here nor there. How then could he boast of having absolved himself from all sensual instincts and worldly involvements, when he has all the weaknesses narrated above.

14. She was not at that time in the dress of a sanyasi but at the same

time she was not snatching anybody's wealth nor was she trying to pollute, involve in passions etc. If still someone takes her in that direction, it was his own fault and not her's.

She accordingly coached the raja to still learn all, where he was lacking as illustrated by her and then only claim that he was above all worldly indulgences and was on way to attain salvation. The raja kept quiet listening to so many weaknesses in him. This only shows that self-analysis and self-realisation is a must before boasting of any achievement and before condemning others finding some faults in them.

On Yudhisthra asking about how Shukdeva attained vairagya, Bhishma told that it was his father Vaysa Muni, who coached him to adopt vairagya after telling him to—

1. Always act as per Dharma.
2. Have control over all senses and sensual feelings.
3. Always speak truth, live with truth, simple, non violent, doing tapsya etc.
4. Leave all kinds of cheatings.
5. Always care for one's weaknesses.
.6 Act as per dictates of shastras pertaining to one's Dharma.
7. Try to attain salvation, which could be possible through vairagya.
8. Earn such a wealth as could not be snatched by raja, not shared by others, nor left after death.

Such wealth is for attaining salvation through vairagya. It becomes individual's own property which goes with the person and not left here after death whereas other properties are left here only. The person complying with 'grihastha' Dharma could become Prajapati, or have a place in swarga but does not attain salvation, which is a tougher path and can be attained with complete restraint from worldly indulgences and control over passions. After salvation only one is relieved of rebirth and redeath otherwise continues to die and reborn in one specie or the other. One, who leaves the passions and pleasures and perform bodily tapsya in forests, can attain anything he wants to have. One should, therefore, think that he is self-contained and there is none to assist him, to follow him, to feed him, to coach him etc. In this universe, even the rich people get treatment from others as they wish and in the case of poors, no one continues to live with them. Then how can one think of depending on others, when one's own body's parts do not function if they are not adequately fed. Having heard all this, Shukdev left the house, having developed vairagya and went to a cave in a mountain to perform tapsya with a view to attain salvation.

Thereafter once Shukdeva saw Narada muni in his ashrama. He worshipped him and then Narada coached him further about vairagya, sadachar and spiritualism. Narada told him that—

1. Shastras were the best panacea in removing all troubles, all doubts, and care for utmost well-being of the people and one who follows vedas and shastras, attains best brain leading to all happiness in life.
2. One should not remember the happenings of the past because their remembrance does not permit a person to renounce the universe.
3. One should take it bad if involvement in universe escalates.
4. One, who, worries for the past, he neither attains Dharma, nor wealth nor appreciation and is in pains only.
5. The people who do not worry even on the death of their sons are courageous although in principle one should not worry for any loss.
6. In case of any bodily or mental ailment, one should try to remedy it and if it is not possible to cure it then one should not worry for it.
7. The best panacea for any pain is not to remember it again and again as by remembering it, it only increases and does not decrease.
8. Therefore, the mental agony should be treated by brain and bodily ailments by medicines. It is possible if one has knowledge of shastras and should not cry like children.
9. Beauty, youth, life, wealth, freedom from diseases and company of relations are non-lasting. Therefore, one should not get involved in them.
10. A person should not worry for the troubles and on the contrary one should rather find a way out to eliminate them.
11. There is no doubt that quantum of sorrows is more than the quantum of happiness but all, out of weakness, indulge in satisfaction of passions and do not like to face the death.

12. One, who stops caring for sorrows as also for happiness, he gets absorbed in Brahma.
13. It is difficult to earn money and then more difficult to protect it and still more difficult to spend it. Therefore, in all situations, money is bad. Therefore, one should not worry on its loss.
14. By attaining wealth one does not feel contented and starts hoping for more and in the chain he dies. So contentment is the best way of remaining happy.
15. The wealth has a loss; every rise has a fall; every meeting has a departure and the end of life is death.
16. The life continues diminishing. When one's body itself is not everlasting then what is in the universe that should be taken as perpetual.
17. One, who crosses worldly involvements and gets absorbed in God, he after completion of his life in this universe, attains salvation and is relieved of all pains of life for ever.
18. One, who gets relieved of sorrows and does not fall prey to any passion, he gets relieved from all pains in life.
19. One gets pleasure during indulgence for satisfaction of sensual feelings only and not afterwards whether he is a rich or a poor.
20. One, who detaches oneself from respected and other people, and wanders about in a modest way, he only is happy and he is learned.
21. One, who is absorbed in spiritual attainment and is away from worldly passions and involvements, is happy in the universe.
22. It is not necessary that one shall be able to collect money by hardwork. Some people get wealth sitting idle and some do not get even after hardwork. Therefore, after efforts, if one does not get money, he should not worry.
23. Some people yearn for a son but do not get one; some get but he is unworthy. While some enjoy and become successors to a lot of wealth of the parents, some destroy it even after getting it. So it is not always advisable to have offspring as it can be bad too.
24. Some people keep good health, others fall ill and get cured while there are still some, who cannot be cured even by doctors. Therefore, it is all ordained by God. In this connection one should take lesson from birds and animals, who never get any

treatment for ailments and are generally free from ailments.

25. Everyone tries to go higher and higher in his position in the universe but there is a limit to it. Similarly, after death too one goes to the Loka according to his deeds in life and nothing less or higher.

26. Everyone wants wealth, but all are not very wealthy. Similarly, everyone does not have a wife or offspring. Some do not want to fall in the trouble caused by having a family while others still want to have a large family.

27. So there are different choices of people, different gains and losses; some depend on effort put in the same and some by virtue of fate—good or bad.

Then there is the discussion between God and Narada Muni about God's incarnations. As already indicated, God comes incarnate in various forms, whenever there is mitigation of Dharma by rakshasas etc. and the rishi are not safe. To revive Dharma, he kills the rakshasas and protects rishis, etc. Some of such important incarnations that have already taken place and those which were yet to take place are—

1. Matsya at the time of creation of earth by salvation out of water.
2. Kurma or Kachhapa when the god extracted Amrit out of ocean, then as Kachhapa he held the mountain on his body.
3. Varaha, when the entire earth sank in ocean, then as Varaha, God brought it back in its position.
4. Narasingha, when Harinakashyap rakshas started annoying people and to save Prahlad from his clutches, by killing the rakshas as Narasingha Bhagwan.
5. Vamana to cause downfall of Bali, when he wished to have swarga under him. Then by three steps he measured entire Brahmand and sank Bali in Patal.
6. Parsurama to kill the kshatriyas, who had started indulging in bad activities harassing the people, extracting money from them and wasting the same on their leisures and pleasures.
7. Rama Avtar to kill Ravana etc. rakshasas, who had started killing rishis and harassing people.
8. Krishana Avtar to kill rakshasas, like Kansa, Jarasandha, Shishupal etc. who were in abundance in Duapur yug and to establish the rajya of Dharma.

9. Balrama Avtar in Duapur along with Krishana to help in annihilation of rakshasas.
10. Kali Avtar in kalyug when the earth shall be full of adharmik people.

These are only some of the Avtaras. Besides, these God have been visiting this earth from time to time to save his bhaktas like to save elephant, to fulfil the desire of Dharma etc. In fact God is there within the human being. He only has to make efforts to find him.

12
Anushasan Parva

Yudhisthra continued his discussion with Bhishma on Dharma, Varnashrama institution, Ishwar-Jeeva relations, duties of the raja, duties of the praja etc. and Bhishma had been telling him everything so that Yudhisthra got rid of the worry of having been responsible for killings of crores of people in the battle including all Kaurvas, Pandavas' own sons and many great rajas and now started looking after the affairs of the rajya. But still Yudhisthra did not feel consoled. He said that he was responsible for bringing Bhishma to such an awful condition of lying on the arrows for such a long time with all attached sufferings. He preferred Duryodhana, who died in the battle-field and did not have to worry for all the killings etc. Bhishma told that he had never been independent in his thinking or doings. He was rather a tool in the hands of death, time and God, who gets all these killings taking place. He should not, therefore, blame himself for all these killings. In this context he narrated the incidence of a snake having bitten a boy to death. The snake was caught by a charmer and brought to the father of the boy to unable him to kill the snake, who had brought his son to death. Father, however, had compromised to the death as in fate and told the charmer that by killing snake his son would not be alive again. The snake spoke like human beings and told that it was death, which was responsible as the boy's death only instigated him to bite the boy. Death also said she was not responsible as the death time desired this to take place. Death time also told that he was not responsible as the Karma of the boy desired this to be done. So ultimately it is the Karma, which is responsible for everything taking place.

कर्मदायादवांल्लोकः कर्मसम्बन्धलक्षणः
कर्माणि चोदयन्तहि यथान्योन्यं तथा वयम्। (1/73)

It is Karma, which follows the human being like his son and grandson and it is Karma which is responsible for happiness and sorrow in one's life.

Yudhisthra had asked how a 'grihastha' could attain salvation. Bhishma replied that 'grihastha' is one of the four ashramas in Hindus i.e. about 25 years long way of life in which a person owns wife, offspring, a home, earns money to run the house. It is the foremost duty of the 'grihastha' to entertain the guests and those, who come to ask for 'bhiksha'. In other words one 'grihastha' has to feed three persons, one each in brahmcharya, vanprastha and sanyas. So morally a 'grihastha' should entertain all guests, bhikshukas etc. and this Dharma enables a 'grihastha' to attain salvation. But bhiksha does not mean giving a part of food only. A 'grihastha' is obliged to give anything asked for by a bhikshuka, even one's life. Once Sudarshana had asked his wife to entertain all guests/ bhikshukas even if they ask for her life and once to test them a brahmin asked for Sudarshana's wife's body which she agreed to offer unhesitatingly showing that satisfaction of a beggar was the biggest task of a 'grihastha'. So satisfaction of a beggar was protocolic obligation on a 'grihastha'.

Then Yudhisthra asked which of hard work and fate was superior. Bhishma narrated the talk of Vashistha and Brahma in this connection, when Brahma stated that at first a seed sprouts, then come leaves, stalk, full tree, then flowers and then fruit. Therefore, the fruit comes from seed and so the result is according to one's deeds. There cannot, therefore, be a result without a seed having been sown. Seed, therefore, is the fate and its result can be had after having put labour in sowing, watering and protecting the same till it yields fruit. As the yield of fruit depends on good labour put in it and no fruits can be obtained if intentions are bad and one does not put labour and want fruit without any labour. So good and bad results are according to the kind of labour put in. Although fate has a role too but fate can only help a person attain result with labour put in it and there can be no fruits without labour even though one has the seed i.e. fate with him.

शौचेन लभते विप्रः क्षत्रियो विक्रमेण तु,
वैश्यः पुरुषकारेण शूद्रः शश्रूषया श्रियम्। (6/16)

Brahmin earns by good moral conduct, kshatriya by his strength, vaish earns by hard labour and shudra by serving the people of the other three varnas. So the labour is followed by fate and fate alone, not accompanied by labour, does not give anything. So it is the labour which gives the result and labour put in bad deeds gives bad results. In every life one gets the result of bad or good deeds in previous life.

Yudhisthra asked about who is able to be rich. In religious terms it is asked where Lakshmi (The Goddess of wealth) resides. It is said that Lakshmi resides in the homes of the persons, who are fortunate to have her, by dint of doing hard work, remaining fearless, being very intelligent, well-versed with their vocation, non-lethargic, grateful and having control over their senses. Similarly, ladies should be having the above qualities along with entertainment of guests, beggars, worshipping God and be kind to all human beings. These are general good qualities for a man to possess and the persons with these qualities would be rich. This is protocolic requirement having been given religious touch. The money earned by foul means shall not stay long as either it is wasted out or the persons earning money with foul means shall be caught some day and lose everything so far earned. Bhishma further told that a man should resort to leave ten kinds of actions to be successful in universe. (1) Violence (2) Theft (3) Rape (4) Talking false (5) Back-biting (6) Talking lie (7) Ill talks (8) Extracting other's money (9) Enmity toward others (10) Not believing in the result of one's deeds. One should avoid these ten kinds of actions by body, speech or mind. Conversely, one should involve oneself in the actions opposite to the above misdeeds. There is detailed narration of the temporal punishment one has to face on involving in above misdeeds.

During the discussion between Yudhisthra and Bhishma, Yudhisthra asked about the efficacy of Shiva, who had been told by Bhishma as having been worshipped by Brahma. In that context Bhishma told that Shiva is very great. Even Shri Krishana had worshipped him for attaining a son equivalent in strength to him from his queen Jambwanti. Krishana then went to a mountain and performed tapsya to please Shiva. Now for performing tapsya, one need to have the guidance of a guru. So Krishana went to rishi Upmanyu and requested him to tell the way to please Shiva. Here it is a matter of protocol only which is depicted by the entire episode—

1. Krishana was himself God and even he was worshipped by Shiva in his childhood. So in a way Shiva accepted Krishana as his God. Similarly, to give importance to Shiva, Krishana proceeded to mountain to worship Shiva like Rama worshipped Shiva before he proceeded to Lanka to fight with Ravana and Shiva had been the worshipper of Rama so much so that Shiva separated from Sati on her having formed herself as Sita to test Rama and Shiva

had come to know of this fact. Rama had also asked his praja to worship Shiva.

2. Worship of Shiva by Krishana can also be with a view to remove misgivings amongst Shiva and Krishana Bhaktas treating them as separate entities.

3. The route to attain God is through guru. Although Krishana knew how to worship Shiva but still acting as a layman, he went to Rishi Upmanyu to guide him reach Shiva. Upmanyu too knew Krishana as almighty God but since he had come to him as an ordinary man and requested him, Upmanyu acted as a guru and gave him proper guidance. He could even forecast that by worshipping Shiva in a particular way. he would reach Shiva in six months.

4. Krishana performed tapsya for six months according to the method told by rishi Upmanyu and Shiva and Parvati did come to bless Krishna.

5. Shiva gave eight boons to Krishana and Parvati too gave another eight boons including birth of thousands of sons, from thousands of queens and non-defeat in battles etc.

6. Krishana had to adopt the way of worshipping Shiva with a view to show to his queen Jambwanti that for her sake, he had to please a God to be blessed with a son from Jambwanti equivalent in bravery to Shiva.

7. The particular way of performing tapsya has been narrated. This shows that for proper tapsya, one had to go to forests or mountains etc. or in an isolated place and perform tapsya after taking advice from a guru. Krishana was a 'grihastha' and he could not perform that tapsya living in the universe.

8. All the rishis have narrated their experiences about how they met Shiva after tapsya and the boons attained by them from Shiva. Shiva is said to be the best of all gods in granting boons.

Yudhisthra asked that sons are a means for attaining salvation and that the life of a person not having a son is considered as of no avail.

In this connection Bhishma narrated the discussion of Narada and Markandey. At first it was told that a woman is never independent in her life as in childhood she has to live under the control of her parents, in youth after marriage she remains under the control of her husband and in old age under the control of sons. Marcandey told that Dharma gets diminished with the time. In Satya yug it was hundred percent Dharma in all and everywhere, in Treta yug, it was seventy five percent; in Duapur yug, fifty percent and in Kalyug, it shall be twenty five percent only. In Kalyug, people shall have short lives, less intelligence and shall be bereft of Dharma and truth. No consideration of varnas shall be there and accordingly no institution of varnashrama Dharma.

Narada then told that if a daughter is born in the house, she must be married, when she comes of age. In that case, one earns Dharma and if not married then one is sinner with every month passed in unmarried condition. The birth of a daughter should not, however, be discarded as the daughter is incarnation of Laxmi and should, therefore, be treated with dignity and one should take it as advent of good time. The son should be married with a girl of his varna as in that case there is always proper understanding and the 'grihastha' life becomes prosperous and pleasant. A 'grihastha' should earn for the livelihood in the forenoon and should then engage in Dharma jobs and after that only during the night, should engage in satisfaction of passion but even then should not very much indulge in the same. He should respect brahmins, gurus, brethren and other relatives and be benevolent to all. The 'grihastha' should give alms to learned brahmins only. A person, who is rageless, Dharmik, true and having control over his senses, should be treated as a worthy brahmin. For giving alms also, time is fixed. After taking bath in the morning, alms relating to gods should be given, in the afternoon alms towards ancestors should be give and in the noon, alms should be given to deserving human beings. The alms given without proper time does not go into any reckoning. The alms should be given pleasurely and not taking as a burden and should be clear from all sorts of insects etc., if the alms given are in the form of foodgrains etc. No alms should be given to a doctor, a pujari (priest), a pretentious person or a drunk one, the brahmins, who perform yagyas on behalf of shudras, who is a paid teacher, who has married a shudra girl, who perform rites for the deads, who lends money on interest, who indulges in jobs of the other varnas etc. A 'grihastha' should act on a given time-table for the day. In this way our shastras have prescribed even the smallest details in human life. The first three hours of the day are called morning hours. One should perform tapsya, pooja etc. during this period; in the next three hours, one should attend to normal jobs of the 'grihastha' in the next three hours, one should again take a bath and perform worshipping etc.; the next three hours of afternoon time should be devoted to jobs like alms-giving etc. for the ancestors (who are dead) and the next three hours are evening hours and during this time again one should perform worship of gods etc. All worship, alms-giving etc. should be as provided in vedas by the persons of all the three top varnas. Telling a lie is adharmik for a brahmin and twice that for a kshatriya, and four times that for a vaish. An invited brahmin should not take meals at other's house. He should not take meals without having taken bath. He should not be given alms if he wants to have the same on making excuses or telling lie. A brahamin not having store of foodgrain, must be fed. Alms should be given to such brahmins as want the same for performing yagyas etc. The women and girls, who only ask for meals, must be fed.

Our Tirthas are the places of worship. These are the places of spiritual protocol. These are generally on the banks of rivers. These are the abodes of rishis, muni etc., who pass spiritual sermons to the people of the universe. who visit the tirthas. A visit to the places of pilgrimage entails visit to the ashramas of rishis and the benefit of their sermons. One takes bath in the river in open and it gives a feeling of one's purifying oneself. These are meeting places of the relatives, who live at distant places but come to have pilgrimage at these places. Further, these places being away from the normal residence of the 'grihastha', enable him to get out of the daily rut for a change.

There are many such places on the bank of river Ganga viz. Hardwar, Rishikesh, Prayag, Varanasi, etc. There is detailed narration of the sacred rivers in India. According to Hindus, Ganga provides—

(1) Salvation to the people taking bath in Ganga and residing at its bank.

(2) People taking Ganga water donot fall ill of any abdominal diseases as Ganga water has germicidal elements.

(3) One feels pleasure after taking bath in Ganga.

(4) As per religion, all sins are washed off after taking bath in Ganga.

(5) Ganga water helps in rich harvest.

(6) One can have darshan of rishis and listen to spiritual kathas leading to salvation at the bank of Ganga.

(7) The breeze at Ganga banks cure many ailments like T.B. etc. as such breeze becomes germicide.

Yudhisthra asked about the persons to be respected in all the Lokas. Bhishma told that those, who worship/respect Varuna, Sun, Agni, Rudra,

Kartikeye, Laxmi, Saraswati, Vishnu, Brahma, Brihaspati, Moon, Water, Earth are respectable persons. It only shows that only gentlemen are respectable for others. Futher, those who are involved in tapsya in forests; who study vedas; who are benevolent towards all beings; true, brahmcharis living in gurukuls and living on bhiksha; who are not jealous of others; brahmins, who have controlled their senses and work for the well-being of the mankind; raja, who cares for his praja, are treated as respectables. Also those, who protect the beings and who have taken refuge under them are to be respected. In this connection an instance of Raja Ushinar has been given. Once a pigeon under fear of an eagle came and took refuge under the raja. Then eagle came and claimed the pigeon as he had been flying after him and it was his food. Raja offered any number of birds, animal etc. but the eagle insisted on the same pigeon. Then raja offered his flesh equivalent to the pigeon. This had been accepted. The raja cut his flesh and put in the scale but still pigeon continued to be heavier. Then raja himself boarded the scale. Since this was only a test by gods, the raja got salvation. The persons, who always have an eye on alms and greed, are not to be entertained. Out of the persons, known for long and those, who come for alms on a day, who is to be preferred from the protocolic point of view, as firstly the person already living with him, would have been already known whereas the new incumbent might be a superior person.

Yudhisthra asked about girls' marriage. Bhishma told various kinds of the marriage of the girl.

Types of marriages—

1. Arranged marriage: Should be arranged by father. The father should find out a boy, who should be of good conduct, from high family, well educated and being suitable physically from marriage point of view. Such marriage with the girl is the best marriage. Dowry should also be given in the marriage but not in consideration of the marriage. This should be given to enable the girl to set up her new house after marriage.

2. Love marriage : Then there is love marriage (Gandharva marriage), in which the boy is selected by the girl. Such a boy too have to have the liking for such a girl.

3. Manishi marriage : In this marriage, the parents of the girl take money from groom's parents in consideration of the marriage of their daughter. This is considered mean type of marriage.

4. Rakshas marriage : In this marriage, the girl is taken by force after killing/beating the parents/relatives of the girl.

5. Prajapatya marriage : In this marriage, money is given by the parents of the girl to the parents of the boy in consideration of the marriage. In present days such marriages mostly take place.

Arranged, Prajapatya and love marriages are considered to be good kinds of marriages and Manishi and Rakshas marriages are condemnable. The marriage should take place within the people of the same varna. The offspring from such marriage take the vocation of the father at the time of birth itself. The marriage of the girl should take place after she has started periods and in case the marriage takes place earlier, then the bride should be brought by the groom to his house after she has entered the periods. The offspring from the married couple is considered as legitimate and where it is by rape etc. then it is illegitimate. The marriage is considered to have taken place after saptapadi. Even today, the marriage in Hindus is complete after saptapadi only. Such a marriage should be performed with vedic mantras.

पाणिग्रहण मन्त्रणां निष्ठा स्यात् सप्तमे पदे,
पाणिग्रहस्य भार्यास्याद् यस्य चादिद्भः प्रदीयते। (44/55)

The groom should take the bride in marriage according to above vedic method with saptapadi, handed over by the father of the girl.

As per vedas, if money is taken from the groom's parents for preparing ornaments and clothes of the bride and such a money is not taken by the parents of the girl for their use, then it is not Manishi marriage and is considered correct marriage although the best marriage is where such ornaments and clothes are prepared by the parents of girl themselves. The girl should, however, be properly attended to in the in-laws' house. If she is not so attended to and is discarded, then she shall always be worried and in that case, shall not produce capable children. That is why it is said that where women are respected, there gods live.

स्त्रियो यत्र च पूज्यन्ते रमन्ते तत्र देवताः,
अपूजिताश्च यत्रैताः सर्वास्तत्राफलाः क्रियाः। (46/5)

Such was the respect afforded to the women in our vedas and shastras. Where the women remain unsatisfied and worried, that family is wasted out.

Yudhisthra then asked a very peculiar question. He stated that according to shastras, a brahmin can have four wives—a brahmin, one kshatriya, one from vaish and another from shudra. From out of four sons, born from them, who is eligible to succeed the father's property? Bhishma told that brahmin, kshatriya, vaish are three upper castes and a brahmin can marry in these three varnas. There is no provision in shastras of a brahmin marrying a shudra girl but out of greed or passion one can have her but sleeping with a shudra girl take him to Narka. A son born out of the brahmin succeeds major portion of his ancestral properties. Then the remaining property should be divided in ten parts. Again out of these ten parts, four should go to the son of the brahmin. The kshatriya is entitle to have three parts out of these ten parts, and vaish should have two parts. Although there is no provision for giving any part of ancestral property still since because of the sin of the brahmin, a shudra son has born, he is entitled to the remaining one portion out of the above ten parts. The son born of the shudra girl by the brahmin is not recognised as brahmin but the sons born out of the brahmin, kshatriya and vaish girls are treated as brahmins. Even if the brahmin has no sons from the girls of other varnas, the shudra son should not get more than one-tenth share. The sons, however, do not get any share out of the streedhan given by the brahmin to his wives. The daughter can have share from the property of the mother received by her from her father as for this purpose there is no difference between son and a daughter. On Yudhisthra asking that when the sons born of brahmin, kshatriya and vaish girls are treated as brahmins then why should there be a difference in the allotment of shares in ancestral property. Bhishma told that even amongst three wives, there are certain rights available to brahmin only such as arranging for brahmin's bath, yagya, dressing up, serving meals, clothing, ornaments. Further there shall always be genetical difference in the sons born of kshatriya and vaish girls although they shall all be brahmins. Therefore, there is difference is sharing the property too. Here protocolic questions arise:—

1. Why should a brahnim be allowed to have four wives, when shastras provide for one wife for all other than rajas? Rama even said that raja too should have only one wife.

2. Why should there be difference in share of property when they are all brahmin's sons?

3. Where shastras speak of proper marriage within same varna, then why should there be a provision for inter-varna marriage and given recognition too.

Like brahmins, kshatriyas can have two wives—one from kshatriya and another from a vaish but there is no provision for a wife from shudra by kshatriya. For kshatrya too the property is divided into eight parts—four being taken by kshatriya's son and three by vaisha's son and remaining one portion to go to shudra's son, if any, although not recognised in the case of ksahtriya. In case of a vaish, the property be divided into five parts, four going to vaish girl's son and one to shudra's son. Shudra cannot have more than one wife and that too from shudra family and his all sons are entitled to equal share in father's property. Further, out of several sons of any varna, the eldest son gets one extra part than the other sons. The above provision shows how detailed our rules had been for the purpose of division of ancestral property indicating exhaustiveness in enactment of all kinds of laws, rules and regulations. There is also narration of the social position of the sons born out of the inter-varna matches such as a son born out of a brahmin and kshatrani is soot; a son born out of a kshatriya and vaish girl is 'magadha' and a son born out of vaish boy and shudra girl works as carpenter and a son born of shudra and girl of kshatriya is 'nishad'. All such offspring is called 'cross breed'. The sons born of women of brahmin, kshatriya and vaish by a shudra are called chandala. The son left by the parents attains the varna of the parents, who brings him up. Similarly, sons born of semens of other male from one's wife, attain the varna of the father in whose house he is born.

In the context of birth of Parshurama, Bhishma told Yudhisthra that Chavan Muni once came to know that a girl of Kushik Raja shall spoil his family by marrying in Rishi family. So he decided to finish Kushik Rajya. He came there. The raja, as per protocol, received him. The rishi told that he wanted to stay there for sometime. The raja and his queen welcomed the rishi in mahal, gave him asan to sit, washed his feet and worshipped him and served meals and told that they both were at his service. The rishi told them that he was going to sleep and should not be disturbed, rather they should continue serving him. The rishi slept for 21days. The raja and queen kept sitting there day and night without taking anything. Then the rishi got up and went away. In the evening, he was again back and again slept for 21 days keeping the raja and queen in his service. After that he asked to pull the chariot in which he shall be sitting and go around the town. The raja and queen pulled the chariot and the rishi whipped them to the point of bleeding. Not only this, the rishi distributed a large amount of his wealth to citizens. But the raja and the queen continued serving him unhesitatingly. The rishi was then pleased and asked them for a boon. The raja asked why he had done so with him. The rishi told that he had come to destroy him but could not get a chance to pass on a curse and was now happy and that in their third generation they shall have a brahmin son and went away. This shows the protocol between a raja and the rishis. The raja had to place everything at the disposal of the rishi and at times the rishis were very cruel too but ultimately the end was welcoming. Similarly, in the case of Harishchandra, Viswamitra wanted to test him and he was in the process put to a lot of trouble but ultimately gained the salvation.

Yudhisthra was still worried about the death of crores of people because of him involving crores of ladies having lost their husbands and sons. Bhishma told that by tapsya one gets swarga, good image, praise in universe, long life, high position and all leisures and pleasures in life. By 'ahinsa', one gets beauty; by learning, high family; by taking fruits and roots, one gets rajya and by living on leaves, one gets swarga; by giving alms, one gets wealth etc. He narrated many such gains from various tapsyas. So all these gains by various kinds of good works have been indicated in our shastras. Then there are the results of construction of well etc. for thirsty people. Bhishma also narrated various kinds of alms and the qualities of high class brahmins and beggars and persons fit for giving alms and their results. The kshatriyas have to undertake very tough jobs involving killing of many out of enemies and criminals and punishing many found to have committed crimes in the rajya. The raja in turn should give alms to brahmins and others needing the same as also perform many yagyas, construct roads, wells, hospitals and other welfare works for the benefit of the public. Further, he is not considered to have committed sin in killing the enemy and his people and the criminals as in doing so he had only been acting as per tenets of Rajdharma and with a view to protect the life and property of his people. In turn, the raja gets a part of the result of the good works done by the praja being in peace because of the protection provided to them by the raja. Donation of earth/land is considered to be the best donation to anyone by the raja or vaishas, who are owners of land.

Then there is the narration of various kinds of alms to be given by the raja and the method of giving those alms and the description of persons to whom such alms should be given and the result of those alms/donations. The donation of food to the hungry and water to the thirsty is considered to be the best of all donations.

Yudhisthra asked about the importance and result of undertaking fasts, pledges, studies, compliance of Dharma, alms-giving, reading of vedas, service of parents, brahmcharya etc. Bhishma told him that the persons, who undertake any pledge and complies with the same till end as per tenets of shastras, get salvation. Even while in universe, one does attain the resultant benefit of compliance of tenets of Dharma, and performance of yagyas etc. A person having control over his senses, gets the desired results. It is stated that different persons adopt different ways of reaching Him. Some live in forests; some think of him in their houses; some feel pleasure in serving the guests. They all go to almighty in their own way but what is required is real absorption in Him. Those, who remain brahmcharis from birth to death, have everything at their disposal in this universe as well as after death. Those, who serve their parents, brothers, gurus etc. also attain salvation. But whatever one does should be as specified in shastras. Bhishma indicated that after his father's death, he performed shradha. At that time, he saw a hand coming out of the asan. He recognised it as his father's hand asking for the 'Havi' but he did not give 'Havi' to that hand and handed over through 'kusha' only as per shastras. Then all his ancestors appeared and approved his action as per shastras and for not having moved sentimentally.

Yudhisthra asked about the origin of gold and why it is valued so much. Bhishma told that in the dreams, his ancestors had asked for donation of gold. Gold is received from the vassal states in presents and gold is given in alms in yagyas and for any other help. Gold is considered as a sacred metal. It has come out of fire and so it is purest form and always shining like fire. Donation of gold is said to be the best as with gold one can have anything in exchange and is easy for being stored with no rusting etc. Therefore, the gods, rajas, ministers, etc. all wear golden ornaments. Once asuras had been annoying the gods and Tarkasura, who was born out of the semens of Shiva was very powerful and could not be defeated by gods. They all went to Brahma, who arranged for the birth of Kartikeye from Shiva's semen so that it was equally brave and so able to kill Tarkasura. Since Kartikeye was born from Shiva's semen and from fire and so was gold, both are considered to be brothers. Parshurama became purer after the donation of gold and attained salvation.

There is detailed narration about shradha remembering the dead ancestors. In Hindus, the ancestors, who are dead are considered to be visiting their homes particularly on their death days and in the month of Aswin. So there is a provision of performing shradha on these days with a view to keep the dead ancestors happy. For this purpose, donation is given to brahmins. The brahmins have to be selected ones. They should preferably be from the home town/village of the family because those brahmins would be known to the ancestors. Such performances are held in Hindus with a view to —

1. Remember the ancestors on those days and follow the guidelines indicated by them and the principles/ideologies followed by them so that the people could progress by following their ideologies.
2. Another purpose of shradhas can be to part with some of the earned wealth to others in the shape of alms and donations.
3. Donations are particularly given to brahmins as brahmins do not do other jobs for pecuniary yield. So, on the occasions of festivals and shradhas, they are given clothes, ornaments, food etc. for their livelihood.
4. The provision of festivals and shradhas can also be with a view to enable all family members to get together for the celebration. Such occasions, therefore, give chance for such a get-together.

In fact first shradha was performed by Nimi muni on the death of his son Shirman, who too was a great tapasvi.

He called brahmins and served them food and gave some donations too. Then he himself felt whether he had done a wrong thing. Then his grand father Atre (since dead) appeared and approved his action to please all deads in the family. Such a shradha, he was told, was first held by Brahma himself and, therefore, there was nothing wrong in it. Since then the shradha is performed with a view to remembering the dead ancestors and their deeds to be followed upon. There is a detailed procedure for holding such shradhas. There are so many things which are not served in food, and so many qualities to be noted in the brahmins invited for such shradhas. With shradhas, one is supposed to be getting blessings of the dead ancestors. So these blessings might be the following of the deads and good principles followed by those ancestors and the resultant gains therefrom. So at first the shradhas were started by rishis but subsequently followed by the people of the three top varnas and detailed rules were made out about their performance. The brahmins, who are learned in vedas and teach vedas to others, are not supposed to be taking the meals of shradha so that other people could take advantage of the same and the vedas teachers are already busy in their vocation. When one performs shradha, the first right is that of the dead ancestors, then of gods and then the other members of the family and the remaining can only be taken by the family of the performer.

Then there is the quality of donor and the donee. Donation should not be accepted from a bad character. Similarly, donation should not be given to a bad character brahmin. Regarding whether or not to accept the donation, there was a meeting of several rishis after Shivi had given his son Shaivya in donation to a brahmin and there was famine. Then Vrishadarbhi (a raja) said that donation had been specified to help the brahmins to make their both ends meet and to help them in case of famine etc. He was prepared to donate whatever he had to brahmins. He could even donate villages in donation. The rishis said that the donation by the raja appeared attractive in appearance but its result would be disastrous as it shall put the brahmins in greed and worldly passions. The donation accepted by a brahmin bereaves him of his tapsya to that extent.

Vashistha muni said that acceptance of one gold mohar causes the loss of tapasya equivalent to the one hundred thousand mohars.

Kashyapa said that even if one gets all the animals, women, gold, foodgrains available on earth, one shall not feel satisfied. Therefore, it is better to be contented and have no thirst for these things.

Bhardwaja said that one's thirst goes on increasing as one gets the worldly leisures and pleasures. The remedy is to get rid of the same.

Gautama said that nothing in the universe can satisfy any person.

Viswamitra said that after one wish of a person is satisfied, he wishes for something else and in this way the wishes go on multiplying and one is never satisfied to finality.

Atre said that passions cannot be satisfied by enjoying the same but go on escalating as consumed.

Jamadagni said that by not taking alms, the brahmin can keep his tapsya intact.

Arundhati said that some people consider wealth necessary for Dharma but she considered tapsya as more important.

Pashusakha said nothing is better than the wealth gained while complying with the tenets of one's Dharma. This fact is known to brahmins too and, therefore, it serves brahmins.

These rishis did not have any greed inspite of having been tempted by the raja and, therefore, went to the best loka. One should not, therefore, have any greed in mind as greed causes all sins, passions and troubles. A person gets the result of his deeds. One does not get the result without any deed and has to face the result of all his deeds. Good deeds give good results and bad deeds give bad results. One should, therefore, control one's sensual feelings and then his deeds shall be good only leading to attainment of salvation. Further, one should have company of good persons only as one is known by the company one keeps. The top man in the universe is he, who even thinking of Dharma, wealth and passion does not involve himself in Adharmik actions. Similarly, on top are the persons, who are very charming and all women get attracted towards them but still donot indulge in that passion. So a married men complying with tenets of Dharma are the best men in the universe.

Yudhisthra then asked about the tenets of 'grihastha' Dharma. This is relevant to the human beings of present day. Bhishma told that similar question was raised by Krishana before earth and the earth had replied that —

1. The 'grihastha' should worship the gods, dead ancestors, rishis and guests. Gods and dead ancestors have to be worshipped by yagyas, havans, shradhas and guests by serving them meals, foodgrains etc.
2. One gets longer life by leading a good conduct life. He gets wealth by good conduct and gets praise in this universe and after death.
3. On the contrary, the bad character has a shorter life.
4. By good conduct, one attains Dharma.
5. A person complying with tenets of Dharma and keeping busy in public welfare jobs, is liked by all around him.
6. Those, who are atheists, lethargy, non obedient to guru and shastras, of bad conduct and not knowing Dharma, are with short life.
7. Rage ruduces life. Marriage in other varna leads to uncomfortable position in this universe and after death.
8. Violence, telling lie, cheating others, affects the life span of a person.
9. A 'grihastha' should rise early in the morning, engage in Dharma and money-making, take bath and then perform pooja etc. Similarly, in the evening again perform pooja and should keep busy during the day in running the house-hold.
10. A 'grihastha' should not indulge in women, other than his wife.
11. A 'grihastha' should dress up himself in the forenoon. He should not travel with strangers. In case he comes across a brahmin,

cow, raja, old man, pregnant lady or an invalid person, then he should keep aside to give him way.

12. He should not annoy others nor should be rude or crude to anyone as the ill talks, cause more serious injuries than caused even with sword or arrow.
13. A 'grihastha' should avoid a jealous or a proud person.
14. The 'grihastha' should keep studying vedas, shastras etc. and act on their contents.
15. He should take bath before sleeping in the night and should not sleep upto sun-rise.
16. A 'grihastha' should neither see towards any other woman, nor sit or sleep with her and should keep control on his senses.
17. While sleeping, he should check up the bed properly and should not sleep on broken or loose bed.
18. He should not take bath naked nor should take bath in the night and should not sleep naked.
19. The meals should be taken facing east and should not disregard the food.
20. Should perform yagyas, havans daily with vedic mantras and should eat sitting and not standing or walking nor should urinate standing.
21. Must wash hands after taking meals and before taking meals.
22. Any old man visiting him should be properly welcomed, asked to have asan and should see him off when he leaves.
23. He should neither catch hold of anyone by hairs nor should cause any injury on forehead; should not rub head with both hands and should not pour water on head or forehead time to time.
24. Should not take eatables prepared with tip (and oilseed).
25. Should not study vedas till one has taken bath.
26. Should urinate and ease facing north during the day and facing south during night.
27. Should not develop quarrel with brahmin, kshatriya or snake.
28. Should not enter into discussion with guru in rudeness.
29. Should put wet sandal on forehead after taking bath.
30. Should not take meals with anyone in one plate.

31. Should not eat curd and sattoo during night and should not take salt from palm as also should not eat non-vegetarian dishes nor should curd be taken after meals but during meals.
32. Should keep quiet while eating.
33. Should serve same meals to all sitting for meals together.
34. Should not have inter-course during day-time.
35. Should help the poor and infirm in the family.
36. Should not have over-eating in the evening.
37. After brahmcharya ashrama, one should get married with an educated, noble girl belonging to high family and produce children from her. The offspring should be sent to gurukul for education. The daughters should be married with capable boys belonging to high families.
38. Should keep aside from an old Sanyasi, loyal to husband and lady belonging to shudra or to high varnas.
39. Should not indulge in love with any unknown girl.
40. Should worship all gods, brahmins, rishis, gurus and respect all elders. Should obey them all too.
41. Should not go to other's houses uninvited.
42. The raja should always care for the well-being and protection of his people.
43. Should not go near his wife during periods and should have intercourse after four days. He shall have a daughter on conception on odd days and son on even days.

On Yudhisthra asking about the body of human beings. Brihaspati told that the body comprised of earth, water, fire, air, space, mind, brain, and soul. Also they all go on watching the compliance of Dharma by him. Skin, bones, flesh, semens and blood leave the soul after death and it is only the Dharma, which follow the soul. Therefore, only the Dharmik person attains salvation. Another person, after having completed the enjoyment by virtue of good deeds, comes back in the universe in the deserved specie and goes on like this till he gets salvation. The being is born by semens of the man. The semens in turn are created by the food taken by the being and processed by the body comprising of earth, water, fire, air, and space along with mind. Then during intercourse with the women, these semens take form of the being in conception and then that conceived matter takes shape of a body with the admixture of the above said six elements and the matter becomes one body. This body only suffers or gets pleasure. Then in the cycle the soul leaves this body of six elements and is reborn according to its good or bad deeds with the help of the semens in another body. Before conception, the soul or the subtle body suffers because of the bad or good deeds in previous life. An adharmik soul has to suffer after death and is reborn as animal or bird depending on the deeds in previous life. Then there is narration of the species attained by various persons like those of donkey, horse, insect, sparrow etc. as per their deeds in life and the periodicity of life in each specie. One, who causes sins and follow the path of adharma, goes to hell. One should, therefore, keep the mind under control and should not allow the mind to cause any sins and resort to compliance of tenets of Dharma applicable to his varna and ashrama. Such a person enjoys life in this universe and then attains salvation, never to come back to this universe. One is Dharmik if one follows the path of non-violence, acts as per vedas, thinks of the almighty, has control over senses, and service of the guru. One, who follows non-violence, he passes on affection, pride and jealousy to others and attains salvations controlling his passions and rage. One, who treats others, like himself, is liked by God too. One should think while causing violence by attacking others that others too could attack on him in a similar way. The violence is caused by mind, speech and action and meat-eating too is violence e.g. desire to take meat is violence by mind; telling others to eat meat is violence by speech and eating meat is violence by action. Therefore, one, who takes meat, is the greatest sinner. For full development of oneself, one has to leave the path of violence. One, who purchases meat, he causes violence by usage, and one, who kills animals, causes violence by action. One, who does not eat meat but kills animals for other to eat, causes violence by action. One, who eats meat and subsequently leaves eating it, is also within the Dharmik persons. In Aswamedha yagya, horse is killed. This too is violence although it is washed off by yagya, alms etc. It is a fact that meat-eating leads to rage, passion, greed etc. all kind of addictions and who does not eat meat remains happy. Brihaspati further told that apart from non-violence, truth speaking, tapsya, are the other deeds, which lead one to salvation. Bhishma told that —

1. One, who wants to increase his flesh by eating others' flesh is the greatest sinner.
2. One should consider others' life like one's own. As one does not want to kill oneself so should he hate killing others.

3. Taking pity on other beings is the greatest Dharma.
4. Saving someone's life is biggest donation. Then the taking of one's life is automatically the greatest sin.
5. One, who takes meat enjoys it for a while only and the others lose life for ever.
6. One, who eats someone's meat, is eaten by him in next life according to the theory of 'Karma'.
7. One, who does not involve himself in Hinsa (Violence) keeps himself busy in other good deeds and enjoy the result thereof.

In all our Puranas, the principles of Dharma are narrated either by God himself or by some rishi etc., Once, when Shiva and Parvati were sitting on the Kailash, Parvati asked for the information for the benefit of the mankind, about the duties of men of each varna and in each ashrama. Shiva told that for a democratic set up, God had first created brahmins out of the four varnas of Brahmin, Kshatriya, Vaish and Shudra, and fixed their duties too.

ब्राह्मणाः क्षत्रिया वैश्याः शूद्राश्चेति चतुर्विधम्
ब्राह्मणा विहिताः पूर्वं लोकतन्त्रमभीप्सता। (141/131)

Brahmins are born out of the mouth of God. Their actions, therefore, are from mouth such as studies, coaching others, performing yagyas and taking donations for livelihood. They have to be busy in tapsya and compliance of their Dharma. Kshatriya Dharma is to bring up the subjects. He takes one-sixth part of the produce by people and in return the raja ensures their protection from outside aggression and internal criminals. He respects brahmins. The raja's main Dharma is control over senses, self-studies, yagyas, donation, bringing up his people, punishment of criminals, action for affording justice to people, speaking truth and acting true, helping the poor and invalids. The vaish have to resort to grazing of cattle, agriculture, trade, running industry, holding yagya, donations, honouring guests and respecting kshatriyas and brahmins. The shudras have to serve the people of the other three varnas. He should control his senses and serve the guests.

In ashramas, 'grihastha' ashrama is at the top. In this the 'grihastha' has to keep himself pious externally and internally too, remaining happy with wife, performing yagyas, worshipping gods, self-studies, earning livelihood as per Dharma. The vanprasthi has to detach himself completely from worldly passions and involvements. He is to handover the 'grihastha' to his wards and go to forests and eat whatever is available there and spend his time in Iswar bhakti. After vanprastha, one enters into sanyas. In this the vanprasthi leaves his ashrama and coaches Dharma to the people but does not accept any alms/ donations except bhiksha for the day only. In brahmcharya, the person goes to gurukula for studies. He learns all vedas, shastras, serves the guru, lives on bhiksha, had a very simple and pious life. There is equality amongst all persons in the gurukula whether one is a rajkumar or a vaish or brahmin or shudra. After preliminary education, one opts the vocation of his opted varna i.e. a brahmin continues studying vedas and shastra, a kshatriya learns principle of governance and warfare and vaish learns about trade etc. One, who is not able to accommodate himself in any of the above three varnas, becomes shudra. There is provision in shastras that the person of a varna should continue compliance of his varna-dharma and if he is not able to make his livelihood following his varna-dharma, he could opt for the next below varna and then he is recognised as the person of that varna. In this, the brahmin can act as kshatriya and kshatriya as a vaish. Similarly an kshatriya can opt to work as brahmin too as Viswamitra had become brahmrishi although initially he was kshatriya. Then such person is recognised in his changed varna only. The raja has to ensure that the people of all varnas act as per their respective varnadhramas only. Those, who act as per their varnashrama Dharma, attain salvation after leading a peaceful life in this universe.

Parvati then asked about the duties of a raja and Shiva told that the raja is an important part of the mankind. When there was chaos and anarchy in public and everyone killed the other one, Brahma created Manu as the raja, who narrated detailed duties of a raja.

Shiva also narrated the various kinds of good or bad deeds in one's life and their results in next life covering all kinds of actions. Such detailed analysis is not available anywhere else in granthas of any religion. Due to shortage of space here it is not possible to narrate them all. But it is a comprehensive narration of all protocolic relation and result of deeds—bad or good—caused by a person and this is a process which continues from one life to another an so on.

From this narration, it shall appear that even the smallest ailment, achievement or joy or sorrow in one's life is the result of some action in the previous life or in the past days of this life itself. Like Indian Penal

Code describing punishment for all kinds of crimes, there is indication of the result of good or bad deeds in the code made out in our shastras. Even with such comprehensiveness in the punishments narrated by our rishis in shastras as also for the crimes in our samritis like Arthshastra, Inder Samriti, Brihaspati Samriti etc., the English could afford to call us barbaric having no such codes with us. In fact English had come to rule India after six hundred years of Mohammedan rule, when Shriat had only been applied in courts of law and all Hindu granthas/samrities had been destroyed. They were, therefore, not aware of the existence of such extensive narration of judicial system in the realm of this universe in Hindu shastras or the English did not want to give credit to our having been so much learned in the vocation of governance although if we see minutely, we will find that whatever is available in Evidence Act, Criminal Procedure Code, Civil Procedure Code and Indian Penal Code, would seem to be similar as it exists in our shastras and samritis and it shall not be wrong if we say that Enligh might have taken it from our shastras/samritis only. Shiva had also told that for the crimes for which a person is punished by the raja in this universe, he is not punished for the same crime again after death by Yamraj or in the next birth. Here the principle of one punishment for one crime has been accepted.

ये नृपैर्दण्डिता भूमावपराधापदेशतः
यम लोके न दण्डूयन्ते तत्र ते यमदण्डनैः (145)

Then there is the question of destiny/fate and action by the individual. If everything has to be as per destiny then what is left for the action/hardwork by individual. Shiva replied that destiny does not help a man, who does not act. Therefore, all actions are based on fulfilment or otherwise by the assistance of destiny.

नरस्याकुर्वतः कर्म दैव सम्पन्न लभ्यते,
तस्मात् सर्वसमाराम्भे दैवमानुषनिर्मितः। (145)

Parvati then explained the protocolic and social relation between husband and wife and what a wife should do to maintain cordiality in the family.

1. She should have best conduct in temperament while speaking. Her sight should please the husband; she does not even think of any person other than her husband; always remains pleasant before the husband; she considers her husband as God.

2. The husband and wife should live in complete harmony and comply with tenets of their respective Dharmas.
3. She should submit to the wishes of the husband.
4. She should serve her husband in whatever position he is —poor, ill, invalid, tired etc.
5. She should look after the household properly to the satisfaction of her husband and bear children in the house.
6. She should have complete confidence in her husband.
7. She should get up early in the morning and dress up the house, perform yagya after taking bath, prepare food for the husband and family.
8. She should serve her parents-in-law properly taking them above her parents.

On her request, Shiva then narrated the efficacy of Krishana the God. It may be mentioned that Krishana took Shiva as his God and Shiva considered Krishana as his God. It has already been mentioned that for having an able son, Krishana had worshipped Shiva at the mountain for a long period and pleased him. Here Shiva is explaining the efficacy of Lord Krishana. Such an interchanged narration of Bhakta and Bhagwan eliminates the difference between the Shaivites and Krishnaites. In Ramcharitmanas too Rama has worshipped Shiva at Rameshwar and Shiva has considered Rama as his God, so much so that when Sati (Shiva's wife) became Sita to test the bonafides of Rama, Shiva separated her having become the wife of his God. Shiva said that Krishana is above Brahma. He is shyam complexioned and have the brightness of the sun. He kills the gods' enemies, respects rishis, munis and all gods worship him. Brahma has born from his abdomen, and he is born from his forehead. All stars have born from his hairs and all gods from his pores. He is the creator, feeder and annihilater of the universe and mankind. He has born in the earth for the sake of gods' benefit. He is called by many names. He affords refuge to all beings, helps the poors , he is almighty, omnipresent and the child of Devki-Vasudeva and Nanda and Yashoda. He is Shiva's God and anyone, who takes refuge under him, gets everything, he wishes. He went on praising Krishana.

Bhishma then asked Yudhisthra to go to Hastinapur and accept sinhasan and to rule as per Rajdharma. He said that because of Duryodhana, Dushashana, Karna and Shakuni, so many people, horses, elephants etc., have been killed. Dharitrashtra etc. all started worshipping Krishana. This brings to an end the dialogue between Bhishma and Yudhisthra. It is stated to have been narrated for the welfare of the people at large since Yudhisthra was already aware of all these tenets of Dharma. This has covered almost all aspects of bhakti, yog, shankhya, Raja-praja relations, Rajdharma, Varnashrama Dharma, father-son, husband-wife, brothers' relations, way of attaining salvation after having lived in the four ashramas etc. i.e. the complete Hindu philosophy in detail. Still while leaving, Yudhisthra asked Bhishma to tell him one God, under whom one should take refuge and worship him leaving all other gods, to attain salvation. Bhishma told that the one God, who is above Brahma is Vishnu, who comes incarnate in human being form from time to time to annihilate rakshasas and to help rishis perform their tapsya fearlessly. He has thousands of names, which have all been narrated in Mahabharata. Bhishma then remembered and praised Krishana. Krishana praised Shiva. As already indicated, Krishana was Shiva's God and Shiva was Krishna's God. So they worshipped each other. Then Yudhisthra left for Hastinapur with all members of his family after taking permission from Bhishma as required under protocol, thanking him for the detailed sermon to him, which enabled him to accept the Rajsinhasan after having been out from the confusion created in his mind by the killings of crores of people including his brothers, gurus, elders etc. Bhishma told him to go to Hastinapur, rule as per Rajdharma, keeping the well-being of the praja in mind always, worshipping all gods; removing the confusion from his mind; and keeping the ministers' advice in view while taking all important decisions. Yudhisthra went so Hastinapur and asked all to go to their respective houses.

He gave lot of wealth to the wives, and sons, whose husband/fathers had been killed in the battle and started ruling the kingdom as per tenets of Dharma.

Next day Yudhisthra again went to Bhishma with his brothers and paid respects along with Dharitrashtra and Krishana. All the rajas not killed in battle were also there to pay their last respects to Bhishma. Bhishma saw them all. He had been on the arrows' bed for 58 days and now time for his death had come as sun was now in favourable direction for him to leave this body. He asked all not to worry for him as whatever had taken place was a must. He told Dharitrashtra that all had happened because of the foolishness of his sons and that now Yudhisthra shall pay him all respects and he could live with him treating him as his son. Then Bhishma remembered Shri Krishana. Shri Krishana allowed him to go to

Vasu Loka, the best of all Lokas. He then gave up this body through yoga, asking all to be true to Dharma as truth could only grant them salvation. Then all rites on funeral were performed by the Pandavas, when all rajas, Krishana and Dharitrashtra were present.

13
Aswamedhika Parva

After the final rites of Bhishma had been performed in Ganga, Yudhisthra got shocked and fell. He ws attended by other Pandavas. Then Dharitrashtra told him that he should not worry as he had come out successful in the war and should now enjoy the rajya with his brothers. It was rather for him to feel shocked as all his sons had died and he had lost rajya too not accepting the advice of Vidur. Vidur had correctly anticipated that Duryodhana should not be pampered as he shall destroy the entire rajya. But he, having fancy for Duryodhana, did not agree to his advice. Then Krishana too advised him not to lose heart and start rajya job. But then Yudhisthra again back to square number one, after having heard Bhishma for such a long time, insisted on going to forests and spend the remaining life in tapsya etc. Krishana advised him to forget what had happened and to do what is required now. But he would not compromise. Then Vyasa Muni too consoled him saying whatever had happened had been as per God's volition. Further, if he still thought that he was responsible for so many killings, he should conduct Aswamedha yagya. But Yudhisthra said that for Aswamedha yagya a lot of donations/ alms had to be given and with the treasury being empty and it being not possible to ask for presents from the young rajkumars, their fathers having already died in the battle, it was not possible to hold the yagya. Vyasa then told that Maharishi Maruta had conducted a yagya after collecting a lot of wealth and since the entire wealth could not be spent in the yagya, a lot of it had been thrown by them in the North. That wealth should be enough to conduct Aswamedha yagya.

But before resorting to Aswamedha yagya, Yudhisthra was advised to come out of his confusion. Krishana told him that one has to face two kinds of ailments—one bodily and another mental. Cold, heat and wind exist in body and all bodily ailments arise out of the imbalance in these three. Similarly, Sato, Rajo and Tamo are the three gunas of mind. These go on changing. Shri Krishana advised him not to think of the killings in the war. He should rather think that because of the annoyance caused by Kaurvas in gambling through cheating, in insulting Daropadi in removing her clothes and then in sending the Pandavas out in exile for 13 years and the sufferings during that period, which had to be faced by them through Jayadratha, who had kidnapped Daropadi, the humiliation Daropadi had to face in Virat Nagar and subsequently Kaurvas not agreeing to part with their part of rajya, the war was a necessity and once the war took place, the killings had to take place, either of all Pandavas or of Kaurvas. Now the Pandavas having been victorious, they should think of taking up the further job of governance rather than thinking of the part, which was not reversible now.

The battle with Bhishma and Darona was over and now Yudhisthra had to win over in the mental battle, which he was to fight alone as neither his brothers nor servants could help him here taking into account that coming and going of the beings continues. Further, if Yudhisthra abdicated himself from rajya, he still shall not have peace, as the happenings of the past shall still keep him upset. The only way now, therefore, was to forget whatever had happened and to prepare himself for future course of action. The entire worldly philosophy rested on 'MINE' and 'NOT MINE'. Once a person comes out of 'MINE', then he is on the path of salvation. So till Yudhisthra gets out of the thinking that 'My brothers or my gurus, or my elders have been killed', he cannot have peace. What was necessary, therefore, is to get rid of 'My' or 'Mine' and then only shall he enjoy the life whether in rajmahal or in forests. The first thing for him now was to hold Aswamedha yagya as such yagyas enable one to forget the past happenings because of the diversion in entertaining various rajas, brahmins, rishis, munis, gods etc. from which one gets enlightenment towards a prosperous life in this universe. Then with the gold he got from Maruta's yagya, preparations were made for the Aswamedha yagya. Yudhisthra came back to Hastinapur along with Dharitrashtra, his brothers and Krishana.

Yudhisthra consoled Dharitrashtra and started ruling his kingdom according to the tenets of Dharma as had been done by Rama, Prithu etc. In his rajya :

1. There was nothing without the sanction of Dharma.
2. Entire praja too was following their respective Dharmas as they had followed in Satya yug.
3. Yudhisthra lived peacefully alongwith his brothers although there

were reigns of Kalyug getting in.

4. There was rain in time, sufficient foodgrains production, none was having chronic ailment, none died premature, no son died before father, none was hungry or having any physical or mental ailments.

5. Yudhisthra was always prepared, without any lethargy, to help the women, children, old people, invalids, ailing persons and in the compliance of varnashrama Dharma.

6. He protected the praja from all aggressions and criminals.

7. There was practically no crime of theft as everyone was having enough, no cases of rape as women were honoured and no foreign aggression, as Yudhisthra was the overall lord of the entire universe.

8. Even the animals had been contributing their part of remaining in cordiality amongst themselves. Cows gave lot of milk and the forests and ocean gave whatever was available with them.

9. There was no famine as foodgrains production was ample. All bad habits and bad addictions of the past were over. Even gods hankered to live in such a country, leaving their abode in swarga.

As already indicated, there are three mental gunas in a person— sato, rajo and tamo. Their balance is rather difficult but one has to try to have maximum of sato and rajo and least of tamo. The three are in isolation as also dependent on one another as also act against one another. Non-decision, lethargy, greed, pride, thinking of the result of any action, atheism, jealousy, enmity, rudeness and crudeness in behaviour, to be sinner, no-control on senses, insulting gurus, parents, and elders, no donation, rage, cruelty to animals, wasting time in useless jobs, no mercy, non-compliance of tenets of Dharma etc. are all tamogunas. One gets the specie according to one's Karma in previous life. Even birds, animals etc. could become human beings and vice versa as per their Karma. One should, therefore, come out of the tamogunas to the extent possible.

Beauty, happiness and sorrows, heat, cold, luxuries, being upset, strength, brave, exercise, being quarrelsome, killing animals etc., fighting, affection, bringing up of the family, caring for worldly involvements, cleverness, thirst for power and money, dependence on others, sufferings, self-studies, yagyas, repentance, eagerness'to have more and more, theft, violence, awakening, dancing and rejoicing are all rajogunas. Rajogunas are a link between tamogunas and satogunas. One should make constant endeavor to take rajogunas to satogunas, rather than to tamogunas.

Happiness, pleasantness, progress, enlightenment, non-miserliness, giving alms, mercy, courage, contentment, simplicity, truthfulness, equality, remaining same in sorrows and happiness, no rage, no jealousy, no prejudices, piety, hardwork, bravery, purposeful actions, intelligence, self-education, control over senses, non-lethargic, humblenss, brahmcharya, non-attachment to worldly involvements, sacrifice, compliance of dharmik tenets, yagyas, vratas, tap and Dharma are all satogunas. The increase in satogunas leads to salvation. In human beings basically there is more of satogunas and less of rajogunas and still less of tamoguna but by their actions and indulgences, they destroy the equilibrium and increase tamoguna by more and more indulgence in worldly passions and getting away from tenets of Dharma. The mind always try to indulge in aversions but it is brain which checks the mind from such indulgences and converts it into good actions leading to rajo or satogunas.

Upto this time, Krishana had stayed in Hastinapur. Now Yudhisthra was well set in governance with the help of his brothers. Krishana then intended to go back to Dwarka. Shri Krishana was praised by all Pandavas and Kunti and attributed the victory to him only. Krishana then took leave of Yudhisthra and others and proceeded. Lot of wealth was given to him by Yudhisthra on his departure. They all accompanied Krishana for a long distance. Then Krishana took leave and sent them all back. Krishana also advised to act as per Dharma, which could take anyone to swarga. Such a person has to take meals only once in a day for an year; live like a brahmchari, keep rage and senses under control; always take bath; should not remain restless; speak truth, not finding faults in others; worship God; give food to brahmins and giving alms after completion of one year. Such a person is absolved of the sins caused during the last ten years. Krishana also told that he comes incarnate for the sake of his bhaktas only. Therefore, one can worship any of the forms of incarnation, and such a person attains salvation.

14
Ashramvasika Parva

Dharitrashtra was upset after the loss of his sons along with Gandhari. But Yudhisthra had made it a point to afford proper service and to see that all privileges are enjoyed by him as were enjoyed before the war. All Pandavas and Yuyutsa were always available to him like his own sons. He was consulted in all matters of governance—first he was quite experienced in governance and second to make him feel that he still was a part of the government. Similarly, the ladies, including Daropadi, Subhadra etc. served Gandhari and Kunti equally. Yudhisthra used to offer all kinds of costly beds, clothes, ornaments and other consumables as were available to rajas. Vidur used to attend to all his religious and social requirements. He used to get sufficient funds for being spent on donations to brahmins and others. All the rajas, who visited Hastinapur, were asked to pay homage to Dharitrashtra too. Yudhisthra used to tell all his people to serve Dharitrashtra so that he did not miss his sons. All followed his sermon except Bhima, who was not able to forget his behaviour with Pandavas.

Dharitrashtra had been holding religious discussions with rishis etc. as usual, and had been living comfortably. Yudhisthra used to tell his ministers that he respected Dharitrashtra like his father and used to provide funds to him as required. Dharitrashtra in turn used to give adequate donations to brahmins and others.

Yudhisthra was always worried lest Dharitrashtra gave up his life in shock of the dead children. He, therefore, provided to him all leisures and pleasures as were available to him, when he was the raja. Dharitrashtra too used to be affectionate to Pandavas like his sons. Gandhari too used to give alms to brahmins etc. Dharitrashtra in this way got more respect than he got even from his sons. Yudhisthra had become very popular in his praja as he used to behave with vaishas and shudras as with brahmins and kshatriyas. It is here that equality amongst all in praja is proved in our ancient time even when the mankind had been divided into four varnas,

> ब्राह्मणानां यथावृत्तः क्षत्रियाणां यथाविधः,
> तथा विदूशूद्रसधानाम भवत् स प्रियस्तदा। (2/24)

In this way Dharitrashtra loved Yudhisthra but whenever he rememered his son Duryodhan, he was reminded how Bhima had killed him and so he was not happy with Bhima. Bhima too used to hate Dharitrashtra in the core of his heart although outwardly he was quite obedient to Dharitrashtra, might be because of the orders of Yudhisthra—and Dharitrashtra could know this fact through his confidants etc. In this way, fifteen years had passed and then because of Bhima's behaviour, he got vairagya. Yudhisthra and others were not aware of Bhima's behaviour towards Dharitrashtra. Dharitrashtra had been thinking and cursing himself why he did not accept the advice of Vidur, Darona, Bhishma, Krishana etc. not to follow Duryodhana. Vidur had even told him to kill Duryodhana right from his birth otherwise he would destroy entire Kuru Dynasty.

But after fifteen years, now he had attained variagya to leave the universe and to live in forests as vanprasthi along with Gandhari. One day Dharitrashtra told Yudhisthra that he was happy with his behaviour but the last days of his life required him to proceed for vanprastha as is adopted by all as per Dharma and he too shall be a party to that Dharma as raja gets a part of the good deeds of the praja. Yudhisthra became very upset hearing it and objected to his going to forests otherwise he too shall leave the rajya and go to forests along with him as he considered him as his father, guru and raja and all- in-all. He even offered the rajya to Yuyutsa, who was his foster son if that could make him happy. He also stated that he did not consider himself as raja and considered Dharitrashtra only as the overall raja of the kingdom. But Dharitrashtra told him that he had made up his mind for tapsya and so should not be checked now. This in fact is the normal sequence of varnashrama Dharma. Even if no battle had taken place, the raja had to leave the rajya and proceed for vanprastha so that the scn got the rajya in time rather than getting the same by dethroning his father as Aurangzeb had done to his father Shahjahan, who was kept in captivity till death. When the dialogue was going on, Ved Vyasa came there. He advised Yudhisthra not to stand in the way of Dharitrashtra proceeding for vanprastha at that age to attain salvation as per tenets of Dharma. After a lot of discussion, Yudhisthra was made to agree to let Dharitrashtra go for vanprastha.

Although Yudhisthra knew all Rajdharma, yet Dharitrashtra, being more experienced, he coached Rajniti to him while preparing to leave for forests. Dharitrashtra told that he was happy with his service and would tell him the things of benefit to him and the rajya. He advised that:—

1. He should rule as per tenets of Dharma and should never have an inkling of pride of having become the Chakravarti raja as rajya could be protected by adopting the path of Dharma.
2. He should consult learned people on the governance of the kingdom.
3. He should depute his confidant spies in the kingdoms of his enemies/other rajas to have all information about those rajyas relevant to his rajya and should not permit anyone working as spy of other kingdoms in his territory.
4. The capital should be properly protected with high walls all around and having strong doors at places, which should be protected by brave persons. There should be six walls, one after the other, around the mahal.
5. Persons of confidence should only be posted on his personal security and he should take care to see that proper food was served to him (not contaminated or poisoned).
6. He should keep himself protected while walking, taking meals, taking rest and while sleeping.
7. The ladies in the rajmahal should be protected by old people of confidence.
8. Only such brahmins should be appointed as ministers as were learned, knowing all vedas and shastras, religious-minded, knowing economic rules. He should not have prolonged consultations with any minister.
9. Secret matters should be discussed with one or two ministers in solitude, closed room, jungle etc. but no consultation should be held during nights. Not even the animals or birds be allowed to come to secret consultation chambers as any leakage of secrecies could put the raja to great trouble.
10. For imparting justice, learned people of confidence should be appointed. They should be contented and spies should he engaged to keep a watch on their conduct.

11. He should prepare such codes as prescribe appropriate punishment for all kinds of crimes so that the punishment was awarded as per those codal provisions and not by whims of the judges.

12. Those judges, who took bribery; had others' women for enjoyment; were in favour of awarding harsh punishment; gave biased judgements; were rude and crude; takers of others' wealth; destroyer of gardens and sarais, and causing harassment, insult to the people of all varnas, should be punished by death sentence or heavy pecuniary punishment as warranted by each case.

13. In the morning, he should get up early and after taking bath, should have consultations with the people responsible for maintaining the accounts of income and expenditure. Then should take his meals. Then he should meet the army-men and commanders to boost their morale. He should meet the spies and ambassadors in the evening.

14. He should draw his programme for the day before sun-rise and should go to visit the town incognito during nights and in the noon.

15. He should keep his treasury full all the time and the treasure should be taken as per tenets of Dharma and not by undue extraction.

16. Those, who found faults in governance and were against the raja, should be ascertained through spies and got killed.

17. The senapati should be perfectly devoted and of confidence, always prepared to give up his life for the sake of the rajya.

18. He should keep an eye on the conduct of his own people and high officials and ministers.

19. The learned people, scientists and inventors should be adequately employed and incentives granted to them on their achievements.

20. He should be aware of the enemies, rajas and mediators.

21. He should be able to differentiate between his foes and friends. The enemies generally want to win over his ministers, governors, army commanders, fort protectors. Therefore, proper watch be kept on their conduct by deputing spies.

22. When one is stronger than the enemy, then he should attack on

him and when enemy is stronger then one should enter into an alliance. One should carefully analyse, when to attack on the enemy.

23. When the enemy was down and desired to enter into alliance, then alliance should be resorted to after taking gold, silver, land, and keeping the rajkumar of the enemy in his kingdom.

24. The raja should act with prudence in case of any trouble in consultation with his ministers.

25. The raja should try to create division amongst the enemy.

26. The raja should develop friendship with good people and should put bad elements behind the bars.

27. When a raja was not able to face the enemy, then he should offer gold, wealth etc. and send him back.

28. The raja should keep an eye on all agreements pertaining to war and peace with other rajas. Friendly relation on war with a raja should be decided based on the strength of the enemy vis-a-vis his own.

29. During the war, efforts should be made to create discontentment amongst the commanders of the enemy. He should take help of other friendly rajas when the enemy is stronger.

30. He should try to cause division in the enemy, or cause some disruption in their system.

31. The raja should keep in tact his army force, wealth force, friends' force, brothers' force etc.

32. The raja should act as per the four cardinal principles—sam, dam, dand and bhed (साम, दाम, दण्ड, भेद) in dealing with the enemy.

33. The raja should set out with his mighty force for conquests. This shall keep the army in tact.

34. The raja should put his spies in the army of the enemy so that he was able to know all their strategy and acted accordingly.

35. The raja should give adequate rewards and incentives to the commanders and troops of his army, and should recruit only strong persons in his army.

36. At the top of all, the raja should take care of his health and of his protection at all times.

37. Following the above principles of Rajniti, the raja shall be popular in his praja and lead a peaceful and comfortable life. Yudhisthra told Dharitrashtra that he shall keep in view the advice given by him.

Dharitrashtra came out of the rajmahal along with Gandhari. His praja came to see him. He distributed alms amongst the brahmins and others and sought their permission for proceeding to forests on vanprastha. This is the protocol followed by the rajas. At first Dharitrashtra sought Yudhisthra's permission as he was the raja and then advised him the rajniti to be followed to become a successful raja and then gave alms/presents to public and then sought their permission to leave for vanprastha. He begged to be excused in respect of all troubles caused to them by him and his son during his regime taking that he was now an old man, whose all sons had been killed and he was the successor of the dynastic rule of Kaurvas. Now Yudhisthra was taking care of the rajya and keeping everyone happy. All felt sorry on Dharitrashtra leaving the kingdom for vanprastha and were very sad. They all appreciated his reign when he treated them like his children. According to our Dharma, the raja treats the praja as his sons and the praja treat the raja as their father. Each one is prepared to give up his life for the other. The people said that they were quite in peace and comfort during his rule and the rule of his son Duryodhana. Now they wished Yudhisthra to rule for thousands of years as they shall not get such a raja again. He had no short-comings and cared for the praja in the best possible way.

Next day when everything was set for Dharitrashtra to depart for forests, he sent Vidur to Yudhisthra to give him some wealth with a view to enable him to perform 'shradha' of Bhishma, Darona, Bahlika, and his sons and others, who had died in the battle. Hearing this, Yudhisthra and Arjuna were happy but Bhima, who still did not like Dharitrashtra, being the father of Duryodhana, who had caused so much misery to them, did not approve of any payment being made to him. Arjuna pacified him saying that he was begging for the money from the rajya for 'shradha' purposes only and they should agree to his petty request. Yudhisthra appreciated Arjuna's view-point as they themselves had to perform that 'shradha'. Yudhisthra agreed to pay the money for 'shradha' to Dharitrashtra and told Vidur to apprise Dharitrashtra that he was the owner of the entire wealth with him in the rajya and even said that even he was at his disposal. Vidur apprised Dharithrastra of the feelings of Yudhisthra towards him. Such feelings with the enemy are unthinkable anywhere in the universe and are the climax of protocolic relations—politically, socially and financially. Dharthrashtra paid alms to brahmins and others and performed 'shradha' of all those, who had been killed in the battle along with Pandavas. Dharithrashtra then left for the forests along with Gandhari leaving Pandavas crying. The praja followed Dharitrashtra but he consoled them and returned them to the kingdom to care for the proper Dharma being followed by them in the regime of Yudhisthra. Vidur and Sanjay followed Dharitrashtra.

Yudhisthra asked Kunti to return to mahal but she stated that she shall go with Gandhari to forests and that he should take care of Nakula, Sehdeva, Daropadi and other brothers and their wives. Yudhisthra was very upset hearing this from his mother and could not speak for a long time and then said that he could not live without her and could not allow her to go to forests. He had attained the rajya by killing so many people on her orders conveyed through Krishana, then how could she now depart from the rajya like that. But she did not listen to her sons and continued proceeding further with Gandhari. She said that they had been badly defeated in gambling and in the situation, it was necessary to boost their morale, particularly when his brethren had been humiliating them. Now she wanted to perform tapsya in the forests, living with Dharitrashtra and Gandhari. Pandavas returned to Hastinapur and Kunti, Gandhari and Dharitrashtra proceeded further towards forests. Dharitrashtra and Gandhari persuade Kunti to go back and enjoy the rajya rather than going with them in tough forests but Kunti did not surrender and all Pandavas and their wives returned to Hastinapur crying for them. Kunti, Gandhari and Dharitrashtra got engaged in tapsya in the forests.

Whereas Dharitrashtra and others settled in forests and started tapsya along with other rishis, Pandavas, their wives and the people of Hastinapur were very upset on the departure of the three from the kingdom. They had been worrying how the old raja and queens shall be living in tough forests. The Pandavas were not able to devote themselves in rajya work. In the situation, Yudhisthra decided to visit the forests to see Kunti and others. Daropadi and other ladies too prepared themselves to see Kunti. Yudhisthra ordered his senapati to prepare for going to forests. Vehicles and men were prepared and loaded with essential commodities. They also allowed the people to accompany, as wished to see the old raja. People started on horses, elephants, chariots etc. Yuyutsa and Purohit Dhomya stayed back in Hastinapur to protect the kingdom. They all proceeded and crossed all rivers etc. enroute. On reaching near the ashrama, they got down from the vehicles. The tapasvis came there to see Pandavas and the Pandavas paid their respects. Seeing the three,

Pandavas started crying and Kunti embraced them. Then Gandhari embraced and then Dharitrashtra embraced them after they paid respects. Yudhisthra introduced each one to Dharitrashtra, who blessed them. Then Dharitrashtra asked about their well-being and that of the praja and Yudhisthra enquired about their well-being as per protocol. The Pandavas and others saw rishis' ashramas and paid respects and in turn got their blessings.

The Pandavas lived in the forest for a month. Then Vyasa Muni came there. Vyasa checked up from Dharitrashtra whether he was now fully absorbed in tapsya and did not worry for the dead sons etc. Some other rishis too came there. Yudhisthra worshipped them all. Then many religious discourses were held. Vyasa then said that Dharitrashtra and Gandhari were always shocked on their sons' death. Daropadi was sad on her sons' death. Subhadra was sad on Abhimanyu's death and so on. Vyasa said that he had come to fulfil their present desires. He asked for the same. Dharitrashtra said that he was happy in the company of all rishis etc. but he was sorry for the deaths caused because of the folly of Duryodhana, and those deaths had been causing him great distress. He started crying, followed by Gandhari too. Then Gandhari told that Dharitrashtra was still feeling the death of his sons sixteen years back and Daropadi was sad on the death of her sons and brothers, father etc. Others too were sad because of some death or the other. Kunti mentioned about the birth and death of Karna. Vyasa told that God could make anyone conceive and such conception is not treated against Dharma. Vyasa told that Gandhari and Dharitrashtra shall see their sons during night, Kunti shall see Karna, Daropadi shall see her sons, Subhadra shall see Abhimanyu, and so on. After that they should forget the deaths and be happy in their tapsya etc. This was God's job and had to be done as all gods had come on the universe in human forms. The Kauravas were rakshasas and had to be killed by Pandavas, who were gods. They all went to Ganga and took bath in Ganga in the evening and after pooja etc. sat together. Vyasa Muni called all Kaurvas and Pandavas killed in the battle. Then all deads in thousands came out of Ganga river. They were all with godly clothes and ornaments. Dharitrashtra and Gandhari could also see them by special power granted to them. All those, who appeared there were above sins, rage, affection etc. They all met with their respective relations. All were very happy. They were now all bereft of their sorrows. After the night, they all went back to their respective Lokas through Ganga water. People of various countries were surprised to know of the visit of the deads. This also confirms the Hindu belief of transmigration of soul. Janmejaya was also surprised to know of the visit of the deads in heir previous form. Vaisampayanji then explained to him that the soul does not come to another form till it had availed of the result of all deeds in the universe—good or bad. After death, the human body gets destroyed but the soul continues with the subtle body and that is what had appeared before the Pandavas and Dharitrashtra etc. The soul continues to have link with the previous body till it enters a new form after having availed the result of good and bad deeds. One should not, therefore, worry for the dead as each person has to go according to his set time and is reborn after setting the account of the deeds of this life. Therefore, all relations are momentary in this universe. Then Janmejaya requested for his dead father too being shown to him. Vyasa obliged him also. Parikshit appeared there and after sometime vanished. Then on Vyas's orders, Dharitrashtra asked Pandavas and others to go back to Hastinapur and get busy in the governance of the kingdom forgetting all worries about the deads. Dharitrashtra, not worried now, came back to his ashrama with Gandhari and Kunti and by tapsya attained salvation having seen his sons having attained salvation by death in battle-field.

Therafter once Narada came to Hastinapur. Yudhisthra asked him if he had ever seen Dharitrashtra. Narada told that he had learnt that Dharitrashtra, Kunti and Gandhari had died having been burnt in wild fire. All in Hastinapur startred crying on that and then on Narada's advice went to forest and then to Ganga and performed funeral rites of Dharitrashtra, Gandhari and Kunti and gave alms to brahmins and others.

15
Mausala Parva

Thirty six years after Mahabharata battle, Yudhisthra started having bad omens. After sometime, Yudhisthra came to know about the death of all Yadavas fighting amongst themselves as a result of the curse passed on them by brahmins. All Pandavas were shocked to know of the incidence of death of all Yadavavanshis. On Janmejaya asking how their deaths took place because of the curse, Vaisampayanji told that once when some rishis had come to Dwarka, a few rajkumars put some clothes an Samba's abdomen and put lady's clothes and asked the rishis whether that lady shall give birth to a male or a female child. The rishis could know the fact and told that she shall deliver a piece of iron (Musal), which shall kill all Yadavavansis. The rajkumars got frightened. They told the happening to Raja Ugarsen, who got the 'musal' ground and threw in the sea. The 'musal dust' came on sea shore in the shape of foam and a special grass grew. That grass became spears, when touched and all Yadavavansis fought with those spears and killed one-another. Then Krishana remembered that after Mahabharata battle, Gandhari had passed on a curse on Krishana that as all her sons had died because of him, all Yadava vansis shall also die and, therefore, all those deaths were because of that curse. Krishana sent intimation of the killing of Yadavas amongst themselves to Arjuna, who immediately came to Dwarka. Krishana sent all ladies to a safe place. Krishana then telling the ladies that Arjuna shall come to protect them, he himself went to forest in search of Balrama. Krishana saw Balrama having left this mortal body. Krishana too sat in a samadhi under a tree. A hunter came there and mistaking Krishana as some wild animal, killed him by his arrow. When the hunter came closer to Krishana, he felt sorry for his mistake but Krishana consoled him and left this mortal body and went to his Loka.

Hearing the death of Yadava vanshis. Pandavas became very sad.

Arjuna went to see Krishana after taking permission of his brothers. Arjuna could only see sixteen thousand wives of Krishana there. They started crying after seeing Arjuna. Arjuna too started crying and became unconscious. Rukmani and Satyabhama came and when Arjuna performed last rites of all Yadavavansis and left for Hastinapur with proper escort on elephants, horses, and chariots, entire Dwarka was sunk in the sea. Arjuna took all women and stayed on the way during night in Panchnad Pradesh. The tribal people of that area got tempted seeing many queens being taken by Arjuna. The robbers in thousands attacked on Arjuna and told them to go back otherwise they all shall be killed but they did not retreat. Then Arjuna took his Gandeeva but forgot to operate it. He forgot the use of all godly weapons. Others escorting the women also failed to check the robbers, who looted all the queens of their ornaments. Arjuna felt such a defeat at the hands of the robbers. Arjuna then went to Kurukshetra with the ladies and their ornaments as could save themselves from the clutches of the robbers and settled them all there. The only rajkumar Vajra saved in Dwarka, having accompanied Arjuna, was coronated as the raja of Indraprastha. Some queens burnt themselves in fire; some stayed with Vajra and remaining started tapsya in forest.

Arjuna then went to Vyasa's ashrama. He paid respects to Vyasa muni and stood before him. Arjuna was very upset on his defeat by the robbers. It was the same Arjuna, who had killed crores of army-men and commanders and brave rajas in the battle of Mahabharata. So it is all the time, which changes the faculties of a person. Vyasa Muni asked the reason for his being so upset. Arjuna told that Krishana and Balrama had left the mortal bodies and because of the curse of brahmins, all Yadavavanshis had killed one another. Their separation had become intolerable for him and further he had been defeated by Ahirs of Panjab and he could not protect Krishana's queens with his Gandeeva having lost the knowledge of use of all astras and he became helpless and all ladies with him had been robbed. Vyasa Muni told him that all Yadavavanshis were parts of Krishana and had gone with him and that he should not worry for them. The ladies were all 'apsaras', who had been cursed by Astavakra Muni that they shall go in the hands of robbers and then get salvation. Therefore, that should not cause any worry to him. His sarthi was God himself and had come as incarnate as Krishana. Vyasa told that his job was now over. All rakshasas had been killed and the God's job had been done through him and that now the Pandavas should opt for vanprastha and attain salvation through tapsya. Arjuna took leave of Vyasa Muni and went to Hastinapur.

16
Mahaprasthanik Parva

Arjuna came to Hastinapur and told the entire happening that took place in Dwarka. Yudhisthra accepted this as the work of the destiny, which had to be accepted and could not be escaped. He entrusted the rajya to Yuyutsu and coronated Parikshit. He coronated Vajra as the raja of Inderprastha. The Pandavas offered their homage for Krishana and others. In Hindus, the varnashrama institution has to be accepted by all. This shows the extent of sacrifice in these people. Pandavas in no time left the rajya and adopted vanprastha. Many alms were given to brahmins and others. The praja, However, did not accept such a decision. But Yudhisthra was clear in his decision. The Pandavas and Daropadi put on the tapasvi's clothes and left for the forests. All people started crying for them. Yuyutsa, Kripacharya and others went with them for some distance as per protocol and then returned. Pandavas were accompanied by a dog too. They walked in a sequence, Yudhisthra was followed by Bhima, Arjuna, Nakula and Sehdeva and then Daropadi and then the dog. When Rama, Lakshmana and Sita went to forests, Sita was in between Rama and Lakshmana as Sita had to follow Rama and not Lakshmana and then Sita had to be protected from all sides. If Sita were at the end then there was fear of her being attacked from behind as many rakshasas were there in the forests. Here the sequence had to be in above order because—

1. Daropadi, being the wife of all Pandavas had to follow them all.
2. They had to move in order of seniority. Daropadi was at the bottom-most in seniority, she could therefore, come after all others.
3. For the purpose of security, she was followed by a dog, who provided full protection. In case of any fear, the dog would bark

and make all others alert.

4. Rama etc, had been going to the forest to kill the rakshasas. They, therefore, could be attacked by rakshasas any time. Sita, therefore, had to be provided a cover. This was not the case here as Pandavas had to go as vanprasthis and there were no rakshasas left in the universe after Mahabharata.

On the way, Daropadi fell. Bhima asked for the reason. Then Yudhisthra told that she was wife of all the five Pandavas but she liked Arjuna more. Therefore, she had fallen down. The Pandavas proceeded further. Then Sehdeva fell. Yudhisthra told the reason for his fall was that he was very proud of his beauty. Yudhisthra advised to proceed further as everyone had to face the result of his deeds—

"यस्य यद् विहितं वीर सोऽवश्यं तदुपाश्नुते।" (2/17)

Then Arjuna fell. Yudhisthra told that Arjuna was proud of his strength as 'Dharmvir'. He said that he shall finish all enemies in one day but he could not do so. He had also humiliated many brave warriors. Therefore, he had fallen. Then Bhima fell. He asked Yudhisthra the reason for his fall. Yudhisthra told that he was proud of his bravery and he used to eat so much as could feed many. Yudhisthra proceeded further along with the dog. Here we find that all Pandavas and Daropadi had fallen because of some sin on their part and they had all fallen in order of the seniority only. So since all were sinners, they fell in order of seniority. Then Indra came to take Yudhisthra on his chariot but Yudhisthra asked for his brothers and Daropadi being taken too. Indra told that they all had already gone to swarga. They had gone leaving their mortal bodies here but Yudhistra shall go with his body too. Yudhisthara then asked for his dog being taken too as he had been very loyal to them. Indra told that he had attained salvation and should not care for the dog, who had to face his destiny and then dog could not be kept in swarga. Their discussion continued. Ultimately dog, who was in fact a god, came to his form and praised Yudhisthara for his affection for the dog. Yudhisthara was taken to the best of the Lokas. He saw Duryodhana there but could not find Pandavas and Daropadi. He asked the messenger to take him to his brothers. The messenger took him to 'narka', where all other Pandavas, Karna and Daropadi were there. Yudhistra asked how Duryodhana, who had been a cheat throughout, could get swarga and his brothers and Daropadi, who cared for Dharma were in 'narka'. Then he was told that everyone had to pass through swarga and narka according to his good or bad deeds.Where good deeds are more, then one is put to 'narka' first to face the result of bad deeds. Where bad deeds are more, then he is sent to swarga first to enjoy the result of good deeds first. The Pandavas and Daropadi and Karna had finished the result of their bad deeds and would, therefore, come to 'swarga' now. He had been taken to 'narka' for a short period as he was instrument in the death of Darona by saying that Aswatthama had been killed knowing fully well that he was referring to Aswatthama , the son of Darona, who had not died and it was an elephant only, who had been killed. Now that was over and he was to now live in 'swarga' for ever. Then all Pandavas, Daropadi and Karna came to 'swarga'. This is how as per Hindu belief, all have to face the result the Karmas (good or bad deeds) in the universe getting 'swarga' or 'narka', as the case may be and then come in new lives in the species awarded to them as per their Karmas. So the soul has at first to face the result in Parloka and then get the destined specie in this universe in the next life.

Let us bring this book to an end here and care for the next life hereafter.

Index

G

H

I

J